The History *of* Virginia's Navy *of the* Revolution

By

Robert Armistead Stewart

Southern Historical Press, Inc.
Greenville, South Carolina

This volume was reproduced from
a personal copy located in the
Publisher's private library
Greenville, South Carolina

All rights reserved. No part of this publication may be
reproduced, stored in a retieval system, Transmitted in
any form, posted on to the web in any form or by any
means without the prior permission of the publisher.

Please direct ALL correspondence and book orders to:
www.southernhistoricalpress.com
or
Southern Historical Press, Inc.
PO Box 1267
Greenville, SC 29602-1267
southernhistoricalpress@gmail.com

Originally published: Richmond, VA 1934
ISBN #978-1-63914-039-8
All Rights Reserved
Printed in the United States of America

PREFACE

Virginia's Navy of the Revolution, largest of all the State navies, has never received due recognition for the important—and in view of the essential credit established in Europe by shipments of tobacco—perhaps the determining part it played in the contest. The present work aims to present the story of this Navy, its achievements and also its failures, as fully as extant records admit.

The sources and authorities comprise: MS Journal and the Letter Book of the Virginia Naval Board, and miscellaneous documents concerning the Virginia Navy; Auditor's papers (dealing with the State commerce in 1776, 1777, and 1778); Letter Book of Thomas Smith, State Agent; Executive Papers—all the preceding deposited in the Virginia State Archives in Richmond; Hening's "Statutes at Large," Volumes IX, X, and XI; "Official Letters of the Governors of Virginia," Volumes I, II, and III, published under the general editorship of Dr. H. R. McIlwaine, Virginia State Librarian; Revolutionary pension claim papers in Washington (eventually to be deposited in the National Archives Building) and documents among the Naval Archives; the *Virginia Gazette;* the *Virginia Historical Register;* "Maryland Archives"; "North Carolina Records"; finally, a series of articles entitled "The Virginia Navy of the Revolution," published anonymously in the *Southern Literary Messenger*, of 1857, but known to be the work of Dr. W. P. Palmer, of Richmond, who was also the compiler of the "Virginia Calendar of State Papers," published in 1875.

The episodes of Chapters VIII and XVI of the present work have been drawn from the *Messenger* articles; the narrative is wholly rewritten.

The conventional fashion of printing the name of a vessel has been departed from in the following narrative. The definite article preceding the proper name leaves no room for ambiguity, and, in the present writer's judgment, the page presents a more pleasing appearance without the quotation marks or italics commonly used for the purpose in view.

ROBERT ARMISTEAD STEWART

Richmond, Virginia, December, 1933.

CONTENTS

Chapter I. THE GUNPOWDER PRELUDE	5
Chapter II. THE NEW NAVY GOES INTO ACTION	15
Chapter III. CAPTURE OF THE JENNY BOAT, DUTCH UNREST, AND THE REVERSE OF VAN BIBBER	22
Chapter IV. THE CAREER OF THE MOSQUITO	34
Chapter V. OVERSEAS ADVENTURING	43
Chapter VI. GOVERNOR HENRY BUILDS HIS HOPES ON HIS MOST CHRISTIAN MAJESTY	51
Chapter VII. THE TARTAR, THE DRAGON AND THE TEMPEST	57
Chapter VIII. OUTWITTING THE MARAUDERS OF THE INLETS	61
Chapter IX. THE UNCONQUERED LIBERTY AND THE DOOM OF THE DOLPHIN	68
Chapter X. NAVAL DESCENT UPON THE "SINEWS OF THE REBELLION."	73
Chapter XI. AN UPCOUNTRYMAN PILOTS THE ADMIRALTY	80
Chapter XII. PICAROONS AND PUNCTILIO	86
Chapter XIII. ARNOLD THE DESTROYER AND THE SEQUEL TRIUMPHANT	93
Chapter XIV. THE LAST OF THE PATRIOT AND THE MARQUIS LAFAYETTE, PRIVATEER	108
Chapter XV. FRENCH OVERLORDSHIP	120
Chapter XVI. BATTLE OF THE BARGES	128
AFTERWORD	135
ROSTER OF THE VIRGINIA NAVY OF THE REVOLUTION	137
INDEX	273

CHAPTER I

THE GUNPOWDER PRELUDE

Intrigues that revolve about gunpowder figure in the foreground of the early Revolutionary strife in Virginia. The removal of this precious article of destruction from the Williamsburg Magazine, by Dunmore, resulted in the march of Patrick Henry and his Minute Men upon the capital, and the consequent transfer, on June 5, 1775, of the seat of Royal Government to his Majesty's ship Fowey, off Yorktown.

Powder was once more an issue the following autumn. John Goodrich, Sr., of Nansemond and of Isle of Wight counties, shipowner and merchant, sprung from a family seated in the Colony for nearly a century and a half, was supplied by the Virginia Committee of Safety with a sum in bills of exchange, to procure from the West Indies powder for the use of the Colonists in arms. This commission the elder Goodrich committed to his son William, who, under extraordinary circumstances, succeeded in transporting fourteen hundred pounds in safety. The incident having come to the attention of Dunmore, he took action as reported in the *Virginia Gazette* of October 21: "A large sloop from St. Eustatia mounting 16 six pounders and a number of swivels, is said to be gone up the Bay with a large quantity of powder. Mr. Goodrich, of Portsmouth, whose vessel Lord Dunmore suspects of having brought in a supply of that article lately, is confined in irons on board a man of war."

Now, in the affair of the gunpowder, William Goodrich's brother Bartlett played a bargaining role. In addition to the gunpowder he had obtained from the Liverpool ship at Antigua British linens, shipped the forbidden goods in his schooner Fanny to St. Eustatius, and having there altered the marks from British to Holland manufacture, expedited the material, in violation of the Act of Importation, to his father John Goodrich, in Virginia, who, on the Potomac River, had them exposed for sale as Dutch goods.

Getting wind of this equivocal transaction, the Isle of Wight Committee of Safety made report to the Convention, and Bartlett was called before the ruling body for question. The altered marks he conceded without hesitation, contending, however, that inasmuch as the Liverpool captain declined to part with the powder, unless the linens were taken as well, he had, for the public good, risked compromising his position in the Colony by yielding to the captain's demand. The goods he had consigned to the master of the Fanny; the powder was turned over to his brother William for immediate transport.

This explanation and plea the Convention regarded with great and indeed not unfounded mistrust, and accordingly resolved that the Goodrich brothers had deliberately violated the Association forbidding the importation of British commodities into the Colonies.

Meantime, Dunmore, having drawn from William Goodrich his side of the matter, dispatched a boat to the West Indies for corroborative reports. He then caused John Goodrich and John Goodrich, Jr., to be seized and held in custody on one of his ships, but he later released the two on parole, under their engagement to give no further aid to the "rebels" and, by way of guarantee, to report to him on shipboard every tenth day. And so persuasive were his Lordship's methods that, in very short order, despite the detentions and precautionary actions of the Committee of Safety, the Goodriches, father and sons, were openly ranged on his side.*

In view of the menace on the water from foes within and without, the Virginia Convention, taking its cue from the recent action of Congress, resolved "And for the greater security of the inhabitants of this colony from depredations of the enemy by water Be it Ordained That the committee of safety shall

---

*In April, 1776, John Goodrich, in command of the armed sloop Lilly, seized in Ocracock Inlet a sloop belonging to North Carolina, and afterwards captured a schooner in the Bay. Goodrich had three boats in Dunmore's service at this time. In May Goodrich was taken, and for at least eighteen months held close prisoner in Charlottesville. In May, 1776, Bartlett Goodrich was captured with his vessel mounting four carriage guns and six swivels, on a return voyage from the West Indies. Bartlett was sent to Bedford, and later to Amherst. Both John Goodrich and his son Bartlett escaped before the end of the year 1778, when they are found in active service of the enemy.

and they are hereby empowered and required to provide from time to time such and so many armed vessels as they may judge necessary for the protection of the several rivers in this colony, in the best manner the circumstances of the country will admit; and, to that end, to raise and take into pay a sufficient number of officers and men, as well sailors as marines * * * That where the land service will admit of it, and the officers and soldiers of the regular force shall be willing to enter upon any temporary expedition in such armed vessels, they may be allowed so to do" *

In January, the month in which Washington appointed Manley commander of his Boston fleet, Lord Dunmore, on the second, opened the occurrences of the year 1776 in Virginia by bombarding and firing the waterfront of Norfolk†. But from his Lordship's further aggression a prospect of early relief had been reported from Philadelphia, where Richard Henry Lee now sat on the Naval Committee of Congress. In October, 1775, there had been authorized the formation of a Continental fleet of armed vessels, and on December 22 Esek Hopkins, of Rhode Island, was confirmed as its head. Even before the news of the bombardment of Norfolk had reached the members of Congress that body had directed the new Commodore "if wind and weather possibly admit, to proceed directly to Chesapeake Bay in Virginia against Dunmore," unless he found the enemy greatly superior. And early in February Hopkins' fleet, after successfully contending with the ice in the Delaware, formed off Cape Henlopen, and on the seventeenth struck out to sea.

Meanwhile, Virginia was beset with additional cause for disquietude. On February 10 the Committee of Safety had report of the arrival of a hostile 50 gun man-of-war in Virginia waters, and, six days later, the *Virginia Gazette* more informatively announced: "We have undoubted intelligence,

---

*Hening's Statutes at Large, Vol. IX, p. 83.

†The statement found in many American histories that Dunmore "destroyed Norfolk" is not strictly exact. As a result of the British bombardment and the fires started by landing parties 54 houses were destroyed. On the other hand, Virginia State troops were responsible for the destruction of 863 houses, up to January 15, 1776, and 416 were later destroyed by order of the Convention. "Journal of the Virginia House of Delegates", 1835.

that the man of war lately arrived in Hampton road is the Roebuck of 44 guns, Capt. Hammond, lately from England, but last from Halifax, in Nova Scotia." Yet so secure was the Virginia Convention in its confidence of aid in the offing that on February 10, the day before a dispatch was sent to the Virginia Delegates in Congress announcing further hostile arrivals in the guise of two frigates and two other ships, the Committee of Northampton County was requested "to employ at public expense one light Swift Sailing Vessel to ply on and off the Capes and give intelligence to the Phila fleet of the Strength of the British Navy here & to continue the same 10 or 12 days."

Whether or not the swift-sailing vessel made contact, as was hoped and desired, cannot now be determined; yet, in Williamsburg, there must have been a startled awakening when it was learned that the expected deliverers, without so much as a single shot against Dunmore and his Roebuck, had found the season particularly favorable for an expedition against the unguarded island of New Providence. From this time forward, affairs in the Chesapeake were to be allowed to take their own course.

But Virginia was using every exertion toward her own defense and salvation. Preparations in the upper Potomac, under the vigorous and skillful supervision of George Mason, of "Gunston Hall," and of John Dalton, are reported in a letter of April 2, 1776, to the American Commander-in-chief: "We are building the row-galleys, which are in considerable forwardness but are not yet fitted up and we are exceedingly puzzled to get cannon for them. And have purchased three sloops for cruisers, two of them being only from forty to fifty tons burden, are to mount eight carriage-guns each, three and four pounders: the other the *American Congress* is a fine stout vessel, of about one hundred and ten tons burden, and has such an easy draft of water as will enable her to run into most of the creeks, or small harbors, if she meets with a vessel of superior force. She mounts fourteen carriage-guns, six and four pounders, though we have thought of mounting two nine-pounders upon her main beam, if we found her able, as we think she is, to bear them; her guns are mounted and to be tried to-morrow. We have twenty barrels of powder and about a ton of shot ready—more is making; swivels we have not, but she may make a tolerable shift without, until they can be furnished. We have got some small arms, and are taking every measure to increase them, and hope to be fully supplied in about a week more. Her company of marines is raised and have been for some time exercised to the use of the great guns. Her complement of marines and seamen is to be ninety six men. We are exerting ourselves to the utmost, and hope to have her on her station in less than a fortnight; and that the other vessels will quickly follow her, and be able to protect the inhabitants of this river from the piratical attempts of all enemy's cutters, tenders and small craft." And for this new Potomac flotilla a Commodore was promptly provided.

On March 27 Lieut. John Thomas Boucher, of the Maryland Schooner Defense, solicited the permission of the Maryland Council of Safety to resign his commission in order that he might assume, at the instance of Col. Mason and Mr. Dalton, the command of the Virginia Potomac Fleet, "which will be more beneficial to me", as he in justification declared. Boucher's resignation was readily accepted with the best wishes of the Maryland Council, and James Nicholson, future commander-in-chief of the Continental Navy, was appointed to the Maryland Defense in his stead.

Boucher, with his broad pennant flying from the mast of the Congress*, found himself sailing at the head of fourteen ships of every description, including sloops of war (Scorpion and

---

*In the land bounty papers of Dr. George Hunter's heirs is found a statement by John Hughes, of Alexandria County, apprentice to Thomas Moxley, that he was employed, in 1776, as a ship carpenter on the Congress, Scorpion, and other vessels. Mrs. Hannah Hunter made affidavit that she and Mrs. Bridget Fleming made for the Congress "the colour called a pennant."

In 1776, the officers, line and warrant, of the Congress were: John Boucher, Commander; Wm. Skinner, 1st lt.; John Thomas, 2d lt.; George Hunter, doctor; Chas. L. Broadwater and Daniel Triplett, midshipmen; Rich. Richards, gunner; John Richards, gunner's mate; Robt. Cary, boatswain; John Dunleavy, clerk; Joseph Catherine, steward. Marines: John Allison, capt.; Robt. Windsor Brown, 1st lt.; John Moody, 2d lt.; Samuel Marbury, 3d lt.; John Biffen, serg.; John Adams, corp.; John Hany, corp.; Henry Rhodes, corp.; Vallantine Peers, lt.

Liberty), row-galleys and tenders. Of this fleet the schooner Liberty (later known as the Hornet), under Capt. Richard Taylor*, was the first to take toll of the enemy. She surprised and secured in the Rappahannock River four merchant-men— the Oliver, the Lark, the Susannah, and the Speedwell, the last-mentioned of which was added to the Virginia Navy, armed, and sent to the West Indies for powder and supplies.

The Rappahannock had also been the scene of an engagement, near Bowker's Wharf, in which one of the Goodriches† had been in command of the enemy. The hostile vessel, a tender, sailing down the river with a prize schooner under convoy, ran ashore on one of her tacks. This mishap was the signal for those who, from the shore, had been following the movements of the ships, to make an immediate effort to seize the stranded schooner before the rising tide eased her off. Small boats at hand were speedily filled with volunteers under the leadership of Messrs. Banks and Walker, men of proved courage and enterprise, and pushed off in the direction of their quarry. The prize was readily overtaken, boarded, and recaptured. In the face of a heavy fire from the tender the small boats were drawing alongside in a bold endeavor to board her, when a flaw of wind filled her sails, and she glided out of the trap and out of the reach of assailants in craft unequal to a pursuit.

Among those who distinguished themselves by their "gallant and intrepid behavior" appear the names of Charles

---

*Richard Taylor, of Orange County, was chosen, on March 27, as commander of the Liberty (afterwards the Hornet); Edward Woneycutt, 1st. lt.; James Gray, 2d. lt.; James Blaws, midshipman; Henry Lyburn, pilot.

†John Goodrich, in April, in command of the armed sloop Lilly, seized in Ocracock Inlet a sloop belonging to North Carolina. The Lilly, somewhat later, acting as a tender to Lord Dunmore, captured a schooner in the Bay. John Goodrich, Sr., who had three boats in Dunmore's service, was captured in the late spring, and for at least eighteen months held in close confinement in Charlottesville. John Goodrich, Jr., kept under observation by the Committee of Safety for some months, was soon in action with Dunmore. In May, 1776, Bartlett Goodrich was captured with his vessel, mounting four carriage guns and six swivels, on a return voyage from the West Indies. He was held prisoner at Bedford, and later sent to Amherst, but eventually made his escape. Bridges, another son of John Goodrich, Sr., was in command of one of Dunmore's tenders in the Potomac.

McCarty, of Richmond County, John Edmondson and Nathaniel Crow, of Essex, James Montague, of Middlesex, and the leaders, Banks and Walker.

A short time after these happenings on the Rappahannock, Captain James Barron* in the Liberty and Capt. Richard Barron in the Patriot, cruising off the coast, brought to, after a brief chase, a sail bearing towards the capes of Virginia. The prize turned out to be the British transport-ship Oxford, from Glasgow, having on board two hundred and seventeen Scotch Highlanders. The vessel's original objective was Boston. Along with several other transports she had been captured, however, by Captain Biddle, of the Continental Navy, off the Newfoundland Banks. With prize officers on board and under convoy of Biddle she was being hurried to the nearest port in the United States, when captor and captive were driven apart by rough weather. As the Oxford swept southward the crew, finding themselves out of range of hostile fire, rose and overpowered the Americans in charge, and were shaping their course to join Dunmore in Virginia, when they fell into the hands of the Barrons. The captive Scotchmen†, or at least such of them as were seafarers, were later invited to enlist in the Virginia Navy, but how many acceded to this condition of freedom, without being pressed, is not in the record.

The capture of the Oxford was succeeded by the seizure of the brig Fanny by Richard Barron in the Patriot, and the same captain, in July, during a cruise off the Capes of Virginia, gave chase to and overhauled a sloop Providence-bound, with a cargo of pineapples and limes, and bearing, in addition, numerous gifts for British officers in America from their friends and kinfolk at home, and, in the matter of muniment, two carriage guns and fourteen swivels, presumably unmounted, in view of the sloop's reported failure to resist the attack.

Another incident of the spring is worthy of mention. In March Lieut. Richard Dale, who had joined the Virginia Navy

---

*James Barron had previously captured the Goodrich sloop Dorothy.
†For arrangements for the disposal of the "Oxford" prisoners see "Official Letters of the Governors of Virginia," Vol. I, p. 149.

under Capt. John Barrett, late the preceding year, was taken prisoner near Sandy Point by the British ship Liverpool, and confined on a prison-ship in the harbor of Norfolk. Here he was persuaded by a former schoolmate, a Tory, to take part in an expedition against the people of the Rappahannock, during the course of which he was wounded in an engagement with pilot boats. But the future commodore of the United States Navy soon returned to his first loyalty, and gave abundant evidence of his devotion to the cause of his country by his service on the Bonhomme Richard and on other vessels of the Continental Navy, with distinguished reward.

While the few armed ships in commission in Virginia's new Navy were playing their parts with no little credit, the spring saw further preparations for meeting the foe. The brig Liberty and the schooner Adventure were purchased; the ship-yards were busy with the building and equipping of galleys*; marines and seamen were recruited; officers appointed; and finally the management of the Navy was entrusted to a Board of Naval Commissioners. Shortly after the last-mentioned move of the patriots towards greater efficiency the British sea-forces in Virginia made a change in their base.

Late in May, Lord Dunmore with his whole fleet left Hampton, in the neighborhood of which one of his tenders had recently taken a cargo of arms and ammunition from Martinique, sailed to Gwynn's Island, and here he disembarked, and entrenched his white and black troops to a number approaching five hundred. "In this sickly situation those pirates and renegades," the *Virginia Gazette* of May 30 circulated a

---

*From Minutes of the Committee of Safety: March 27, Phil. Chamberlayne appt. first mate of Capt. Muter's cruiser ("Hero"). March 29, Banj. Pollard appt. 1t. marines; March 29, cruiser for York River, commanded by Capt. Lilly; April 1, Capt. Eleazer Callender appt. to command of 2d cruiser (the "Defiance") to be employed in Rappahannock River, and Capt. Green, first mate; Celey Saunders appt. capt. of one Row Galley to be employed in Rappahannock River, and W. Saunders, 1st lt.; James Marsden appt. capt. of 2d Row Galley in the Rappahannock; April 5, Ordered that 2 vessels be provided for James River, one to carry 2 six pounders & 6 four pounders and that Max. Calvert's Schooner be one of them**to be fitted out under the direction of Capts. James Cocke and Isaac Younghusband; April 29, Capt. Francis Bright appt. of first armed cruiser directed to be fitted out on the Eastern Shore, and Capt. Robt. Cooke of the second.

common report, "on their evening after landing amused themselves with a promiscuous ball, in which a certain spruce little gentleman opened with one of the black ladies."

Soon, however, his Lordship's followers found little time for diversion. Several weeks later, the besiegers on the mainland made a furious attack on the tenders, including the sloop Lady Charlotte (mounting six carriage guns, six swivels, and a cohorn) and a badly armed pilot boat, under orders from Capt. Hammond to prevent, at all costs, the Americans from reaching the island. One of the shots from Gen. Lewis's batteries passed through the Dunmore, and considerable other damage was done to the fleet. "If we had had," speculated John Page in a letter to Jefferson, "only two more 16 pounders and Powder & Ball in plenty we might have destroyed the Dunmore & all their Tenders. The Fowey did not attempt to assist the Dunmore, the Otter preparing once to fire but received a shot between wind & Water on which she went off on a careen."

The next day, Thursday in the afternoon, the "African Hero", as Richard Henry Lee had ironically dubbed this descendant of the Royal Stewarts, re-embarked his motley band from an untenable camp, in which the conditions were later described as appalling. The discomfiture and departure were announced, on July 13, to Daniel of St. Thomas Jenifer, President of the Council of Safety of Maryland: "As the Enemy's Fleet has been driven from their Station and their Force obliged to abandon Gwyn's Island, and we are informed they will endeavor to possess themselves of some place on the Eastern Shore of Maryland, we have thought it prudent to give you the earliest intimation thereof. A battery of 2 eighteen pounders played on their ships and in a few rounds forced them to leave; 4 nine pounders silenced their Batteries, raked their camp, and threw them into the greatest confusion, on which our men as soon as Boats could be procured past over to the island, which the enemy abandoned with precipitation carrying with them all their cannon except one; two of their tenders fell into our hands."

After an excursion up the Potomac Dunmore's fleet, somewhat battered by stress of weather, anchored off St. George's Island, where, as Lee foretold, "the brave spirit of Maryland" did not long leave him in place. However, the Maryland campaign, under a midsummer sun, was not without privations and hardships, as Capt. Price, from his Upper Camp, Saint George's, indicated to Jenifer, on July 29: "This is a Shocking Country everything scarce Water we are Oblidged to hall near three Miles no Liquor but bad Whiskey to Drink."*

On the twenty-first of this month the Earl of Dunmore, in a letter to Lord George Germain had already announced, by implication, the impending close of his career in his rebellious Dominion: "I have taken the opportunity of advising all those who have put themselves under the protection of his Majesty's ships to proceed to such places of safety as they shall think proper. Some go immediately to Great Britain and others to St. Augustine."

News of the exit John Page conveyed to the North Carolina Council of Safety on August 8: "Lord Dunmore with his Fleet in Two Divisions has just left our Capes, one of which steered to the Southward and the other with a fair Wind to the Northward."

Some of his vessels, however, planned an early return, and other hostile visitors, not to speak of the Goodriches, remained to be reckoned with.

---

*"Maryland Archives," XII, 138. On pages 24-25 of the same volume is given a list of Dunmore's vessels. The *Virginia Gazette* gave him a far greater number than the forty here listed.

CHAPTER II

THE NEW NAVY GOES INTO ACTION

On July 21, shortly after Patrick Henry, installed as first Governor of the Commonwealth, left his post in consequence of the state of his health, which was to demand frequent recruiting during his three succeeding years' tenure of office, John Page, acting "in his Room", as the expression then was, directed Captain James Cocke, of the "Cruizer Brig" Raleigh, to proceed to the Eastern Shore and thence transport to Williamsburg a large part of the powder recently imported from the West Indies. Captain Calvert of the Norfolk Revenge "Row Galley" was to proceed down the James into the Bay, and, subject to the orders of Capt. Cocke, to protect trade and annoy and distress the enemy "if it could be done with safety."

The Virginia naval force that had come into being would have been capable, according to Page's surmise to Richard Henry Lee, of destroying Dunmore's fleet, the Roebuck excepted, and, unless the enemy were heavily reinforced, would give a good account of itself yet,* and the Lieutenant Governor, further, retailed the freshest Virginia naval intelligence: "We have taken a little Tender, since their Flight, which was cruising off the Eastern Shore, in quest of Provisions. She carried twelve swivels & 18 Men—We have a fine Brigg mounting twelve 4 Pounders under the command of Capt. James Cocke, a brave and experienced Officer now cruising in the Bay—& a Row galley carrying 2 eighteen pounders is gone down James River—but I do not like the Galley she is Clumsey, & I think can not carry the 2 heavy Guns to any Advantage— We expect Lilly [in the Liberty] will cruise next Week."

---

*Lately put into service were the galleys Safeguard, Capt. Elliott (afterwards of the Northampton) and the Henry, built in Gloucester County under the superintendence of Robt. Tompkins, who became its captain.

And the Potomac ship Congress, whose movements in the earlier months had been hampered by Dunmore, now sailed from the river, bearing a commodore who had made up his mind to resign his commission at Williamsburg. On August 30, Boucher informed Jenifer of this intention along with the news that he was about to leave his then station for the purpose of convoying a tobacco-laden brig safe out to sea. In the event the pay were equal to what he received in Virginia and he were permitted to take the Brig Defense to sea he would be willing to accept the captaincy of the Maryland vessel *vice* Nicholson, reported about to resign.

The Congress was lying near Norfolk on September 1 when the surgeon George Hunter wrote in his Journal: "The Como (Boucher) with seven others set off for Norfolk, I should have accompanied him but for the number of sick. About 5 of the evening having waited on board Sandford's brig Adventure Lieut. Skinner and Lt. John Thomas the former & self proposed to return and call at an elegant Brick House that just offered to our view imagining that the best mode of introduction would be to enquire for fruit.

"Sept. 4, 1776—This morning Capt. Allison Lt. Skinner & self at Cranley's point where we saw Col. Broadwater and John Hunter making salt."

On September 6 Capt. Travis of the Manley Galley was ordered to join Boucher off New Point Comfort, and the Congress and Manley proceeded to convoy the Adventure, without incident, as far as Cape Hatteras, but on their return, off the Virginia Capes, they were chased by the Fowey. However, the Fowey failed of her purpose, and Boucher was able to carry out his intention of resigning his command. Lieut. Skinner, promoted to the captaincy of the Congress, was directed in December to bring his vessel to the mouth of Queen's Creek, and, with a cargo, he set out for the West Indies early in January of the following year.

The late summer had seen the row-galley Norfolk Revenge, Capt. John Calvert, cruising the Bay, the captain using all skill and caution to the full extent of his "power & Abilities in Captivating and annoying and distressing such of the Enemy's ships" as fell in his way. Capt. James Cocke was to be joined by the brig Liberty as soon as the latter had taken in ballast. The schooner Adventure, Capt. Wm. Saunders, was directed to make, with due precautions, a cruise to the Capes. At the beginning of August the Rappahannock cruisers "Lewis" and "Page"* were christened by the Naval Board and their officers appointed. And the same month arrived Capt. Pasture in the Molly† from St. Eustatius with 7500 pounds of gunpowder consigned by Van Bibber & Harrison.

In September, when the State was left "naked and defenceless" by the removal of three battalions of Continental troops to New Jersey, every effort was made to assemble all ships for transporting further troops to the Head of Elk. The next month, however, this order was countermanded, and several of the armed vessels were free for West Indian voyages. The brig Liberty was directed to Martinique; the schooner Hornet, Capt. Taylor, to Cape Francois, and the sloop Defiance, to the command of which Capt. William Green had succeeded Capt. Callender, was ordered to Surinam. To numerous trading vessels permits were granted to proceed on their voyages. And, also, the Aurora, chartered and loaded in Virginia by order of the Secret Committee of Congress, was granted a permit to start on her important voyage to Nantes.

In January, 1777, the month in which the Board selected Gosport as the place for building two Continental frigates of 36 guns, authorized by Congress, and the 9th Virginia Regiment had been transported up the Bay, hostile ships were taking the offensive in Virginia waters, and it was anticipated that the Chesapeake would soon become the seat of more serious hostilities. On January 21, Sir John Peyton, of Gloucester, informed the President of the Virginia Council that he had learned from Mr. Edward Hughes, "who was taken by the

---

*Lewis Galley, Capt. Celey Saunders; 1st lt. Stafford Lightburne; 2d lt. Samuel Healey. Page Galley, Capt. Markham; 1st lt. John Lurty; 2d lt. Henry Lightburne.

†On Jan. 20, 1777, the Pilotboat Molly was purchased for 425 pounds from John Pasteur, Charles Bailey, and Samuel and Thomas Watts, Pasture (Pasteur) was continued as captain, and Edward Lattimore was appointed 1st lt. Later the boat was sent out for indigo, to be shipped at Charles Town for the West Indies.

enemy last Wednesday," that there are three ships in the bay-a 60, 50 and a 36 under the command of Commodore Hotham. Sir John's informant understood that these ships were to cruise here, and expect 7 or 8 sail more every day. This intelligence found its way into the *Virginia Gazette* of January 31, with the additional news that a ship-of-war had driven up East River a sloop from Martinique bound for Baltimore.

Stirred by the danger, the Virginia Council gave approval to an apparatus of warning: "That for the safety of the Commonwealth there be immediately set up at the point of land at Cape Henry, a staff fifty feet high at least; a white flag striped red, to be kept constantly hoisted in the day when an enemy appears: that there be also hoisted on said staff a proper light [a lanthorn], to be kept burning in the night time when no enemy is within the Capes, and taken down on the approach of the enemy."

And the fleet was performing its service. In early February the Northampton had a prize to her credit. The Protector was on guard in Wicomico; the Safeguard, near the mouth of Potomac, and the two Rappahannock galleys, near the mouth of that river. Capt. Taylor, with his ship, had been scouting south of Cape Henry.

Important orders were shortly communicated to Captains Sturdivant of the Manley Galley, Calvert of the Norfolk Revenge, Muter of the Hero, Tompkins of the Henry, Markham of the Page, (whose officers, somewhat later, were censured for not keeping "proper watches on Board"), Travis of the brig Raleigh, Celey Saunders of the Lewis, and the Barrons of the Liberty and the Patriot*. And in the emergency Walter Brooke, late of the schooner Hornet (first christened the Liberty), was on March 21 raised to the rank of Commodore, a position vacant since the resignation of Boucher, and the new head, on April 9, was informed by the Naval Board that they, had it "from very good authority that a Fleet of Men of War and Transports may be expected in the Bay any day."

*In the auditor's papers, in the Virginia State Archives, is found mention of the Brig Rochester, in service in April, 1777. Little is known of this vessel. In the same month there is record of the Pilot Boat Lee, stranded on Hatteras.

The "any day", however, was deferred for four months, and in July the Commissioners ventured to order the Northampton, Capt. Bright, duly supplied with marines and provisions, to undertake a cruise at sea not exceeding four months. The cruise must have been cut short by untoward events or, perhaps, not undertaken, for it was Captain Bright who reported that at 9 o'clock on August 14 a fleet of 200 sail was seen standing directly into the capes. One week later the *Virginia Gazette* informed the public that this same fleet had proceeded up the Bay, while a large man-of-war, supposed to be the Raisonable, was "hankering about York spit."

The visitation that portended Brandywine and the fall of Philadelphia created widespread consternation. Uncertainty prevailed as to whether the British ships, after disembarking their troops, might not turn again southward with the design of wiping out the Commonwealth's vessels. To provide against the threatening disaster the authorities urged all captains of ships in the service to exercise unremitting caution and vigilance. The Norfolk Revenge, the Hero, and the Henry at Hampton were ordered to be so stationed that they might seek a refuge at the first signal of danger, and a similar charge was given to Capt. Saunders of the Manley in York River, at the mouth of which the Raisonable was said to be "hankering".

Meantime the Eastern Shore was assailed from the water. Numerous negroes, of a black population that outnumbered the whites two to one, were absconding and being spirited off to the head of the Bay. In order to block these movements of slaves, the flight of Tories, and the provisioning of the hostile fleet, Commodore Brooke, Capt. Saunders, Capt. Markham, and Lieut. Thomas were instructed to put out of reach of inimical hands all boats that might further the enemy's purpose.

Yet in this time of anxiety and alarm Virginia was not without comfort. Under the shadow of the British fleet and the "artifices of the Tories" bent on shaking the loyalty of the Eastern Shore militia, this body was declared to have stood steadfast, one man excepted. The single dissident declined, according to the *Gazette* of September 19, to take the oath of allegiance to the Commonwealth; whereupon his comrades granted him a day "to consider of it", and, finding him still obdurate at the end of this period of grace and reflection, they pulled his house down and thus brought swift retribution upon his head.

On Sept. 12, Henry, whose dejection caused by the disasters at home was mitigated by the prospective defeat of Burgoyne, informed Richard Henry Lee that the presence of the enemy's fleet rendered in some measure impracticable his plan to throw a body of troops on the Eastern Shore, but he was not without hope that the enemy would be forced to re-embark, and continued, doubtless with reference to the officers and crew of the captured privateer Raleigh: "Hearing from undoubted intelligence that our lost officers are imprisoned at N. York, & having one Lieutenant and 3 midshipmen of the Enemy's prisoners here, I've ordered them close prisoners in goal by way of retaliation. I have resisted the first impulse to this, but repeated proof of inhuman Treatment to our people will suffer no longer hesitation."

Shortly afterwards General Nelson had "the greatest reason to expect an attack upon York Town from several ships that lie in the river," but, on September 26, Acting Governor Page was able to assure the North Carolina Executive: "Last Tuesday evening the whole of the Enemy's fleet, which had gone up the Bay, went out of our Capes," departing, as Washington later added, "with attention fixed on other Objects releaving Virginia from further fear for this Campaign." And Page had further apprised Governor Caswell: "The Board having received information that the Ocracock Inlet* has been blocked up, by some of the Enemy's small Cruisers and Tenders, and it being suggested that if the Gallies, which were directed to be built and fitted out at the joint expence of North Carolina and Virginia, or even any one of them, could be expeditiously equipped, that important pass might be easily opened to the

*On Sept. 10, 1777, the Caswell Galley (one of the two galleys built at South Quay on Blackwater), of which Willis Wilson had been captain since Oct. 26, 1776, was ordered to proceed to Edenton, N. C. for cannon, and thence to proceed to her station in Ocracock Sound. The Washington Galley, Capt. Goodrich Boush, which had been building under the direction of Capt. Christopher Calvert, was probably nearly ready for service.

great advantage of these States, and Possibly to the disgrace and destruction of that part of the Enemy's fleet," and, after an expression of his appreciation of Caswell's generous offer of militia aid "on the late alarming occasion", he concluded: "May an affectionate mutual attachment between North Carolina and Virginia ever increase, to the Honor and Security of the United States in general, and of these contiguous sister States in particular."

Now, the Eastern Shore, that had received the protection of Capt. Celey Saunders, in his Lewis Galley, and of Capt. George Elliott, with his Safeguard, was about to be defended by galleys of its own, authorized by the Convention in May, 1776, built on Muddy Creek, and, after being armed across the Bay, stationed in the Inlets of Chincoteague and Metompkin. William Underhill was appointed captain of the Accomac, and Johannes Watson, of the Diligence.

But amidst the preparations for defense there were mutterings within. On November 1st, a petition was presented to the Assembly by officers of the Navy calling attention to "the great injury worked by officers being obliged to quit the service because the pay was insufficient for their subsistence." The petitioners declared that they would continue as long as they consistently could, but prayed for an increase of their stipend.

Yet funds must also be provided for augmenting the navy. In December Richard Henry Lee suggested the building of four galleys, eighty feet long, for the protection of Chesapeake Bay, in view of the fact that prisoners had conceded that hostile men-of-war stood greatly in fear of this species of craft. "Let us cultivate this passion", he had exhorted the Governor of Virginia the February preceding. A suggestion from this capable member of the Naval Committee of Congress commonly bore fruit in an Executive order, and the Naval Board of Virginia was instructed to build the four galleys, accordingly.

And so the year 1777 closed in the Commonwealth—a period during which Virginia vessels had checkered experiences in West Indian and European waters, as the three succeeding chapters disclose.

CHAPTER III

THE CAPTURE OF THE JENNY BOAT, DUTCH UNREST, AND THE REVERSE OF VAN BIBBER

No sooner was it apparent that Britain was determined to employ every recourse at command to reduce to subjection her revolted Colonies in America than to these latter the question of necessities and of adequate armament furnished food for pressing concern. A long-established trade with the British West Indies was forcibly ended. Of Virginia's former sister dependencies Bermuda alone, in her ocean isolation, contrived to reconcile loyalty to the Crown with the barter of one bushel of salt for two bushels of corn, not without some strain and friction, and an interdict by Congress in the later stage of the conflict*.

But Bermuda had neither the will nor the way to exchange munitions, clothing, and medicines for tobacco and foodstuffs. Virginia's staples, deposited at convenient warehouses along the Commonwealth's rivers, must be transported, as opportunity offered, to the island subjects of the Stadholder and of Louis XVI, which subjects, before they turned into outright belligerants, put a liberal construction on the limits of neutrality, and, with more or less calm calculation, became America's unofficial allies.

As brokers for this West Indian commerce Richard Harrison and Abraham Van Bibber of Maryland proceeded early to establish themselves under the firm name of Van Bibber & Harrison, the latter electing Martinique and the

---

*On May 11, 1779, St. George Tucker presented to the Virginia Assembly a memorial, setting forth: "He is a native of the Island of Bermudas, the inhabitants of which, from the commencement of the contest between Great Britain and America, have professed and manifested an attachment to the cause of liberty; that this has drawn down the resentment of Great Britain upon them, and they are too numerous to be supported by the internal produce of their country; that they are now suffering under the complicated misery of tyranny and famine, and praying that an exportation of provision may be allowed from Virginia to that island."

the former, leaving a "comfortable & Plentiful home" gravitated naturally, by virtue of his Dutch tongue and affinities, to the port of St. Eustatius in the Dutch island of that name.

Van Bibber subsequently, in an hour of adversity, plumed himself on having been both conscientious and capable. "I Came here with clean hands and an unblemished character, & be my sufferings what they may none shall have cause to Complain, or Impeach my Integrity, I'd rather give my shirt first."

While Harrison and the faultless and still completely attired Van Bibber acted their delicate parts with discretion, earning in Virginia commissions a total of 1440 pounds accrued by the mid-year of 1777, a competitor had arisen in the person of Mr. John Ball, of Northampton County, Virginia, who, in August, 1776, had gone out to Hispaniola with Capt. Mahony, but finding conditions there not to his liking, proceeded to make St. Eustatius his base.

In Hispaniola, Virginia was represented efficiently by Mr. Raleigh Colston, accepted for one of the Foreign West Indies in November, 1776, who had chosen Cape Francois, at which port he succeeded in maintaining himself with credit until the close of the contest.

Van Bibber, in St. Eustatius, rounding many corners, got along famously for well over a year, and such vessels as contrived to make port he loyally supplied with return ladings after disposing of tobacco, staves, etc., from Virginia and indigo from Charles Town, under the conniving looks of the Dutch Governor and the local magnates, with competent thrift. But June, 1777, put quite another face on the Van Bibber fortunes.

To the man who proved the agent's undoing John Ball had endeavored to open Aylett's eyes on March 25, 1777: "Capt. Ralls has not been to Carolina and from all I can understand will shortly return from hence without his errand."

The Virginian Master, however, shipped his own version on the following day: "I was beat off the American coast in the Latitude of Charles Town so far that I was obliged to bear away for this or some other West India Island,** upon my getting into this Harbour after being chas'd by various vessels which I escaped thro (I believe) the Interposition of Providence more than this Vessells sailing (which in fact she will not do to any degree of perfection)."

On April 2 Vanbibber* pursued for Aylett the theme of the Master of the Jenny Boat: "As to Pastures & his Boat they are boath clever, I wish the same cou'd be said of Capt. Ralls and his Crew. He arrived here after a passage of about 20 days with a Woman passenger. I was at first determined to load him agreeable to your Instructions the same as if he had been to Charles Town & performed his voyage, but was the same day Prevented from it by him & his Crew making publick there Errant."

But Ralls, after discharging his cargo and doubtless the woman in transit, was supplied with funds by Van Bibber and dispatched to Charles Town to consummate his indigo commission. And while the Jenny was thus occupied a prize fell to a Virginian captain, as Van Bibber recounted to Aylett in a letter of April 21: "There is just arrived here the Capt & Crew of a very fine Schooner that Sailed from here about Two Hours before Capt. Saintclare [Sinclair] & was bound for Newfoundland, but Capt Saintclare over Haul'd him that Night & altered the Schooners voyage to Virginia** and landed such of his Crew (as did not chuse to go to Virginia) on the Island of Saba** I am told Capt Sinclares Prize had on board 800 Joes in Speicie 100 hhds of Rum & 24 of Sugar—I do sincerely wish Saintclare & his Prize may arrive safe. He appears to me to be the most deserving Cleaver young fellow that I have seen & a very striking Contrast between him and Ralls. Saintclare on his Arrival †there proposed to me to take his Cargoe & give him his return in goods intended for homewards Cargoe & that he & his Vessel & Crew should be ready to Sail that same day, & he did Sail within 30 Hours after his Arrival here, &

---

*For printed letters of the firm of Van Bibber and Harrison, see the *Virginia Magazine of History and Biography*, Vol. XVI, 163 et seq.; Vol. XVIII, 63 et seq., and *Tyler's Quarterly Magazine*, Vol. I.

†On April 10 Van Bibber had written "The little Boat Nicholson Capt. John Saintclare arrived yesterday with 13 Casks Indigo."

with the least trouble & noise I ever noticed &c Had his Prize in Possession in four hours afterwards.

"Pardon me for Entertaining you with my Remarks & oppinions of your Officers.

"I speak Impartially & only wish you to know those that are worthy of your Esteme."

It was conceivably this success that aroused in Ralls, returned with his cargo of indigo, a sanguine ambition, which without delay came to fruition. Against a prey marked in advance he stole out one dark night in his Jenny Boat for a shadowy waylaying that resulted in a deplorable aftermath. Concerning the whole wretched fiasco Van Bibber, on June 17, poured out his heart to Col. Aylett, with original diction and spelling, in a peculiarly affecting recital:

"No doubt when you View the within Contents you will [feel] as every Christin Ought for me in my present Situation. I am falsely accus'd & Suborned Evidences procured & made Valid against me, but this is too long a detail to Inform you particularly of at present & will only give the heads & Cause of it at present viz—the 21st May Arrived here Capt George Ralls in Jenny Boat, he haveing a Commission I was Obliged to become Security for his good behaviour &c before he could be admitted to an Entry, this being done I received the goods he brought with him & was ready to Deliver him another Cargo the same day if he would have received it but he Delayed until the 23d May without any seeming desire to return with a Cargo as was Intended for him: but came to me the said 23d May and Inform'd me of Sundry Vessels then lying in the Road that was British property & valuable Cargoes that was to Sail soon & in particular one which was to sail that night, which he seemed determined to Capture & at same time Informed me he could return again & proceed with his Cargo & had he possessed the least Clevernys he might have done it all with Safety & not put me in the Shoking Situation I am in, however he left me to proceed on his scheme & did so far well that he went & cleared out his Vessels property, & the same day A Gent'n from Boston Mr Samuel Pain said he had been in Company with Capt Ralls & that he was very indiscreetly bragging of his Intentions of Makeing a Prize, Ralls came to my lodging some time in the afternoon to see me & I verry unfortunately was not within nor did I see him afterwards, but was again Informed he had made Interest with the Capt of an Armed Sloop in this Road to let him have some more Hands, on this Information I was Induced to write & send of a Note mearly of Advise. I never Intended it as Orders neither did he view them as such, about Eight that night he went to Sea & in three hours after being out Captured a Sloop loaded with Cotton bound to Antigua; then it's said Ralls & all hands got Drunk & lay hull too until they were surprised by a man of War & both him & his Prize was taken, then it was that the poor timid wretch endeavoured to Screen himself by Accusing me. And as they have long had a desire to fix something on me that this Government might have some Collour for makeing an Example, it appears that no ways nor means have been omitted to gain what they have long wished for.—The Note of Advise sent to Ralls is figured into positive & Extensive Orders. I am held as a burger of this Island & that Note of Advise is held as Treasonable Against the Prince & States & as Waging War Against Great Britan.—How this will end in this Despotick Arbetary Government God Only Knows, At present I am in fort Orange under Strict Gards of Soldiers & this day Another flag of truce goes up to Antigua to Admiral Young for all the proof he may Alledge Against me Obtained from Sailors in Irons threatened with the Halter &c.

"*** I have long seen this was a Dangerous Government for me to live in or any other person Attempting to Serve the United States of America, but Alass my Circumstances was such they would not let me depart from hence for the large sum of Mony I was Indebted on Acct of the State of Maryland **** it's no verry Dificult task in the English West Indeas to prove any thing in favour of Government. A Sailors Oath is verry sufficient against any ryputable person***.

"As to Business I will mention to you no more than that I have employed proper persons to Act for you in my place who will write you.

"I must detain a Sum in my hands to serve me in this emergency. money Alone moves every thing here their Creed faith & belief is in it, had I but that Great Layer to speak for me Lavishly I might bid defyance to all that could appear against me, but I am poor & have ever been so here tho the ever endeavouring to spin out all I was Interested with to the end with Oeconomy***.

"P. S. I have at different times for Eight or ten months past applied to the Governer here to receive back my Burgers Brief and to consider me as an american or transient person, but he told me not to fear & I even proclaimed my self an American Subject on tryal in Court before the Governer & Council when I was Attacted by Mr. McConnel about the Brigantine the B. Hero Sloop took (which I suppose you are no Stranger to), but this is not noticed now but Intirely layed aside to please the English."

In another lamentation the prisoner rated "the poor mean wretch Ralls" as a "man of very indifferent character" and professed that his own passionate patriotism was such that it "may for ought I know bring me to ignoble death or what is worse Corporal punishment."

In Van Bibber's appraisal of the Virginia Master, Capt. Wm. Graham, writing from Edenton, on July 12, wholeheartedly joined: "Rawles was Certainly a damned Rascal, I had agred to Come home with him but he went away before he said he Should be Ready in order to go on the above Schieme: he came from Virginia to Statia instead of going to Carolina."

The "damned Rascal", in the fervor of his privateering, had been the victim of self-deception. The prize taken by the Jenny and recovered by the British man-of-war Seaford, which, in addition, had overhauled in open sea two Holland-bound Dutch vessels, was believed by the Virginia captain to belong to one Henry Johnston of St. Eustatius, but was the property, as it later developed, of merchants in Antigua, to whom it was promptly returned, on the payment of salvage. Among the effects of the captured Ralls was discovered the note from Van Bibber suggesting a profitable vehicle for the disposal of prizes—which indiscretion on paper came in due course beneath the angry regard of Admiral Young of his Britannic Majesty's fleet in Antigua. Young straightway hotly protested and prevailed over his Dutch Excellency, who was so terrified—if one may credit the comment of the unreserved William Graham—that he would have even stooped to pay indelicate homage to the Admiral's person.

At the first opportunity in bondage, the ex-Master of the Jenny Boat, whose crew "hull too", according to Van Bibber, had deemed it a matter of honor to get ingloriously drunk while resting on their laurels, wrote from Basse Terre, St. Christopher's, an exculpatory letter to Aylett, with a thrust at Van Bibber:

"My duty requires that I should inform you I was taken on the 23d of last month by his Majestys ship Seaford, my men are confined on board of her, except the Pilot & myself who are now on Board the Sylph a 16 Gun Sloop which is to sail tomorrow for England, what they purpose to do with us there I am not able to tell, I landed the Cargo of Indigo & delivered the same safely to Mr Vanbibber**Thro' the intimation from, & his contrivance &c. I met with my present situation & may justly say that the loss of my own & peoples Liberty & the countrys vessel was thro' his doings & may be properly laid to his debit.—I recd from Mr Van Bibber the day before I was taken 18½ Joes which I did intend to have distributed among the Schooners people in part of Wages this, as also my own Money & what property I had on board is taken from me** friendless moneyless & now bound to an Enemys Country where God knows what fate I may meet with and all this thro your agent.

"I do not know of any service which you can do me any other way than the supply of Money to Mrs Ralls at Hampton.

* * * *

"Mr. [George] Watkins, who was my pilot on board the Jenny desires that 3 Months wages may be paid to his son William Watkins of Hampton to his order."

And so Capt. Ralls, whose strength was not equal to his sense of resentment, was borne into captivity in Plymouth, England. Yet, early in 1779, he was back in Virginia, and, after fitting out the Alliance, renewed his former ambitions. But these buds of hope were soon blighted. In consequence of a sharp attack that appeared in "Purdie's paper" on February 3, exposing the captain's lack of discretion and balance in St. Eustatius, Thomas Whiting and Duncan Rose, of the Board of Trade, bluntly refused him the command of the Alliance, the Gouverneur, or of any other vessel trading with the Dutch ports. This verdict Ralls confided to the columns of the *Virginia Gazette* of August 14 of this year, and presumably waited for the current to set in in his favor. At any rate, he was subsequently in service once more, with ill luck still in his train. The *Gazette* of July 27, 1780, records what was probably his final removal from the Revolutionary scene: "A letter from Williamsburg informs us the state schooner Alliance Captain Stratton, in company with Capt. Ralls and Tucker, not far from the Capes was captured and carried off by the enemy on Sunday the sixteenth instant."

To return to Van Bibber, deeply concerned about the issue of his Fort Orange confinement. One of the "proper persons" he elected for carrying on the State's business was a Dutchman with the ingratiating name of Benedict Benevolus, who, to forearm Col. Aylett, revealed on July 8 alarming intestine conditions: "Government here hăs lately been so very rigorous in punishing what some time ago was only thought a venial fault, and rather encouraged, that the state of things is entirely alter'd; and everybody in the utmost consternation stand agast, knowing not how to act; patiently waiting to hear how they may venture to do with safety—You may guess the author of this, he wrote you by the Sloop Virginia Capt Wm Sergeant duplicate P. schooner Betsey, Capt. May, The Present tends to advice you by Green Field in the Molly, who sailed the 5 Currt was Shipped Eight Hundred & odd fire Engines (sic)—The Night following Mr A V B— eluded the Vigilence of the Guard & escaped from fort Orange—his Rout I know not—but I fancy he will visit you as soon as possible."

Van Bibber had used all the instruments at his disposal, but having lost his footing in a country which he had long seen was a dangerous Government for him to live in, lost no time on his homeward-bound course. John Ball, already on the spot, started to guage the situation and patch up a peace in the precarious port that had before it nearly four years of nominal Dutch supremacy before falling an easy conquest to Rodney. However, in respect to further dealings with the Dutch, William Graham confided misgivings: "I would advise you never to send any of your vessels to Statia but to Martinico as the Dutch Governor is frighted out of his witts & by his Orders Van was put into the Fort; and Sundry others would have shared the same fate had he not Pulles Foot (?) because the Admirall pledged he had Caryed on a Correspondence with the Rebels in America & God knows who by the Bye has done as much of this kind of Business as Henry Godet Son in Law of the Governor in partnership with the Governor and out in Statia and more openly and now he wants to Father the Whole on Poor Van Bibber and clear themselves of the whole at his expense, but I think it lies on you to write to the Governor of Statias & acquaint him of your Displeasure of the same as he promised Van all the Friendship he possibly could Expect &c.&c."

Whether or not Aylett, by writing, melted the Governor is not of record, but at any rate the new agent John Ball started out with Van Bibber's benevolent judgment: "Mr. John Ball the gent who you have thought fitted to succeed me & who I think highly worthy of your confidence" he had begun his letter to the Commissary on July 2, from his cell in Fort Orange. Yet Ball's letter to Aylett of a proximate date was not one of reciprocal compliment: "From a mind that places its supreme Felicity in the Possession of an abundance of wealth, it will ever be fruitless to expect either Honour, Integrity, or Public Spirit, as these are virtues of the heart which Riches cannot give, and when they come in Competition with the Predominant Passion will surely give way to it. It would ill become me to give any opinion respecting Mr Van Bibber."

Nor was Ball in accord with William Graham's views as to Dutch perils and pitfalls, as appears from a letter written on October 22, when he was three months old in his new position. After stating that reports from Martinique indicated that war between France and England was very near and that Lord Stormont, the British Ambassador to the Court of his Most Christian Majesty, had taken French leave of the Court, Ball tendered his counsel: "Tho every State ought undeniably to expand its commerce as much as possible, and there may be greater advantages from large Vessels trading to Europe than to these Islands, yet very fast sailing vessels that would carry 50 to 190 hhds would make more money in this than in the European trade, as the voyages here are short and the danger would be little as they could easily keep off any of the privateers, and the ships of War are generally dull sailers. Rum Sugar & Melasses which are necessary for the Navy and Army are to be had upon good terms, and Duck of all Kind, Ozenburgs, Coarse Linen, Russia Drabs, Checks and Stripes, and many other Articles at not more than 10 per-Cent Profit to the Importer from Holland and many of them at less."

To return once more to Van Bibber. When he was snug in America he received, under date of September 10, 1777, from a secretive F. B——, along with an itemized bill, a letter full of betrayingly Dutch double o's, and containing a dark passage, as follows: "Though I am afraid of Tagan at St. Croix Blowing me if he Noos anything of it which I hope he doont. Now my dear Sir you no your Promise to me the night you Came out (the hasard I ran myself of being found out) the Placaat was 2000 fine and as much more for them who found you out."

So the prisoner had contributed liberally, with funds in hand and in promises, to achieving his own deliverance. On November 19, 1777, he presented to Joseph Prentis, ex-judge of the Virginia Admiralty Court, a memorandum of the price of escape: "21 days costs £268.8.9 Current Currency. To Lawyers Counsellors soldiers sailors for effecting his escape both in Statia & St. Croix."

In the "Precipitancy of his flight", as Richard Harrison expressed it, Van Bibber not only left affairs bemuddled in St. Eustatius, but, contrary to Benevolus' prediction, failed to report to Aylett en route. This hot haste he justified in a letter of September 17, entrusted to the carriage of one Benjamin Statler, "an unfortunate person bound to the West injes": "The time I passed through your State was so alarming to a Man Circumstanced as I am with a Family at the Very Place where it is Judged the Fleet was Bound will fully Plede my Excuse for not Vissitting you."

The Maryland Bayport was not, as it transpired, the British objective, and, from its security, Abraham, as member of the firm of Isaac and Abraham Van Bibber, dispatched to the Virginia Assembly a petition praying to be absolved from any responsibility for the lapse of the sea captain, who had been "so imprudent as to make known to the fullest any service that the petitioner had rendered the States of America."

A Committee of the Virginia House sifted the evidence, upheld Van Bibber, and exposed Ralls without mercy: "It appears to your Committee that the Dutch Government having prohibited the Exportation of Military Stores to the Continent of America, there are great Risque & Danger in any person exporting the same from St. Eustatia & could not be done but by great Secrecy & Address. That the said Abraham Van Bibber in transacting Business for this Commonwealth behaved himself diligently & faithfully, and by his Activity & prudent Management contrived to send large Quantities of Arms & military Stores into this Commonwealth; that while he was engaged in this Business, among other Vessels which were conveyed to him upon public Account there was an armed vessel belonging to the Commonwealth commanded by a certain Capt. George Ralls a man of very indifferent character, and much addicted to drinking", et cetera.

Before long, Van Bibber had a mischief-making interview with Col. Aylett, the tenor of which was transmitted to Ball: "Mr. Abraham van Bibber was lately here & expressed much concern at being informed that you had heard he had spoken disrespectfully of you as a Gentleman & a man of Honour, but signified that he was satisfied you would not be concerned in shipping Arms & Warlike Stores to the Continent, and that you were one of choice who could visit the English Islands, when you pleased, & that he did not think you were a friend of

American Independence. You have now opportunity of clearing up this Point, by lending the Agent your aid in Shipping a number of Arms purchased by Messrs Vanbibber & Harrison which I believe are in the hands of James Smith, & such other Military Stores & Arms as he may direct."

Against the innuendo Ball protested with candor and feeling, and Aylett, in a letter of August 29, assured him that the remarks were "merely a friendly hint," and soothingly added, "I am perfectly satisfied with the reasons you offer in Justification of your conduct in St. Eustatia."

Some years later both Ralls and Van Bibber, of the firm of Isaac and Abraham Van Bibber, saw eye to eye a common ground for complaint. In November, 1785, Ralls, in a petition to the Virginia Assembly, declared that when, in February, 1779, he returned to Virginia from his imprisonment in Plymouth, he received pay as Master of the Jenny Trading Vessel in paper, but no depreciation, and on November 16, 1789, Van Bibber likewise appealed for his "depreciation" on the compensation for 208 stand of arms "brought from Baltimore on the vessel that brought the Marquis Lafayette," which arms were the subject of a letter written by Governor Jefferson under date of April 14, 1781.

CHAPTER IV

THE CAREER OF THE MOSQUITO

After the capture of the Jenny Boat came the turn of the little brig Mosquito, whose name has suffered sea-changes—Musquito, Misquetto, even Miscator—under the quills of mariners better versed in navigation than in standards of spelling. Already in service on July 21, 1776, the vessel was captained by Jacob Valentine, of the marines, which landsman branch of the service learned that the beginnings of life on shipboard are painful. A complaint of Marine Lieutenant Meriwether was presented to the Naval Board on October 7: "That the Language of Lt. George Rogers to the Marines is Most Scurrilous Abusive & Profane; That he had at different times struck them Particularly John Reynolds with a peice of Iron when unwell and excused from Duty by the commanding officer." Lt. Rogers, found guilty as charged, was ordered to make to Lt. Meriwether proper amends, but, so far as the record shows, "John Reynolds struck with a piece of Iron when unwell" was left without moral balm for his sensational experience. Nor was this the last instance when seasoned seamen took forceful means of carrying their point with marines in the making.

In October, Isaac Younghusband, formerly of the merchant marine, appears in command of the Mosquito, his crew augmented from the Defiance by as many men as Capt. Callender could spare. Shortly afterwards, Younghusband, unable to carry out certain orders of the Naval Board, on the plea of ill health, was superseded by John Harris, whose wife was a sister-in-law of Dunmore's captain of militia, the Scotch surgeon James McCaw, returned to Great Britain in the Loyalist exodus. Under her new commander the brig was dispatched from Warwick by way of Jamestown to Portsmouth, to be refitted by John Herbert and supplied with stores, in preparation for a cruise of not more than six months.

Lieutenants Byrd Chamberlayne and George Chamberlaine, who had levelled charges against their former commander, Capt. Robert Tompkins of the Henry Galley, were assigned to the brig. Byrd Chamberlayne took the place of the overbearing Lt. George Rogers, on November 21, 1776. George Chamberlaine, after a short service on the Manley, entered the Mosquito on January 28, 1777. Nine of the Henry's crew with hammocks, bedding, etc. were also transferred to the Mosquito, and on the same day that Byrd Chamberlayne was appointed first lieutenant, his brother Edward Pye Chamberlayne was received as midshipman.*

A shifting of marines was likewise determined. On December 4, 1776, Alexander Dick, captain of marines since February 4, received notice at Port Royal that his company of about twenty-five was wanted for the Mosquito. The men were accordingly shipped from Hobbs Hole to Portsmouth on the Manley, Capt. Cocke, who was directed to take on Capt. Valentine's marines in return.

On Wednesday, February 6, the Mosquito with a crew of close to seventy-five, her captain supplied with instructions concerning the disposal of prizes, left the Capes and bore away in the direction of Point Peter, Grande Terre, one of the ports "open to our cruizers", as the Naval Board had been discreetly informed.

Late in March, the adventurer met with success not unmixed with ill fortune. Her initial conquest, the Snow† John, laden with clothing and provisions for Antigua, contrived to slip away from the captor, but that same evening the Virginia

---

*The officers of the Mosquito were: John Harris, capt.; Byrd Chamberlayne, 1st lt.; George Chamberlaine, 2d lt.; Charles de Kay, sailing master; Alex. Moore, midshipman; Robert Hambleton, gunner; Edward Eagles, gunner's mate; John Brock, steward; Jos. Warwick, pilot's mate; Archibald McNickle, surgeon; John Smith, boatswain; Edward Chamberlayne, midshipman. Marines: Alex. Dick, captain; George Catlett, 1st lt.; Edmund Waller, 2d lt.

According to a statement of Wm. Mitchell, private, Lt. Chamberlaine, Moore, Brock, Hamilton, and Warwick had previously served on the Sloop Defiance, along with himself.

†A "Snow" was a peculiarly-rigged species of merchant-man, with a small and short mizzen, and bearing a try-sail instead of topsails and spanner-sheets.

brig fell in with and took the Antigua-bound King's transport-ship Noble, Capt. Addis, from Cork, Ireland, with a cargo of beef, bacon, candles, flour, etc. The prize was convoyed successfully into the port of Guadaloupe, and the valuation of the cargo at 80,000 livres caused each private to welcome in anticipation "60 lois, deducting the portion reserved for the Board of War." Capt. Harris, unable to see to the transaction in person, consigned the commission to a merchant at Point Peter, one M. Soubies, who, according to his own declaration, shipped the greater part of the supplies to Martinique on a boat that fell a prey to a Dominican privateer. For this piratical outrage Soubies contended he was able to exact no redress. It was the conviction of the Virginia authorities, however, that he was seeking to screen himself behind shallow excuses, and, two years later, Capt. John Cox, appointed agent in Martinique, in succession to Richard Harrison, was instructed to spare no pains to bring the French defrauder to terms.

The crew of the Mosquito, destined to receive no share of their booty, were marked, on the other hand, for an ungrateful memento from their late captives of the Noble. "We have just received," a letter of June 5 from Martinique per the sloop Virginia announced, "a letter from Capt. Harris. He left Guadaloupe a few days ago after being detained there a short time by the Small Pox which had gone through his whole crew without much loss except that of time." In after years, the marine Wm. Dishman affirmed that, when the prize was taken, discovery was made that one of the Mosquito's crew had the smallpox, and it was necessary to return "to inoculate the rest." Whether the contagion came by the customary channels or whether it was "small pox taken by inoculation," to use an expression then current, further time devoted to convalescence might have averted the lot in store for the crew. Shortly after the Mosquito left port on the evening of June 4, she espied a sail that turned out to be a British man-of-war commanded by Sir Thomas Pringle (according to Ralph Horn) or under Capt. Collier (if Moses Stanley be credited). Despite every effort to evade a pursuer so superior in weight of metal the little Mosquito was soon overhauled and forced to surrender. On

June 19, James Smith, an agent in St. Eustatius, reported the loss: "Mosquito Brig captured to windward of Barbadoes by the Ariadne Man of War of 20 Guns—The Capt and his hands it's reported were sent home with a number of others (among them Ralls) in the fleet that sailed three days ago from S. Kitts." And, on July 10, the seizure was announced by John Ball, almost in the manner of a remark in parentheses: "I forgot to mention to you that the Mosquito was taken by the sloop Ariadne and carried into St. John, Antigua. Capt. Harris, Capt. Ralls, and a Captain of the Sloop Oliver Cromwell of Philadelphia (who was also taken by a Kings ship) are all sent to England in the June fleet. The Ship which took out the Mosquito failed her much."

So the officers of the Mosquito, commissioned and warrant, but not their "hands", were transported "home" to Fortune (Forton) Gaol, the quondam Queen Anne's Hospital, in Gosport, and their home-coming is thus chronicled in the extant Journal of an American prisoner:

"Muscetor (*sic*) from Virginia committed Aug. 8, 1777.

"Aug 9 (1777) this day came on shore forty nine American prisoners. Among them were three captains of armed vessels, viz. Captain Courter of the 'Oliver Cromwell', Captain Harris of the 'Miscator' (*sic*) and Captain Hill of the 'Montgomery'. The Agent made it his business to make them deliver up their money by the point of the bayonet. There is no such thing as refusing."*

'The Sailors we are told are all in Goal at Barbados," Van Bibber & Harrison announced on June 25, "but the Capt & other officers are carryed to Antigua, from whence they will be transported to England. It seems prisons are there fitted up for the reception of all Americans who have the ill fortune to fall into their hands (no matter where) but more particularly those taken in armed Vessels.—This is a consequence of the last Act of Parliament suspending the Law of Harbeas Corpus

---

*"A Yankee Privateersman in Prison in England. Journal of a Forton Prisoner, edited by W. R. Cutler", *New England Historical and Genealogical Register*, April, 1876 to January, 1879.

& empowering the King to seize & confine whoever he may suspect of Treason or Rebellion."

The hardships visited on the seamen and marines were in afteryears variously related. Moses Stanley declared that he and others were thrown into a Bridgetown prison and kept seven months and fifteen days before they were transported in the Antelope to "Fortune Goal," Gosport. From the Barbadoes prison (other testimony shows) Francis Pickett, Reuben Brooks, and William Chandler of Caroline County were removed to enforced service on a British ship, and the two last-named, seized with fever, died for lack of necessaries.

Ralph Horn, charged with the crime of treason, was kept six days in confinement. On June 17, 1778, the men were distributed, he further recalled, in a fleet of British ships bound for Jamaica and there removed to a Man-of-War, "where six of us drew 4 British mens rations". Two chances to escape presented themselves, but each attempt met with failure. According to Capt. Dick, Horn, after seven months in Barbadoes prison, was removed to the Antelope "on the Course of Brazil". On the ship Prince George several captives were ill used because they refused to enlist, and Horn, failing in his effort to escape, was brought to the gang-way. Three years later this marine was transported in the Romulus to England, and there lay three years more before he was finally released, reaching New Castle on Sept. 19, 1783.

But Barbadoes had not held all its prisoners. M. Soubies, of Guadaloupe, in bad odor because of his "Noble" transaction, affirmed, in 1778, that he had furnished with clothes Virginia seamen escaped from Barbadoes. William Dishman left the island under pleasanter auspices. Detained at Bridgetown until June, 1778, he and other men were distributed among the ships of a merchant fleet that touched at the port. The three Dishman brothers were placed on the same ship and set at liberty on the island of Jamaica. After a period the three were put on a vessel, with permission to work their way to Philadelphia, but, thanks to the intervention of a Scotch merchant on board, they were landed a short distance below their intended destination, then in the hands of the British, and contrived to reach Baltimore safely—on the night, as it happened, of the illumination in celebration of the recent treaty with France.

Dr. Iveson, of the Mosquito, was reported by Harrison, on December 27, 1777, to have arrived in St. Pierre, bearing the news that the remainder of the prisoners in Barbadoes would be released by the first of the year, unless orders should arrive for their further detention. It later developed that the Habeas Corpus Act was to continue another year, and "Harris' people much in want of cloaths" were supplied by Harrison, through a friend, "to the Amount of 20 Lois."

Finally, the Barbadoes prisoners were transported to Gosport, England, where some were held in the hulks and others in "Forton Gaol." Shortly after the newcomers' arrival Ralph Horn received from Capt. Alexander Dick a note urging that an endeavor be made to have all the privates lodged together in the prison, presumably with a view to an *en masse* effort to effect an escape.

Among the first to get out, by whatever means, were Dr. McNickel, Captain Dick, and Midshipman Moore. After an interval William Mitchell and fifteen other privates succeeded in undermining the gaol, made straight for the harbor, seized a small vessel, and safely reached the French coast.

Captain Harris, who, during his imprisonment, had received news direct from Virginia "from one Green[*] a Virginian who has not been very long from his country", was fortunate in receiving the good offices of Dr. James McCaw by proxy and, later, in person.

According to his fellow-prisoner, John Kilby[†], Capt. Harris left Forton under the following circumstances: "At last the day and hour of exchange were announced to us[**] The agent appointed for that purpose, a Mr. Hurum, called all of our names and read to us these words, to wit: 'You all now have received His Majesty's most gracious pardon.' At that time there was a loud cry from many of our men, 'Damn his

---

[*]This was doubtless Capt. Wm. Green, of the Defiance, captured in 1778.
[†]"Narrative of John Kilby", *Scribner's Magazine*, July, 1905

Majesty and his pardon too.' The gates were opened and one hundred of us, the first on the list, (when I say the first on the list I mean this, that as we were committed so we stood on the list, unless put back under the penalty before mentioned), were marched out under guard. There were one hundred of us with Captain John Harris at our head."

The prisoners went directly from Portsmouth to Nantes on a French vessel, and at the French port Kilby and many other seamen shipped with John Paul Jones.

A letter to a now unknown correspondent throws some light on Harris's fortunes:

"Some time in the year 1779, while I was in Fortune Prison in England, I received a Letter from a Doct'r Brehan, who had made his escape from said Prison, that if I shou'd be so fortunate as to make my Escape also, to apply to certain Gentlemen in London who would supply me with Cash to forward me to France, & when I should arrive at Paris to apply to the Honble Arthur Lee Esqr That he would Furnish me with every necessary, for he himself received many favours from said Gentleman—When I arrived at Nantes I wrote to Doct'r Franklin, also to Doct'r Lee in behalf of many of the Prisoners who came over with me in the same Sloop that was in a Distressed condition. I received an answer by the Return of the Post from Doct'r Lee who informed me of his being out of office at that time, but that if I would Draw up a Remonstrance in behalf of those people he would do everything in his power that Doct'r Franklin would relieve them, at the same time expressing himself very feelingly for those poor men who had Risked & suffered in the Cause of American Liberty— While I was in France I had an opportunity of hearing the sentiments of many Gentlemen respecting the character of Doct'r Lee & I must confess I heard with pleasure that he was the true Friend to America & the Honest man & that his Honesty was the cause of his being not in office at that time particulars of which I heard from Commodore Gillon* & many other Gentlemen, but do not well recollect, but it was some-

---

*Commodore Alexander Gillon, of the South Carolina State Navy, went abroad in 1778 to negotiate a loan on indigo.

thing respecting the publick money, I have since seen some American Prisoners that was confined with myself that said that when they got to Paris that Doct'r Lee was their Friend mentioning that Silas Dean was partial to his countrymen upon the whole, as I never before this present session had the Honor of seeing him hope no one will suppose I have any other Interest but Declare what I know to be the truth.

JOHN HARRIS."

Lt. George Chamberlaine and Lt. Byrd Chamberlayne* were back in Virginia certainly before June 25, 1778, on which date they were "given leave of absence for a fortnight", as appears in the Navy Board Journal, and Capt. Dick returned probably early the following year. The last-mentioned officer, on November 22, 1779, presented to the Virginia House of Delegates a petition praying payment of a debt of 1650 guineas contracted through his imprisonment and his subsequent escape and appealing at the same time for advancement in rank.

Capt. Harris†, whose wife had died during his absence, was in Virginia again late in the year 1779. A visit to Richmond was reported in the *Gazette* of January 8, 1780. Re-entering the Virginia naval service as captain of the ship Oliver Cromwell, he continued until his last illness in the spring of 1782.

Lieut. Catlett, of the marines, returned in the spring of 1781, "with feelings so violent from the treatment he had received that he would never have left the service as long as there was a chance of fighting", on the testimony of a former fellow-prisoner, who furthermore affirmed that the sentiment thus expressed was shared in by all.

The Mosquito's sailing-master, Charles de Kay, for whom, on August 5, 1778, the Virginia Assembly had voted a warrant of 46 dollars in specie to repay a loan from Capt. Harman Courtier, remained with some others of the crew in gaol until

---

*Lieut. Byrd Chamberlayne, in command of a small armed vessel is said to have captured a large merchant-man off the coast of North Carolina sometime previous to his service on the Mosquito. Details of this achievement are lacking.

†An article on Capt. Harris, with cut of a miniature likeness, was published by General Walter Drew McCaw, U. S. A., in the *Virginia Magazine of History and Biography*, Vol. XXII, p. 160 *et seq.*

the close of the war. John Paullin and another died in the prison.

About a month after the loss of the Mosquito occurred the capture of the "Cruizer Brigg" Raleigh. This vessel, of sixteen guns, had been in service since the spring of 1776. On July 12 of that year her then commander, James Cocke, was directed to cruise with the Barrons and to transfer with great secrecy a large portion of the powder on the Eastern Shore to Hampton and Williamsburg. On October 24 Capt. Travis was designated to command the brig, in case that Capt. Cocke were willing to resign, and the same day Capt. Wm. Green, of the Defiance, was directed to turn over to the Raleigh as many men as he could spare.

With Travis commissioned captain and Robert Gray lieutenant, the Raleigh, duly supplied and equipped by Capt. Lilly, was sent on a cruise in April, 1777, with the West Indies in view. This goal was never attained. The brig had been but a few days at sea when she was assailed by the British frigate Phenix, and, despite her efforts to outdistance the Briton, she was captured and convoyed to New York. In the hulks in that harbor the Virginian crew was submitted to such rigorous treatment that, upon a representation of their wretched condition, retaliation was ordered upon the crew of the British sloop-of-war Solebay captured by one of the ships of the Commonwealth. John Anderson and Jonathan Barrett were among the members of the Raleigh's crew who died in captivity.

CHAPTER V

OVERSEAS ADVENTURING

The urgent need for supplies and munitions impelled the Government of Virginia, in 1777, to send out vessels directly to France, and the first singled out for this enterprise, with its chances and dangers, were the Congress and the Liberty.

Not long after her return from a profitable voyage to the West Indies Boucher's former flagship, laden with 105 hogsheads of fine tobacco and carrying an invoice of merchandise and muniments for her return, was dispatched to Pliarne, Penet & Company in Nantes. A letter from the Commissary, Aylett, announced that two or three other vessels would soon follow; a top price for the cargo of tobacco was demanded; the brass cannon ordered might be mounted on deck, or, in case they were more than the deck could accommodate, some might be made use of as ballast; Capt. Skinner and his men were to be given a month's pay at Nantes; and, in conclusion, the French house was instructed that "much depends on a Safe & quick return of our vessels from Europe."

Without untoward incident the Congress made her overseas voyage, but the "quick return" encountered unforeseen obstacles. Brass cannon were, for the moment, not to be purchased in France. The ship's detention, it was further explained, arose from the expediency of waiting for longer nights, which "greatly decreased the depredations of privateers in the Channel." Late in August the Congress was "entirely loaded and waiting for the first fair wind", a prospect that must have been long in fulfillment: it was not until October 17 that Pliarne, Penet & Company announced the departure: "We have dispatched your two vessels Ye Congress and Ye Liberty."

Without the brass cannon (later to be furnished by importation from Germany) the Congress reached her home port in safety, towards the end of November, with "a valuable supply of goods", the invoice of which is still to be seen.

Of the further activities of the vessel little is known. There is record that when Daniel Triplett returned to the ship, in 1779, after an interval in the land service, he carried into Philadelphia a prize taken by the Congress *off the Delaware capes. It is also attested that the captain, William Skinner, continued in that capacity until the ship was "laid up", June 1, 1780.

Another transatlantic voyager was the brig Liberty, "a large man of war of 18 guns", which, according to Page, needed, in consequence of her peculiar shape, much pig-iron as ballast. In February, 1776, this vessel under command of Capt. George Gooseley, later successively superintendent of trading vessels and captain of the Thetis, belonged three-quarters to the public and one-quarter to Mr. Wm. Ronald of Yorktown, Ronald's interest was presently reduced to one-eighth, and on March 7 the Council of Safety ordered that "the whole adventure on Board the Brig Liberty," then lying at Cumberland on the Pamunkey, should be taken by the public. Later this same month the brig, with Lilly as master and Thomas, first mate, was fitted out principally for the protection of York River and the inhabitants of its shores.

On August 6, Capt. Lilly, Capt. Travis of the Brig Raleigh, and Deane of the Revenge schooner were directed to join Capt. Cocke and Capt. Calvert of the Norfolk Revenge in Hampton Roads to act in conjunction with them against the enemies of America, "or separately as you think best." This excursion must have been brief, for at the end of the month the Liberty was on her way to take on ballast in Baltimore.

While ballast was being taken in, many of the crew under stress were decamping, as exposed in a petition to the Naval Board, dated Oct. 11, by the warrant officers of the Liberty, Joseph Willson, John Chick, Thomas Coleman, Thomas Bailey, John Royston, who had "determined at the risque of their lives" not to remain silent longer, but to protest against the "Arbitrary Tyrannical unmanly & illiberal behaviour and treatment of their commander Capt. Thomas Lilly occasioned

---

*There was in the commercial service a sloop Congress under the command of Capt. Robert Pulley.

by the desertion of the Common Sailors who could not and would not submit, the Complement of Seamen being reduced to four and one Boy. Whilst they lay at Baltimore thirteen sailors and four marines deserted."

"As freemen," proceeded the protestants on the Liberty, "we think it the essential right of Free Mariners to speak openly. That your petitioners the Warrant Officers were compelled to the Duty of Common Sailors."

The gunner, John Chick, declared that "when very sick he was called up wantonly to load & charge the guns." Massenburg, sailing-master, complained of contradictory orders. Coleman, the pilot, had had his crosses and clashes with Lilly. The genteel John Royston revealed that, when the brig was at Baltimore, the marines and common sailors were huddled into a miserable loft infested with sinister insects and obliged "to Diet & Lodge together without distinction." Not having received one shilling of pay, he was forced "to sell his cloaths to raise Money to pay his Washing Woman" her score. The messmates faced "food cooked intolerably bad & were refused the small privilege of being allowed to dress it themselves."

Capt. Lilly, whose attendance was required at Williamsburg, won the day and the Naval Board decided that the charges were not sufficiently proved. Yet permission was given to petty officers with grievances to remove from the brig, and some immediately did.

Capt. Lilly, in straits, was directed to ship four of the captured Oxford's Scots as Virginia seamen, if they gave him a favorable ear, and, on November 4, Capt. Brooke of the Scorpion was charged to turn over all the sailors he could spare to the Liberty*, that had an immediate voyage in view. It was doubtless on this cruise that the ship Jane, with a cargo of West Indian goods valued at £6,000, was seized by the Liberty. The Jane's captain, David Wallace, was given

---

*Officers of the Liberty, under Capt. Lilly, at this time were: Thomas Herbert, 1st lt.; John Rogers, 2d lt.; Alexander Massenburg, 3d lt.; John Wilson, sailing master; John Bingham and Timothy Laws, midshipmen; Dawson Cook, acting midshipman; Robert Culley, carpenter; Samuel Mercer, boatswain; Thos. Coleman, pilot; John Chick, gunner; James Douglas, master-at-arms.

permission to join, on parole, his family in England; the Commissary of Stores was requested and empowered by the Virginia Council to purchase the Jane. Later, Lilly was once more making an effort to fill out his complement, but he was soon diverted to other activities. On April 8 he was directed to repair to Pepper Creek and see to the finishing of the galley there building, and of this new craft, planned for a prisonship, he was appointed the captain.

To the command of the Liberty Lieut. Thomas Herbert, known as "Silverfist" from a metal device he employed to take the place of the left hand he had lost, succeeded, and with a cargo of 105 hogsheads of tobacco and 7200 staves the new captain was ordered to proceed on a voyage to Nantes. On August 26 the mercantile house of Pliarne, Penet & Co. wrote that the Liberty had safely arrived in the river.

The cargo unloaded, the French firm, with commercial enterprise but without license from the Virginia Government, proceeded to arm the brig for reasons explained: "We have furnished Capt. Thomas Hervey (Herbert) with six pieces of ordnance that he may defend himself." "Silverfist", however, did not restrict himself to defense, but, with the example of the daring John Paul Jones under his eyes, issued from Nantes to try his luck at privateering himself, and, in due course, "divers prizes" were taken. Touching one of his adventures, which brought him mishap, he himself, seventeen years later, bore evidence: "On the 22 day of—[took] the Brig I. D. Ann belonging to Malaga in Spain bound to the port of London in the course whereof the petitioner had his left knee broken by the dismantling of one of the Brig Liberty's guns, which so disabled him that he could not walk for a considerable time without assistance*."

This capture, under a prize master, was dispatched to Martinique, whence Richard Harrison wrote to Aylett on December 21, 1777: "I have the pleasure to Inform you that the Brigantine Idea and Ann, a prize taken by the Liberty, Capt. Herbert, has got into a safe port of this Island. She is

---

*Petition to the Virginia Assembly, Nov. 13, 1794.

loaded with Raisins, Figs, Wine &c from Malaga to England, but as the Invoice & other papers were destroyed, I cannot tell what the Quantity of either until she is discharged, I have sent craft alongside to Receive the Cargoe, and propose sending the Brigantine forward to you with a Lite Load of Salt if she is in a condition to proceed & the Salt can be provided. As the Prize Master tells me she is a Stout Vessel & deeply charged & I promise myself a tolerable market for the goods** be pleased to direct in what manner to apply the Proceeds of the Musketos Prise which I have now some hopes of Recovering, having engaged our general himself in the matter."

Before long, however, Harrison discovered that raisins in frails are short-lived in a sub-tropical climate and planned to dispatch a consignment to Boston. Contrary to the earlier impressions, the captured brig proved to be in "such a wretched Situation" that even a "Lite load of Salt" might bring her to grief.

After sending the Brig I. D. Ann on her determined way, "Silverfist", despite his new physical handicap, pursued his success by taking the so-called "Portland prize", whose indirections were set forth in a letter of January 31, 1778, from Samuel Phips Savage, President of the War Office in Boston, to the authorities in Virginia: "We take the earliest opportunity to Acquaint you of the Arrival of a Prize Sloop taken by Capt. Robert (*sic*) Herbert in your Privateer Brigantine Liberty, the Circumstances of which as given in by the Prize Master Mr. Seth Cobb, are as follows, On the 5th of November the Sloop near the Rock of Lisbon on her Passage from Malaga to London laden with Lemmons and Raisins was Captur'd the prize Man'd, keeping on board two persons belonging to her, and the Prize Master order'd to proceed to North Carolina, after keeping Company Two days with the Brigantine, was by a Gale of wind Sepperated and after attempting to get to her Design'd port was forc'd by a Series of Misfortunes into Mount Desert, one of the most Eastern Ports of this State from whence he proceeded & with Dificulty got into a Town to the Eastward Call'd York, part of which time for Want of Suitable Provisions the people were obliged to eat Raisins for the

Support of Life, not a Man board Except the Master and Mate fit for duty and the Sails almost blown to Pieces, he there protested, and taking a Pilot on Board left that Port, Design'd for Boston, but was forced into Squam a back Port on Cape Ann where he had the Additional Misfortune to get on a Bar, which oblig'd him partly to unload his Vessel from whence the Master came to Boston by Land and apply'd to the Members of this Board for advice and assistance***"

* * * *

Evidence points to two additional prizes to the Liberty's credit. Lt. James Meriwether, of the marines, is said to have been placed as prize master on an Irish vessel that the Virginia brig captured, and another affiant bore witness that a British ship bound from Liverpool to Quebec, laden with naval stores, was brought safely into Little York under the care of Joseph White, the brig's master-pilot.

Yet Capt. Herbert himself encountered his greatest peril in port. Near Hampton he was run aground by the enemy, with the consequent loss of his papers and the near loss of his cargo, "prevented, at the considerable expense of Capt. George Muter of the Hero Galley, from falling into the hands of the enemy," and Capt. Lilly was awarded fifty pounds by the Naval Board, "for getting off the Brig Liberty and most of her cargo." Capt. Herbert himself entered a claim to reimbursement for money advanced to the men on the cruise.

In the year 1778 a second overseas voyage was in contemplation for the Liberty, repaired at Frazer's Ferry "upon a principle of frugality," as disclosed in a letter of Thomas Smith to Capt. James Gray, formerly of the prison-ship Gloucester, directing him, with words of warning and wisdom and promises of professional advancement, to embrace the first favorable opportunity to proceed to Nantes with his brig, "launching into an Element filled with Enemies whose unrelenting Hands you have felt the weight of**keeping always upon the defensive your situation as to Men & Arms is at Stake, but as to the State a safe Voyage will be a great step towards laying a foundation for your future welfare. On return come into Chincoteague, Matompkin, Machpungo or Sandy Shoal, but give preference to Cape Charles for reasons I have personally observed to you, the Idea of Ocracock & Carituck frights me, they are places every person acquainted with them should avoid."

It may be inferred that the projected voyage was never accomplished. Towards the end of the year the Liberty, Capt. George Rogers, with his brother John Rogers second in command, was captured by a British cruiser, off Buckroe. Her officers and crew were taken to New York, and in prison there Capt. Rogers and the surgeon, Joseph Harrison, died.*

Still another ship that crossed the Atlantic was the Greyhound, the record of which is unhappily meagre. The brigantine was built at Minge's Ferry under the superintendence of Capt. Edward Wonnycutt, who became the new vessel's commander. Late in November, 1777, she set out for France with her cargo, bearing incidentally Patrick Henry's reply to William Lee, who had solicited the State's business in Europe. A second communication to Lee, dated December 15, suggested that as "the Brigg Greyhound is a very swift sailing vessel she had better return here loaded with salt than be sold."†

Before February, 1778, the brig was once more in Virginia, and was soon engaged in salvage operations, as disclosed in a letter of the State Agent Thomas Smith to Mr. Archibald Richardson, on April 10, "no time is to be lost going down to Suffolk, thence in quest of the Brigg Greyhound, Capt. Ed. Wonnycutt, who, I am informed, is assisting to raise the

---

*Alexander Massenburg remained in prison until 1783. Armistead Culley, the ship's carpenter, is said to have frequently recounted his sufferings in captivity, after his return to Virginia. His brother, Robert Culley, affirmed that the Liberty was taken to Halifax.

The Brig Liberty should not be confused with the *Boat* of that name commanded by Capt. Richard Barron, which never fell into the hands of the enemy. Then there was the *Sloop* Liberty, engaged in the Trading Department. This last-mentioned vessel (at one period called the Independence) was, late in 1776, under command of Aaron Jeffries, with John Archer lieut. *vice* Wm. Gray. Later, her captain, Walter Brooke, was succeeded by William Ivy, and Ivy was followed by Capt. Bayne (or Baynes), who made frequent trips to St. Eustatius and to St. Croix during the succeeding two years.

†A Schooner Pilotboat Greyhound was in the Virginia commercial service before the Brig Greyhound was built, It was presumably this trading vessel that George Rogers commanded for some months after leaving the Mosquito.

Defiance Galley commanded by Capt. Wright Westcott." Not long after this a mysterious calamity had befallen Wonnycutt's vessel; on June 22, Smith, writing to the same correspondent, referred darkly to "the unfortunate Greyhound" and hinted at some culpable lapse on the part of the captain, without committing himself to details.

So far as appears, no further attempts at direct overseas contacts were made in Virginian bottoms. On November 29, 1777, the Council had recourse to the following plan: "That we endeavor to establish a credit in France for whatever Goods we may want in future, to be shipped in French Vessels & as French property to Cape Francois & re-shipped there in our swift sailing Boats, engaging to pay for the said Goods by shipping Tobacco sufficient for that Purpose in any Vessels our Correspondents may send for it."

And this method was, in the future, pursued.

CHAPTER VI

HENRY BUILDS HIS HOPES ON HIS MOST CHRISTIAN MAJESTY

The year 1778 dawned ominously, with the British in occupation of the deeper waterways of Virginia—"they lord it here at present," candidly conceded the Governor—throttling with a 64-gun ship and four 24-gun frigates the commerce of the Commonwealth.

And one ship fell to them by the treacherous dealing of a body of militia "assembled as well for the purpose of protecting the said vessel as for preventing the Enemy's making depredations or receiving or procuring provisions." In January the French Snow Elégante was the victim of this extraordinary treachery. "A certain Captain Yerby of Lancaster County," ran the indictment, "did in a false Traitorous & wicked manner aid and assist British Ships of War [lying in Rappahannock] in taking & making prize of a Ship or Vessel being French property which trading in this State was entitled to its protection."

The justly outraged Captain Collinau of the Elégante presented a memorial to the Governor, who publicly expressed his horror, directed the Treasurer to indemnify the French captain to the amount of five thousand pounds for vessel and cargo betrayed, and urged severe measures against Yerby and those implicated with him.

This was, for the time, an isolated case. The Army and the Navy were, almost to a man, unwaveringly loyal, but of their ability to cope with the force of circumstance Henry entertained more serious doubts.

The preceding autumn (November 4, 1777) Richard Harrison, from St. Pierre, had written to Virginia: "2000 French troops lately arrived. These troops I imagine will rest idle till the Spring, when it is probable there will be some work carved out for them. I would not, however, wish my Countrymen to confide too far in Such an Event—Their own Manly Exertions will be the surest means of Success, and their Success, the surest means of gaining them friends."

Governor Henry, however, made no secret of the fact that, unable to stand alone, he was only too ready to supplement "manly Exertions" with succor that lay over the water. "I have no expectation," he confided to the Agent in France, William Lee, "of facing British power without their aid and co-operation," and he further stressed a suggestion that, inasmuch as Virginia had not a sufficiency of ships to transport tobacco overseas, France should be solicited to sent out swift sailers, which might put into Smith River, north of Cape Charles, to take on tobacco in exchange for their cargoes. Munitions of war with the exception of cannon might, in his judgment, be transported with comparative safety to Raleigh Colston at Cape Francois, and thence transferred, for importation into Virginia, to the Commonwealth's fast-sailing vessels.

At this trying time Henry had cheering news of an accession from over the water. In May the 50-gun Brave Fier Roderique, of Rochefort, formerly the King's ship "Hippotame", visited the waters of Hampton, from the mercantile house of Beaumarchais and Company at Nantes, her arrival hailed, perhaps with some coloring, by the agent Chevallie, as "one of the most fortunate events that could have happened, absolutely necessary to her [Virginia's] preservation as a State." This windfall, laden with supplies and munitions including cannon, had successfully flouted the stormy protests of the peppery British Ambassador, Lord Stormont, within, and the hostile privateers in waiting, without. Providentially, Chevallie's enthusiasm was not damped by foreknowledge that as late as 1793 he would be appealing to the Virginia Assembly for a debt that even then, as he claimed, was not fully discharged.

As a protection to further friendly visitors three State galleys were detailed, upon a sudden resolve of the Navy Board, to guard the North, or Cape Charles, Channel, a force which, it was conceded, would furnish slender resistance to a concentration of hostile vessels. In the face of the perils in the Bay negotiations were in progress with Governor Johnson for the dispatch of Maryland galleys to co-operate with those of Virginia for the protection of trade in the inner waters.

And the difficult Ocracock Inlet was to have a protector. In April Capt. Willis Wilson, with 145 men on his Caswell Galley, announced to the Governor of North Carolina that he was now properly fitted to proceed to Ocracock Bay, and on May 20 he was able to give assurance from his station there that the place was not at all infested with hostile cruisers, adding, "I shall exert myself to keep it so." But this fortunate state of affairs was not of notable duration. On June 29 the North Carolina Executive was informed by Capt. Eaton that cruisers were constantly hovering about the coast and that "Gutteridge (sic) with a brig in company had the week before driven two vessels into a small inlet against Hunting Quarter."*

The month of May, 1778, brought a series of distressing disasters. The Defiance, Captain Green, was captured, but the details are now entirely lacking. On May 28 the Norfolk Revenge, Capt. Wright Westcott, was sunk in Nansemond River, with a loss of prisoners, including Lieut. Edward Morton, who died in captivity. Capt. Westcott and those of his officers and crew who escaped were directed by the Naval Board to proceed directly to Jamestown, and the captain of the trading vessel "Peace and Plenty" was charged to salvage everything worth saving from the wreck of the hapless Revenge.

Something sinister befell the Lewis. The story as recounted by one attestant is as follows: The galley, stationed in York River, was assailed by a superior force. The commander retreated up the river. The enemy pursued. The fleeing vessel turned into Carter's Creek and, by favor of the high tide, ran into a millpond on a level with the outer water in consequence of the collapse of the dam. In this hiding place the enemy discovered the galley and set her afire. The officers and crew

---

*"North Carolina Archives," Vol. XII, p. 560. Capt. Hance Bond and Lt. Samuel Gardner raised a company of marines for the Caswell. In November following, the Naval Committee of Congress wrote to the Boston Naval Board: "At present we consider it an Object of Importance to destroy the infamous Goodrich, who has much infested our coast, cruising with a squadron of 4, 5 or 6 armed vessels, from 16 guns downward from Egg Harbour to Cape Fear, North Carolina."

saved themselves from capture by flight to the neighboring woods.

The one flaw in this picture is the fact that the Lewis appears in the records time and again after this period. What actually happened can only be guessed.

And now French vessels on a more militant mission were announced to be skirting the coast. In mid-July a report was current in Williamsburg that a French fleet of sixteen, believed to be that of D'Estaing, had fallen in with five English men-of-war, two of which they sank, captured two, and ran the fifth one ashore. It was "confidently believed" that the visitors had taken pilots aboard and sailed for New York. Apart from the truth or inexactitude of this agreeable rumor, the vice-admiral of France was beyond question in American waters, and, in the course of events, was feted and supplied with provisions in Philadelphia, encountered Howe and a tempest with indecisive result, proceeded to Boston to refit, and, after experiencing there a checkered reception, set sail in November for the West Indies.

Virginia, left unsupported to deal with her pirates, girded for action. Towards the close of July the request of certain private persons of enterprise for permission to fit out vessels to hunt down the Goodriches found favor in the eyes of the Governor. Two months later Thomas Whiting, first commissioner, announced to the Naval Board that the Tartar, the Dragon and the Northampton, properly manned and everyway fitted for a cruise, only waited for orders, and it was accordingly ordered that these ships-of-war should at once put out to sea "cruising backwards and forwards within fifty Leagues of the Land and using their utmost diligence to capture the Enemy's cruisers particularly those commanded by the Goodriches." And if the Committee thought proper, the flotilla, on return from the first trip southward, was to cruise a little farther to the northward "in expectation of falling in with the Continental Frigates expected at this Station," an anticipation which, so far as the records reveal, remained unfulfilled.

During the autumn, when the news from South Carolina was disquieting, Congress sought from Virginia, to the appreciable embarrassment of the Executive, a contribution of armed galleys, to be fitted out with all possible dispatch as a contingent of the expedition contemplated against East Florida, a plan, which, though still agitated in January, 1779, was, for compelling reasons, discarded. For the information of the President of Congress Henry particularized Virginia's equipment: "We have two vessels called Ship Gallies drawing eight and nine feet of water, carrying about eighteen 3 or 4 pounders; one of them formed for use of two heavy guns in the Bow in still water with men & about six smaller gallies, calculated for the Bay or Rivers, but not esteemed to be Seaworthy." He conjectured, however, that the Galley in Ocracock, if found fitted for sea, might serve the purpose of Congress. For the protection of the South Inlet a substitute galley might serve. Yet, in the end, after taking stock of all possibilities, the Governor singled out the Dragon and the Tartar ships-of-war as Virginia's share of the project.

In November the sea yielded a prize to the patriots. The British ship-of-war Swift, in chase of the privateer Rattlesnake, ran ashore near Cape Henry, and her crew fell into the hands of a hastily assembled band of Princess Anne County militia. The fate of the Swift is not further recounted.

It was probably in this year 1778 that Lieutenant Richard Servant, nephew of Commodore Barron, lost his life heroically, as related in later years by his cousin, Capt. Samuel Barron: "Richard Servant, who had been 1st Lieut. of the armed boat Liberty, under Captain James Barron, was at the period of the incident on furlough and in command of an armed schooner belonging to the brothers James and Robert Barron and other persons, and he was killed in an action off Cape Henry, Virginia, after one of our most remarkably hard fights, but altho the force against him was ten to one—ten armed privateers to one armed merchantman-schooner of about eighty tons, he beat them all off until he so far entered our Bay as to run his vessel ashore about Crump's Hill or abreast of what is or used to be called the 'Pleasure House' (Lynnhaven Bay).

"Before he ran ashore he received his first wound in his right thigh, but as the bone was not broken he kept the deck and probably would have succeeded in his hope to reach Hampton, for he had gained the advantage of the Bay shore, and proceeded along in it only a few feet more than his vessel drew, but when the second shot struck him he knew his absence from the deck would tempt the enemy on board and then all would be lost. He ordered the vessel to run ashore, the militia came down, and drove the enemy off—several of his men were also wounded, and took him off and saved the property.

"The last ball went through his body and in two days after he died. His body was brought to Hampton and buried. A Captain Kemp commanded the Corps d honneur. I was present at his funeral and have not forgotten my tears, nor the bitterness of my feelings, for he was my favorite cousin, and I loved him dearly—he was handsome, amiable and much beloved."

CHAPTER VII

THE TARTAR, THE DRAGON AND THE TEMPEST

These three vessels,* associated in enterprise in 1778, were given their devastating names, presumably with the design of striking terror into their adversaries.

The Tartar, Capt. Caleb Hunter, "Undertaker", was begun in August, 1776, at the Frazer's Ferry shipyard, on Mattaponi River, and her ironwork was done chiefly by Mr. Frazer himself. On July 5, 1777, while the vessel was still on the stocks, Richard Taylor was appointed her captain.

The Tempest, also a product of Frazer's, was of later completion. It is recorded that First Midshipman Benjamin Strother was active in recruiting her crew, that she sailed for some time in Chesapeake Bay, was anchored near Hampton Fort for a period, and later, in a skirmish off Hog Island, captured a British brig, of which last-mentioned action no particulars are given.

The Dragon was an inspiration of Col. Fielding Lewis of Fredericksburg, and in that town her keel was laid in the late autumn of 1776. Capt. Callender, formerly of the Defiance, was assigned to superintend the building of the galley in December, 1776, and on October 9 of the following year he was

---

*Officers of the Tartar at this time: Richard Taylor, capt.; Merryman Payne, 1st lt.; Wm. Richards, 2d. lt.; Wm. Payne, midshipman; John Reynolds, surgeon. A later roll of the Tartar shows in 1779: Wm. Saunders, capt.; Wm. Parker, lt.; John Tupper, sailing-master; Justice Livingston, doctor. The Tempest, in 1778, had the following officers: Celey Saunders, capt.; Michael James, 1st lt.; Wm. Steele, 2d lt.; Benjamin Strother, 1st midshipman; John Robins, 2d midshipman; John Pierce, 3d midshipman; Allen Saunders, boatswain; John Wilkinson, boatswain's mate; Thomas Landrum, surgeon's mate.

Officers of the Dragon, not long after she went into service were: Eleazer Callender, capt.; John Hamilton, 1st lt.; Midshipmen Francis Webb; Alvin Wilson; Joshua McWilliams; and Benjamin Rust; sailing-master Wolling Smith; gunner, Iveson Nuttall; gunner's mate, John Nuttall. Later, Samuel Eskridge, Edward Eskridge, and James Tutt were midshipmen, and Theophilus Field was lt., on the Dragon.

appointed her captain, with John Lurty of the Page galley named first lieutenant.

The Dragon's first year of service was passed on the Rappahannock River, not without stirring incident. It is related that, in a sudden gale at a time when the ship was hourly expecting an engagement with the enemy, one of her masts gave way. Immediately George Daniel, the carpenter, went into the woods close at hand, fashioned a new mast, and had it in place in a few hours' time, and the ship ready for action, to the dumb astonishment of the whole crew. George Daniel grew into a proverb for dispatch and efficiency.

In the spring of 1778 there were larger plans for the Tartar, the Dragon and the Tempest, with the Northampton assisting. In March Captain Callender was ordered to put the Dragon in the best order he could and proceed with her to York. Soon after, Capt. Tompkins was directed to supply the Tartar with six six-pounders from his galley, the Henry. The Tempest was likewise equipped with more muniment. And there was the usual draught of men from other ships to make up the complement of those singled out for action. On April 11 Captains Taylor, Callender and Bright were commissioned to set off to Cape Charles on the Eastern Shore for the purpose of surveying every channel there and determining a station of comparative security for Taylor's flotilla.

The summer passed without any movement of moment, but in September the Naval Board concluded that all was ready for a cruise of importance, and State Agent Smith, possessed of this knowledge, counselled Capt. Joseph Wrenn, of the schooner Defiance intending a cruise to Cape Francois, to secure the convoy of this fleet, from York River as far on his way as might be. With or without Capt. Wrenn under convoy, the Tartar, the Tempest, the Dragon, the Northampton and a tender started with sealed orders ("destination unknown** on an offensive against the island of Bermuda", as one of the participants put it), and in their company went two ships from Philadelphia.

The expedition was briefer than had been anticipated. Several days after leaving the Capes they descried two large vessels* that turned out to be the Roebuck and the Emerald, with a large sloop serving as tender. The enemy gave chase to the more numerous but less powerful Americans. In the course of the pursuit the fast-sailing tender drew so close to the Northampton that she had her quarry under fire and came near cutting her off from her companions. The rest of the Virginia flotilla, however, slackened sail that the slower boat might keep up with them, and soon with the oncoming darkness all, by separating and changing their course, eluded the pursuers and eventually reached in safety their stations within the Capes.

A month later, when Taylor and his flotilla were lying off Cape Henry, the acting commodore had occasion to take the aggressive. A hostile privateer, the Lord Howe, suddenly came in sight and bore down on the Dragon, whose crew housed their guns, concealed themselves for the moment, and let sails hang loosely, some at half-mast. As the Howe came up she discovered her mistake in the character of her opponent, and, discharging a broadside as she ran by, hauled off to escape. Meanwhile Captain Taylor in the Tartar, hearing the firing, sailed up accompanied by his tender, the Boat Patriot of six swivel guns, to "know what it meant," and, on learning the course of affairs, threw twenty-one men into his tender, which was the swifter vessel, and, taking command of her in person, gave chase to the enemy. When he overtook the Howe at about an hour's sun in the evening, he found that she mounted eight four-pounders and carried a proportionate number of men. However, despite the great inequality of force, the American commander "was induced," as he afterwards explained it, "to hazard an engagement in consequence of the great injury to trade from the number of British cruisers plying off the coast."

Now, as the Patriot moved forward to the attack, she ran foul of the Briton, her jib-boom passing through one of the Howe's quarter-deck windows. While the Howe was lying in this unusual position a party from the Patriot attempted to

*One veteran of this affair declared there was but one hostile ship—of 74 guns.

board her, the twenty-seven year old commander at the bow of his vessel cheering them on. The confidence he inspired showed itself in the courage of his men. For several hours the action was supported with the greatest judgment and valor, with a loss of one Virginian killed and eight wounded, including William Jennings, who has left an account of the battle.

Finally, the Commodore, having received in his thigh a musket-shot which in its passage shattered the bone above the knee, was left incapacitated to continue the action and, finding himself unsupported by the other vessels of the squadron, he gave orders to the sailing-master, Brittain, to sheer off from the enemy, who made no attempt to pursue. The Patriot, Lieut. Hamilton commanding, sailed with the seriously wounded commodore under the care of the surgeon, John Reynolds, for the Capes. Why the Dragon failed to come to the aid of the Patriot is not clearly explained, but Taylor is said to have been so angry at what he considered inexcusable neglect on the part of Capt. Callender that he refused to speak to him when the two met the next day. On the other hand, the Northampton, lying under Smith's Island in sight of the engagement, is said to have fired a shot at the British schooner and made every effort to make headway, but, owing to "the prevalence of hostile breezes," found herself thwarted.

Without any mark of disfavor from the Naval Board Callender kept his vessel at Yorktown refitting for about a fortnight and then went on a cruise of the Bay, in the course of which he recaptured from the enemy two Virginia vessels laden with flour. He then sailed beyond the Capes as far as the mouth of the Delaware, "often chasing, oftener chased by the enemy", as a veteran of the expedition tersely recalled.

The first months of the succeeding year found him in command of squadron for the protection of the Bay, with Metompkin Inlet on the Eastern Shore as its base. *

---

*The sources for this chapter are, in addition to the Journal of the Navy Board, the land bounty and pension papers of James Burke, Lewis Hinton, Wm. Jennings, Dr. John Reynolds, Lt. Joseph Saunders, and Capt. Richard Taylor.

CHAPTER VIII

OUTWITTING THE MARAUDERS OF THE INLETS

The events recorded below are not strictly a part of the annals of the Virginia Navy, but, in view of the fact that hostile barges were a constant target for the efforts of the naval force, an exploit against Kidd's marauders may not be regarded as altogether alien to the present narrative.

In order to have a better understanding of the course of the happenings, it is important to get the topography of the region fixed in one's mind. All along the coast both of the Bay side and the ocean side of the Eastern Shore of Virginia stretches, at varying distances from the mainland, a succession of sandbars, marshes, and islands. Between these and the shore at the scene of this episode, lies a comparatively smooth expanse known as "The Broadwater", extending from which small arms, or creeks, indent the shore, many penetrating far inland to a heading of lowground or marsh. Between the islands or sandbars are found channels of various depths, along which vessels must pass from the sea to reach safe anchorage within.

The house of Col. John Cropper, an officer already distinguished in the Continental Line and now at home on furlough, occupied a site on the north side of and close to an inlet known as Folly Creek, which debouched into "The Broadwater" at a point nearly opposite Metompkin, one of the gateways to the ocean. It was through this sea passage that, before dawn one morning early in the year 1779, there entered several barges under the command of Commodore Kidd, a Scotchman with a pseudonym borrowed, it is said, from that notorious corsair who met his end in London a half-century before. Undetected, the invaders approached the mouth of Folly Creek, disembarked, and, using all stealth, contrived to hedge in their most redoubtable adversary. A few moments later the young colonel awoke to find his premises in the possession of the invaders and himself entrapped and a prisoner of war. Straightway the freebooters set to collecting all the loot that they could conveniently carry, and, not content with pillage and plunder, heaped insults and indignities upon the family.

Two sentries with bayonets fixed, stationed at the colonel's bed-chamber door, kept a close eye on the captive. But the rest of the band were prevailed upon by the courageous and self-possessed Mrs. Cropper to withdraw from the immediate premises—not, however, before they had rounded up thirty odd negroes, either coerced or induced by promises of reward to abscond from their master. The marauders, their boats loaded with the greater part of their booty, then loitered on the shore, seemingly in deliberation over their next errand of mischief.

Even during the earlier tumult and confusion the captive Cropper had racked his brain to discover some way to elude his sentries, seek aid without, and, if possible, fall upon the ruffians and destroy them before they could make off with the goods they had stolen. But how was this to be managed? He was scantily clad and without a weapon, and there at the only practicable exit stood guards apparently alert to his every movement. Since he was already stripped of his portable property, to offer bribes would not be likely to meet with success, while to resort to threats would merely provoke summary vengeance. A little later, when the subsidence of commotion revealed that the greater number of the marauders were at a distance from the house, the prisoner's desire issued into action. At what he judged with the eye of a hawk to be a favorable moment he leaped for the door, bounded over crossed bayonets, as the men made sudden shift to bar his progress, dashed through the outer yard, plunged into the mazes of an adjoining garden, and, outstripping his pursuers and happily escaping their fire, gained in a few minutes the woodland beyond. Others of the pirate band, who had spied the fleeing colonel, rushed up from the shore in full cry with the intention of intercepting his flight, but these were brought to a sudden stop by a hitherto unobserved strip of marshland that lay in their path, and were forced to abandon the chase.

In a brief time the agile Cropper had covered the mile intervening between his house and that of a friend. Here he gave the alarm, realizing, however, that time would not admit of the rallying a force sufficient to deal openly with a hundred well armed desperadoes. What was lacking in numbers and strength he determined to compensate by strategy and audacity. Collecting a few fowling pieces, he put the weapons into the hands of a small group of supporters whom he managed to gather from the immediate neighborhood, and resolved to return at once to Bowman's Folly, confident that men apprehensive with regard to securing their spoils would be more subject to sudden panic from an unexpected attack.

With his backing of comrades, then, Cropper pushed forward, exercising more and more caution as he drew nearer to his objective, and having reached, without exciting suspicion, the inclosure of his garden, in which he and his men were screened from observation by outbuildings and fences, he directed a further stealthy advance in order that, from closer range, he might deceive the marauders into believing that a company of rebels, numerous and well-armed, was upon them.

Things developed exactly as he wanted them to. At a signal agreed on, his followers discharged their firearms repeatedly and raised such a salvo of shouts and fiendish yells of defiance that the marauders, astounded at this totally unexpected outburst, were still more confounded to see Col. Cropper himself dash suddenly forth with all the assurance of the commander of a conquering battalion. Assuming fancy for reality, the whole pirate gang turned tail in confusion, and, leaving a goodly portion of their booty on the shore, scuttled away, scrambled into their boats, drew off and pushed down the creek with all possible speed. It was probably long before they learned how sadly they had been outwitted and hoodwinked.

Shortly after this happy occurrence the young colonel returned to the Headquarters of the Continental Army, applied for and was granted, for reasons of health, an extension of furlough, and came once more to Virginia. But even now he was not to enjoy the repose he had counted on. The want of men of courage, constancy and military experience was keenly felt in a region where those disaffected to the patriot cause abounded and the loyal inhabitants were constantly subject to audacious and vengeful annoyances. To meet this situation Col. Cropper, while retaining his commission as a Continental officer, was induced by the Governor to undertake the direction of the Accomac militia. His skill and experience were soon again put to the test.

The dreaded Kidd was still hovering with his flotilla about the shore of the county. Very early in the year 1780 the chief dispatched one of his tenders, a large schooner-rigged barge, to harry the countryside in and about Folly Creek. He had doubtless kept in mind potential plunder left on the shores of this inlet, and was eager, one may assume, to wipe out the stain upon his pirate honor in consequence of the fiasco of his men in that quarter.

The adventuring barge, said to have borne the name Victory, kept to the outer waters until nightfall, that an entry might be made with the greater security. Her crew consisted of some sixty or seventy ruffians and renegades commanded by one of Kidd's lieutenants, whose name is not given. Arrived at Metompkin Inlet, the only practicable channel to the Broadwater for a craft of her draught, the barge proceeded unmolested towards the mouth of Folly Creek, and presently the crew not only gained access to this inlet, which meanders through an expanse of marsh and flat land and almost doubles upon itself, but, their presence still undetected, they had made their way some distance within. Reaching their objective, they dropped anchor, landed, and, before the alarm was fairly given, had already gone about their work of ravage and destruction. Some of the band pushed on to scour the country beyond; others made for Bowman's Folly with the design of pouncing upon their mortal foe, who this time, however, proved altogether too cunning. Yet the work of pillage went on with the full confidence of the gang that, in a brief period, no force sufficient to cope with them could by any possibility be mustered.

While the greater part of the marauders moved further and further from their point of debarcation Cropper was abroad assembling in person and by messengers the district militia. In an amazingly short time he had under his orders a small but determined body of patriots and fearing that, if he should longer delay, Kidd's men might work all possible damage, gain their boats, and make off without hindrance, he lost no time in rushing his company to a point near the mouth of the creek—a locality that demands a word of description that one may understand Cropper's reasoned maneuver.

On the southern shore of Folly Creek and nearly opposite Bowman's Folly was Henry's Point, jutting boldly into the creek and thus commanding its waters both below and above. To accomplish withdrawal by water, the enemy would find it necessary not only to pass this little peninsula, but, in order to avoid the shallows, they must hug its side if they wished to keep in the navigable channel. Fully alive to this, Cropper made his men haul several pieces of ordnance mounted nearby, to a site commanding the channel, while he, with a few trusty followers, concealed himself among the reeds and marsh grass that with small arms they might do as much execution as possible among the crew of the oncoming craft.

The leader's plans did not stop with these provisions. Anticipating the possibility that, despite the disposition of his forces, the enemy might run the gauntlet untouched, he determined to dispute their passage. But how were fresh measures to be taken before the near approach of the barge, the crew of which, now fully conscious of the preparations for their reception, was rapidly regaining the vessel, with a view to expediting retreat. Cropper saw that if he were able to command the sea passage at Metompkin Inlet, he might yet at that point deal his opponents an annihilating blow, even should the arrangements at Henry's Point fail to arrest or to impede their progress. He accordingly dispatched without delay several of the most powerful of his company with specific orders. The service was successfully performed. They actually contrived to transport a cannon across the narrowest part of the Broadwater, and having dragged it with great labor to the designated site, so disposed the piece as completely to command the only outlet for the marauders' craft. Then the men awaited the issue of the forthcoming attempt at Henry's Point, determined to second with all their energies the enterprise of their resourceful commander.

These operations had scarcely been completed when the marauders were seen descending the channel at Folly Creek, obviously in full knowledge of Cropper's devices and with the intention of foiling them. Now as the Victory drew nearer to Henry's Point, the Virginians opened a steady fire in the hope of inflicting appreciable damage before a closer engagement was necessary.

Apparently undeterred, the Victory held on her course, and was presently within range of those posted in the marsh, who, by volleys from their small arms, began seriously to harry the crew. The enemy's position, hemmed in by the narrows of the creek, became one of great peril. Though thus beset, they showed no lack of courage and resolution, returning the fire of those lurking in ambush, and finally, when too hotly annoyed, a group of the seamen, without a moment's hesitation, plunged into the shallow water, and wading across the shallows, made good their footing on the bank. Here a surprise was in store for them. Instead of the numerous band they presumably expected to encounter they found a mere handful to oppose them. These heroes stood their ground as long as prudence permitted, and then, with their leader, retired speedily to a point of safety. But it was only through the bodily strength and devotion of one of his servants in extricating him that Cropper escaped falling into the hands of his vengeful opponents. In his impetuosity in the attack he had ventured out too far in the mire and his leg was swallowed up nearly to the knee.

Meantime the remainder of the barge's crew had, after hotly contested gunfire, succeeded in maneuvering their boat past the guns of Henry's Point, and, having taken aboard their comrades of the landing party, hastened in the effort to make good their escape. Without further interference they gained the Broadwater, and were doubtless already congratulating one another on their rare good fortune, when with astonishment and consternation they detected a new enemy grimly awaiting their approach, on the emplacement at Metompkin Inlet. Whether Col. Cropper had been able to reach this vantage ground in time to take part in this second attack on the Victory is not stated. At any rate, it was through his forethought and initiative that the boat found herself assailed by another menace that resulted to Kidd in the loss of a unit of his flotilla.

The Victory's crew boldly pushed on to the disputed gateway of the ocean. But, as the barge drew within range of the gun on shore, the fire was so accurately directed that the shattered boat started to fill and those who manned her, still suffering from the effects of their recent encounter, were further demoralized. Why the commander did not land his men and make an effort to carry the gun by storm does not appear; possibly his ranks were dangerously thinned and his one hope was to keep the craft afloat long enough to reach a place of security. Such a hope, if it existed, was soon quenched. The Victory did indeed succeed in passing through the Inlet, but hardly had she reached the open sea when she sank, carrying with her to doom nearly the whole of her crew. In this affair neither the casualties sustained by the enemy nor those of the patriots are recorded.

CHAPTER IX

THE UNCOUNQUERED LIBERTY AND THE DOOM OF THE DOLPHIN

Early in 1779 the Governor of Maryland and the Governor of Virginia received in response to their urgent representations as to the necessity of immediate measures towards safeguarding the trade of Chesapeake Bay the assurance that Congress flattered itself that a speedy end would be put to the depredations of Goodridge (Goodrich) and his associates.

Shortly after this heartening forecast from Congress the Virginia Executive, on February 6, was candid with Governor Caswell touching the ineffectiveness of the two galleys built at Virginia's expense in attaining their object of ensuring the safety of trade through Ocracock Inlet, and he further complained that the North Carolina sponsors of this protective arrangement had failed, as he was informed, to duplicate Virginia's contribution in accordance with the original compact.

About this time treachery was at work on one of the State's vessels. While the galley Accomac was lying in Chincoteague under the command of Ishmael Andrews, a British vessel was taken. The captive commander must have been a man of adroitness and most engaging address, for, after a private conversation with Andrews, he was not only repossessed of his vessel, but supplied with powder from the Accomac's magazine as well. And thus equipped, he proceeded to sail straight for Metompkin Bay and put out a landing party that committed many depredations on Col. Custis's estate, before the militia, hastily summoned by Capt. Levin Walker and George Oldham, drove off the marauders. The Americans then got into small boats and followed the enemy as far as Hog Island Inlet, whence they contrived to make off under cover of night and put out to sea.*

---

*This account is from testimony in the land bounty papers of Lt. Robt. Milliner, who resigned from the galley on account of Andrews' behavior. The charge mentioned in the Journal of the Navy Board is "forgery and bribery."

The author of this unbelievable infamy was tried by court-martial and sentenced to death, but the Naval Board "on examining find that the atrocities of which he was convicted, were not cognizable by any of the regulations for the government of the Navy of this State, have thought proper to remit the punishment ordered by the Court Martial have discharged him with ignominy and disgrace from the service, and have turned him over to the civil power for farther trial."

While Congress, designing, at the instance of Gérard, a joint American and French "expedition against the British Colonies to the Northward ** to give the King of France Halifax and Newfoundland," was temporizing with regard to the instant needs of the Chesapeake region, Maryland and Virginia set themselves, unsupported, to the task of defending their commerce. The *Virginia Gazette* of March 26 announced that Captain Callender was to convoy the outward bound vessels clear of the coast, and on April 2 the same organ had the satisfaction of informing its readers "that the squadron under Capt. Callender, is now joined with two large gallies from Maryland commanded by Commodore Grayson and Capt. Nicholson, mounting four 18 and ten 4 pounders each, and well manned: likewise that the Capes have been clear of the enemy for some time past."

The title at the head of this chapter links two memorable exploits of the year 1779—the one a glorious victory and the other a no less glorious loss.

An achievement of the Boat Liberty was recounted by Commodore James Barron, of the United States Navy, in the *Virginia Historical Register*:

"The Schooner Liberty, one of the armed vessels of the Navy of Virginia, was commanded, in the commencement of our revolutionary war, by Captain James Barron, afterwards Commodore Barron, Senior officer of that Navy. The Liberty was the most fortunate vessel in the service, and was the only one, in fact, that ran through the whole contest without being captured by the enemy. Her armament was judiciously arranged, so much so, as to render her superior to British Government vessels of double her size and rate. She was engaged, first and last, in more than twenty sharp actions, but I shall select only one of them for this short account of her.

"In the early spring of 1779, she had an action with the tender to the frigate Emerald, a New England built schooner, called the Fortunatus, of about 120 tons, mounting 10 six pounders, and manned from the Frigate with a crew of fifty seamen; commanded by a Lieutenant named Dickey, a gallant and worthy fellow, as the sequel will show. The Fortunatus came into Hampton Roads in the night during a heavy gale at N. E., and, at daylight next morning, was seen by Capt. Richard Barron (who lived on the banks of the James River opposite the Roads,) getting under way to go to sea again, when he instantly mounted his horse and rode in great haste to Hampton, to inform his brother, Capt. James Barron, of the fact. Volunteers were immediately called for, and as readily obtained from the good old patriotic town, and off started the Liberty in pursuit of the enemy, which she came up with, four or five miles inside of Cape Henry, where a most sanguinary conflict (at least on the part of the English) ensued; which continued for about two hours, during which period most of the crew of the Fortunatus were either killed or wounded, and her fire so much slackened that Capt. Barron was induced to hail her, and request the Lieutenant Commandant to surrender, as he, Captain Barron, had not a man either killed or wounded; and as Lieutenant Dickey was by this time convinced that there was not the least probability of his escape from capture, and the request to surrender was manifestly prompted by motives of humanity, he consented to do so and hauled down his colours. When the boarding officer from the Liberty got on the deck of the Fortunatus, he found that the Lieutenant and four men, were all the crew then able to use a sponge, or a rammer, to load a gun. I ought to state that the ammunition of the Liberty was composed entirely of large-sized musket balls, and 32 of them put in a bag were discharged at every fire from each of her guns, so that 100 of these balls were constantly playing on the crew of the Fortunatus, which will account for the great number of men killed and wounded on board of her, while the fire of the Fortunatus was only five six pounder shot thrown at her enemy in the same time.

"The result of this action was encouraging to the patriots of the Navy of the State; and the officers, crew, and volunteers of the Liberty, sixteen in number, were spoken of in terms highly honourable to them, I wish I could now remember the names of all these worthy persons; it would afford me pleasure to record them along with their deeds in defence of their country. Two of the volunteers I recollect, were Captain Richard Barron, and John King Esq., first Collector of the Port of Norfolk, after the war, and there were several other gentlemen of Hampton whose names I have forgotten. John Gibson was the Gunner. The Lieutenants were so frequently changed in those days, that it is not to be wondered at that I do not remember who they were on this particular occasion. The most of them were masters of merchant vessels, who had been compelled to go to sea in order to obtain clothes suitable to their decent appearance in public.

"The Fortunatus was not considered an efficient vessel for our service and was therefore sold."

The British Lieutenant Dickey was sent as a prisoner to Portsmouth, and will again appear in a scene to which we shall presently come.

The spring that saw this success of the Liberty witnessed also the end of the gallant little Dolphin, which had already had her baptism of fire. The previous year, in the course of a cruise of the Chesapeake, she had made her way as far as Tangier Island and had reached during the night a point near the rendezvous of the enemy without being aware of their proximity. The following morning the British through the haze of early dawn descried the Virginian and, with their two armed barges, made ready to attack. The British ships approached the Dolphin so cautiously and at the same time with such swiftness that she was the target of their fire before her crew were able to man the guns. It was not long, however, before the Dolphin was briskly replying, but in consequence of a considerable reinforcement coming to the aid of the enemy, the Virginian spread her sails, and bore away from the unequal contest. In this brief action the patriots lost five killed and seven wounded, including John Younger, who has left an account of the engagement. The enemy's loss was not less.

And now came the final episode in the career of the Dolphin, with a crew of seventy-five men, commanded by Captain John Cowper, of Nansemond County*. The vessel ready for sea, the intrepid captain set sail from Nansemond Creek in search of outlying privateers. Yet before weighing anchor he had deliberately nailed his flag to the mast, vowing, cost what it might, never to strike it to an enemy. He shaped the course of his vessel over the broad expanse of Hampton Roads, stood away towards Cape Henry, and passed out into the ocean. As the Dolphin's sails became shadowy in the distance watchers at the Cape observed three other vessels take shape on the horizon. Suspense as to the nature of the strangers was brief. Captain Cowper, before he left home, had solemnly resolved that, no matter what the odds against him, he would without hesitation assume the offensive. The Dolphin was accordingly now seen bearing down upon the newcomers, who as promptly closed in to meet the attack. The action which now began was, according to witnesses, a long and apparently doubtful one. Finally, however, the three hostile tenders sheered off and bore away to the eastward, leaving, to the watchers' eyes, no sign of the fourth. It had been a death struggle against hopeless odds. The Dolphin with all on board had gone to her doom.

---

*Philip Chamberlaine, formerly captain of the Hero, was 1st. lt. of the Dolphin; James Cunningham, 2d. lt., and Frank Lennis, 3d. lt.

CHAPTER X

NAVAL DESCENT UPON THE "SINEWS OF THE REBELLION"

On March 27 of the year 1779 Governor Henry addressed to George Mason a jeremiad on the theme of the "various tribes of money makers and stock jobbers of all denominations," who, though affecting to be patriots, were bent on continuing the war "for their own private emolument, without considering that their avarice and thirst for gain must plunge everything (including themselves) in our common ruin. * * Our enemy behold with exultation and joy, how effectually we labor for their benefit, and so far from being in a state of absolute despair, and on the point of evacuating America, are now on tiptoe."

Six weeks later the British were no longer on tiptoe, so far as Virginia was concerned, but they were advancing with a most powerful instrument for a thrust at the "sinews of the rebellion", and of the result of this thrust Sir George Collier sent his account, *May 16, from his flagship, the Raisonable, off Hampton, to General Sir Henry Clinton in New York:

"Sir

After leaving New York the 5th instant with the men of war and transports under my command, I proceeded towards the place of our destination with the most propitious winds, and on the 4th day (from our sailing) made the capes of Virginia. The fleet anchored that night between the sands near Willoughby's point, which they had hardly done, when the most terrible flurry of thunder and lightning, wind and rain came on that I ever recollect; its continuance however was not more than half an hour, and the ships were all so fortunate as to escape driving on shore. At sunrise we saw some rebel

---
*This letter was published in the *Virginia Gazette* of September 25, 1779.

ships and vessels in Hampton road, with their sails loose, who, as soon as the tide admitted of it, got under weigh and ran up Elizabeth and James rivers; our fleet also weighed, and the Raisonable anchored shortly after in Hampton road, her great draught of water not admitting her going farther with convenience.

"I immediately shifted my broad pennant to the Rainbow, and proceeded with the fleet up Elizabeth river, till a contrary wind and the ebb tide obliged us to anchor; the following morning being calm prevented the ships from moving with the floods, on account of the narrowness and intricacy of the channell, and as the intended place of descent was not more than five or six miles distant, and the General, anxious to lose no time, embarked the first division in the flatboats, and covered by the Cornwallis galley and 2 boats, that carried a six pounder at each end, proceeded up and landed without opposition at the glebe, which is distant about three miles from Portsmouth. The Fort fired some heavy guns at the gally which the distance rendered of no effect.

"A favourable breeze having arose, brought the ships up even before the first division had got on shore, and the remainder of the troops with the field artillery, &c. were landed immediately with the utmost expedition, the movements of the army afterwards General Mathew will best explain to your Excellency. The rebels still kept their colours flying at the fort, from which circumstance we judged they intended to make some defence, though we did not expect much. To give them no time however to throw up fresh works, or for waiting to be reinforced by more rebel troops, it was agreed between the General and myself, that the Rainbow should move up with the morning tide before the fort, and that the troops should attack it at the same time on the land side, the enemy however saved us the trouble by quitting it that evening, and we took possession of the fort and town of Portsmouth, as also of Norfolk, which was on the opposite side of the river, without resistance.

"The enemy by this surrender, lost several ships and vessels which fell into our hands, some were burnt by themselves, among which were two large French ships which were said to be loaded with 1000 hogsheads of tobacco.

"Apprehending that many rebel vessels had pushed up the river, I despatched the Cornwallis galley, two gun boats, four flat boats manned and armed, together with four privateers, which had desired to receive orders from me under the command of Lieutenant Bradley, assisted by Lieutenants Hitchcock and Johnson, in pursuit of them. They were very successful in their enterprise, taking and burning a great number of the enemy's vessels, many of which were on the stocks for launching. Amongst the captures was the Blacksnake, a rebel privateer of 14 guns, who, after being cannonaded by the gun boats, was carried by boarding with the loss of some of the rebels, but on our side, two men only were wounded; I had sent some small ships under the direction of Capt. Creyk of the Otter, up the main branch of the Chesapeak, at the same time I entered Elizabeth river, the movements of this little squadron were so judicious, that the enemy were much harassed and distressed. They destroyed many vessels and captured others, among which were two with about 200 hogsheads of Tobacco.

"The Raisonable, remained stationed before the town of Hampton with some armed tenders, blocks up that port, and the navigation of James river; Elizabeth river is already taken effectual care of, and Captain Creyk's little squadron renders the ingress and regress of the Chesapeak almost impracticable for the rebel vessels without their being taken. I have now informed your Excellency of the detail of our military operations by sea to the present time, our success and the present appearance of things infinitely exceed our most sanguine expectations, and if the various accounts the General and I have received can be depended on, the most flattering hopes of a return to obedience to their Sovereign may be expected from most of this province; the people seems importunately desirous that the royal standard may be erected, and they give the most positive assurances that all ranks of people will resort to it, you are too good a judge Sir, of the very great importance of this place we now hold to render my saying much upon that subject necessary, permit me however as a sea officer, to observe that this port of Portsmouth, is an exceeding safe and secure asylum for ships against an enemy, and is not to be forced even by great superiority, the marine yard is large and extremely convenient, having a considerable stock of seasoned timber, besides great quantities of other stores; from these considerations joined to many others, I am firmly of opinion that it is a measure most essentially necessary for his Majesty's service that this post should remain in our hands, since it appears to be of more real consequence and advantage, than any other the Crown now possesses in America, for by securing this, the whole trade of the Chesapeak is at an end, and consequently the sinews of the rebellion destroyed. I trust and hope Sir, you will see this matter in the same important light as I do, and give such directions for reinforcements to be sent here as you may think necessary, in order for our pursuing and improving these advantages which we have with so much good fortune acquired. General Mathew proposing to write to you by this express boat, I shall leave to his pen to inform you of the destruction of the considerable magazines in Suffolk (intended for the rebel army) by a detachment of the King's troops under Col. Garth, and before I conclude my letter, permit me to express my great satisfaction in the choice of the officers you were pleased to name, for cooperating with me on this expedition, as too much praise cannot be given General Mathew for his indefatigable zeal and attention for the King's service, and I have the pleasure in acknowledging the perfect harmony and understanding, which subsist between his Majesty's land and sea officers.

I have the honour to be, &c.

George Collier."

General Mathew found at least one host to welcome him at Portsmouth in the person of Lieutenant Dickey of his Majesty's late schooner, the Emerald. This reception Commodore Barron described in a pendant to his account of the Boat Liberty's exploit.

"Lieutenant Dickey was sent to Portsmouth, then a garrison town, and put on his parole of honor, with almost unlimited privileges; and there he remained, becoming a great favorite with the good people of that place, and enjoying the hospitality of all the genteel families in it, until the invasion by Admiral Collier and General Matthew, in the following May. It will be remembered that at this time the British Army under General Matthew, landed south of Pig-Point, and marched along the river side to the Western Branch, when they crossed over that stream, and Scott's creek, to the woods in the rear of Fort Nelson, then commanded by Major Mathews, who, aware of his utter inability to defend the fort against such odds, was obliged to quit it, and cross over to Washington Point, leaving, however, the colours flying to deceive the enemy and gain time. During this movement of our troops, Lieutenant Dickey had walked out into the country, as was his usual custom, and to that part of it back of the fort, now the site of the United States Hospital, and there he remained until he saw the last of Major Matthews's men embark for the other shore. He then entered the fort, and found himself solus, and commander-in-chief,— and so he continued to be until the British made their appearance out of the woods, and approached the place, when he mounted the ramparts, and hauled down the American colours. The British then advanced, and took possession of the fort, and very soon after of the town of Portsmouth, where Lieut. Dickey now appeared in his new character of Conqueror, instead of a prisoner; and it is gratifying to record that he shewed the utmost kindness and courtesy to the citizens of the town, who experienced all proper protection and comfort through his influence with his countrymen."

But no stories of kindness and courtesy reached Governor Henry in Williamsburg. The British fleet of invasion, according to the first advices, consisted of a 64-gun ship (supposed to be the St. Albans) and fifteen or sixteen larger ships, frigates or armed vessels, and some smaller craft. Executive communications spread the alarm at their arrival, and the consequent unopposed seizure of Portsmouth, with the destruction there of some "Capital Ships" belonging to this State [including the Frigate Virginia, of which Capt. James Barron was commander] and one or two private ones loaded with tobacco. On receipt of the news of the sack and burning of Suffolk the thoroughly aroused Governor issued a proclamation denouncing in bitter temper the predatory havoc and atrocities reported to have been perpetrated on the march to the doomed town—horrid ravages and depredations, such as plundering and house-burning, killing and carrying off stock of all sorts and exercising abominable barbarities. "Seven Frenchmen, it is said, and believed have been murdered in cold blood," he added on partisan testimony, in a letter of May 19 to Richard Henry Lee, who laid the charge before Congress.

The Virginia Assembly of this month, after ripe deliberations on the perils of the situation, dangled, for enlistments, the lure of magnificent promises. On joining, each man was to have a new suit of clothes, and an additional suit, including a pair of "overhalls", each succeeding year of his service. Recruits were to receive $750 and 100 acres of unappropriated land. They were to be exempted from taxation. If a soldier or sailor were disabled he would be cared for, and the families of the slain or of those dying from other causes in service would be allotted relief. And finally came the most dazzling of all the provisions, which Virginia never fulfilled; "And all general officers of the army being citizens of this commonwealth, and all field officers, captains, and subalterns, commanding or who shall command in the battalions of this commonwealth on continental establishment, or serving in the batallions raised for the immediate defence of this state, or for the defence of the United State. And all chaplains, physicians, surgeons, and surgeon's mates, appointed to the said battalions, or any of them, being citizens of this commonwealth*** provided Congress do not make some tantamount provision for them, who shall serve henceforward, or from the time of their being commissioned until the end of the war.

"And all such officers who have, or shall become supernumerary on the reduction of any of the said battalions, and shall again enter the said service if required so to do ***and continue therein until the end of the war, shall be entitled to half pay during life to commence from the determination of their command or service."*

Patrick Henry had no occasion to put these inducements to the test. He retired, for the time being, on the first of the following month. One of his last official communications was a letter to Col. Theodorick Bland, with agreeable tidings: "The enemy are gone to sea."

---

*In 1832, by Act of Congress, the United States assumed this pledge unfulfilled by Virginia.

CHAPTER XI

AN UPCOUNTRYMAN PILOTS THE ADMIRALTY

Of a Commonwealth shorn of the larger part of its fleet and of its stores but free, for a brief space, from agitating alarms Jefferson took the direction with decision and vigor Portsmouth was re-occupied; vessels that had been withdrawn, for security's sake, to the upper reaches of the rivers were emboldened to venture from hiding. The Dragon, Capt. Callender with Lieut. Chandler second in command, laden with rigging, etc. for the new ship Jefferson, found her way from Richmond to the Chickahominy shipyard, and on the Jefferson many of the Dragon's crew were promptly enlisted.

Yet the British had not, as it turned out, left the Capes altogether without vigilants, to their own discomfiture in one instance at least, as disclosed by the *Virginia Gazette* of June 18: "Last Monday two gallies from Maryland engaged a British frigate of 28 guns near the Capes; they took one of her boats and sunk another; the gallies had an officer and some men killed; the frigate taking advantage of a fresh breeze made her escape in a very shattered condition."

The day following the publication of this encounter Jefferson forwarded to John Jay a request for fifty of the letters of marque newly granted by Congress, "for want of which our people have long and exceedingly suffered." And relying on Jay's penetration, the Governor added: "Our trade has never been so distressed since the time of Lord Dunmore as it is at present by a parcel of trifling privateers under the countenance of two or three larger vessels who keep our little naval force from doing anything. The uniform train of events which during the whole course of this war we are to suppose has rendered it improper that the American fleet or any part of it should ever come to relieve or countenance the trade of certain places, while the same train of events has as uniformly rendered it proper to confine them to the protection of certain other parts of the continent is a lamentable arrangement of fortune for us. The same ill luck has attended us as to the disposition of prizes taken by our navy, which tho' sometimes taken just off our capes, it has always been expedient to carry elsewhere. A British prize would be a more rare phenomenon than a comet, because the one has been seen, but the other never has."

As a matter of fact British prizes taken by Virginia vessels were distinctly more common than comets. Jefferson was drawing a long bow in the heat of a not unnatural resentment or perhaps he was referring to prizes taken by the Continental Navy, in which case his statement was significantly true. Animated doubtless by similar feelings, Richard Henry Lee had written to a Continental officer of prominence, on June 26: "The Confederacy & the Boston can with infinite ease destroy the enemies vessels that are doing us so much injury, causing us so much expence by frequent calls for Militia—They have already burnt several private houses and one public warehouse with between 2 & 300 hhds of Tobo. and carried off much plunder & many negroes—Soon as they see the Militia gathering they embark and go to another unguarded place. They have 6 vessels, Otter 16, Harlem 12 Guns Kings Vessels—Dunmore 16, Schooner Hammond 14, Lord North 12 Guns & Fin Castle 2 three pounders, The 4 last are Guntridges [Goodrich's] Pirates ***."*

Neither the Confederacy nor the Boston was stirred by this urgent appeal.

Ten days before Jefferson wrote to Jay, the Galley Protector had fallen a prey to the enemy. Captain Thomas "hove her out" into the Great Wicomico with a view to making repairs. In that situation, when her guns could not be brought into action, the British attacked her. Thomas and his men, resisting gallantly with musketry, were soon driven off by the enemy's cannon, and under cover of the cannon the galley was burned. At the same time the North and South Wicomico warehouses went up in flames. The Protector's crew made

---

*Ballagh's "Letters of Richard Henry Lee," Vol. II, p. 81.

their way to the Chickahominy shipyard, and were there transferred to the Tartar.

In the early summer, during a respite from British aggression, Jefferson, rather surprisingly, sounded his neighbor to the south with regard to a matter of merchandise. The Virginia-built and partly Virginia-manned galleys, Washington and Caswell*, had, as Patrick Henry had pointed out, largely failed of their object. The cost of maintenance was high and the service rendered, inconsiderable. The galley named in honor of the North Carolina Governor, with bottom eaten out and sunk at her station, could "not be hove down to be refitted." The Washington, however, might profitably be acquired by his colleague at a moderate figure.

Jefferson's enterprise created a precedent which the Governor of Maryland speedily followed. He was prepared to make a preferential offer to Virginia, for a suitable return, of two supernumerary galleys. But the Virginia Governor was not to be tempted, asserting that it might safely be conjectured that only "some motive of expediency" could have prompted the Maryland proffer, when, in the common emergency, "to keep our little fleet in order," taxed Virginia's every resource.

In autumn the future looked brighter. About the middle of November the Chevalier de la Luzerne, second minister plenipotentiary of his Most Christian Majesty, dispatched enquiries concerning Virginia's equipment for the reception of a friendly fleet that caused Jefferson to entertain the most sanguine expectations of relief in immediate prospect. By return of courier went the assurance that the Governor would place at the disposal of the "French Admiral or Commanding Officer" harbors and disembarking places at discretion, provisions would be amply supplied, and adequate hospitals organized. For a station and rendezvous he recommended York river as most defensible, with the pertinent suggestion that the farther the visitors could "withdraw up our rivers

---

*On June 9, 1780, Capt. Wilson of the Caswell apprised the Governor of North Carolina that he had waited on the Virginia Naval Board to inform them of the impossibility of getting men at twenty dollars bounty and half a dollar a day, provided they enlisted for three years. Previously he had complained of the inadequacy of the supplies furnished.

into the country the more it would be in our power to assist them against the attack of the enemy."

Before occasion called for performance of these engagements two more perilous years were fated to pass.

And the October session of the Assembly dealt devastatingly with the remnant of the Navy. It was resolved that the Executive, after retaining for commercial purposes such ships as were needful, should dispose of, at the best advantage, at public vendue for ready money the ships Tartar and Dragon and the galleys Henry, Manly, Hero, Page, Lewis and Safeguard. Guns and serviceable material were to be kept for the use of the State. The ship Thetis, the brig Jefferson, the Accomac and the Diligence Galleys, and the Gloucester prisonship were to be continued in service. The Tempest, held until the Thetis* should be ready for sea, might then either be retained or disposed of, at the Executive's discretion. A third boat of the character of the Liberty or the Patriot was to be procured, to serve as a lookout.

But the sales decreed by the Assembly failed of fulfillment, and serious obstacles presented themselves to the fitting out of those vessels voted retained.

On December 4, the *Gazette* heralded from the West Indies overdrawn news accepted as pregnant with promise: "On Monday last arrived at Hampton the Schooner Alliance†, Capt. Henry Stratton, in fourteen days from St. Eustatia, who inform that the English packet had arrived at Antigua, and that the combined fleets of France and Spain ride triumphant in the English channel."

On the other hand, an uncomfortable situation threatened with Spain's Peninsula neighbor. A Virginia privateer of private ownership, under Capt. Joseph Cunningham, had overhauled and seized a Portuguese snow. This occasion for friction was overshadowed, however, by disconcerting news

---

*The Thetis, built at Chickahominy shipyard, was christened, verbally, by the Commissioners on August 28, 1778.

†The Alliance was now one of but six trading vessels in the Commonwealth's service. The decline to this small number was responsible for an order, on December 14, to discontinue the shipyard at Cumberland on the Pamunkey.

from New York; the British fleet in force had put out to sea, not, as it was learned later, for the soon-to-be-ice-bound waters of Chesapeake, but for the open harbor of Charles Town.

The year 1780 brought a memorable spell of weather of the greatest severity—weeks of intense, unbroken cold when the water ceased, in great part, to be a navigable element. The rivers and even the Roads and the upper Bay were frozen from shore to shore. It is recorded, for example, that Capt. William Jennings was able to have his wife and infant son brought from Norfolk to Hampton on a barge propelled over the ice by some of his men. Vessels were stranded or tight bound in the ice. The *Virginia Gazette* reported in its issue of January 15: "The Tempest is on shore between Hog Island and Cobham, a brig and a snow are aground near Mulberry Island, and the privateer brig Jefferson*, is sunk off Jamestown. She was a fine new vessel, just finished and ready to sail on a cruise." A ship under command of Capt. John Rogers had battled with the blasts off the coast, and from the intense rigors of the cold, many of the crew had miserably perished. Lieut. Thomas Snale, severely frost-bitten, was brought ashore, but soon after expired.

On February 4 the War Office announced that the reviewing and receiving of new recruits for the navy as well as the army was deferred owing to the inclemency of the weather, and a few days later the *Gazette* carried the intelligence that the Continental Brig Baltimore and a Philadelphia brig, Capt. Vallance, had gone ashore at Cape Henry.

With the opening of spring the seat of government of Virginia was transferred from the peculiarly pregnable Williamsburg, as Jefferson had augured, to the more securely situated hamlet of Richmond, from which the Executive was forced to withdraw in some haste twice in the course of the year that followed.

---

*In August 1780 Capt. Wm. Saunders was in command of the Brig Jefferson, and Robt. Bolling was lieut. Officers of the brig in December 1779 and January, 1780 were: Richard Barron, capt.; George Chamberlaine, lt.; Robt. Hall, sailing-master; Thomas Grant, midshipman, and Michael Jennings, boatswain.

In their new surroundings, in May when the fall of Charles Town, with the consequent captivity of a number of Virginia troops, had depressed and disheartened the Commonwealth the Assembly, animated by determination, legislated with vigor. With a view to facilitating the business of making war a Commissioner of War, a Commercial Agent and a Commissioner of the Navy (salary 30,000 pounds of tobacco)* under the "controul and direction of the governour and council" were to take the place of the Boards of War and of Trade, now abolished. The militia of the lower counties was to be called out. The Governor was authorized to employ the Diligence and Accomac Galleys†, repaired and re-manned, for the defense of the Bay and the coast. The Thetis, the brig Jefferson, the Dragon and the Tempest were to be refitted for service. Three hundred marines and five captains and fifteen lieutenants to be enlisted at once. A three years' enlistment entitled sailors to the liberal provisions of $1000 bounty and two dollars a day pay; officers of the navy—the master surgeon and surgeon's mate, to stand on the same footing in the matter of pay and of perquisites with regulars of equivalent rank. The Henry Galley was to be repaired and manned for the defense of Hampton, Hampton Roads, and the adjacent water.†

"And whereas it is necessary that no officer should be retained in the marine department but such as are properly qualified, in order therefore to produce this reform. Be it enacted—That a board shall be appointed by the governour, with the advice of the council to consist of the Commissioner of the Navy, and of six of the captains the most approved for their ability, any four of whom together with the said Commissioner of the Navy shall be sufficient to constitute the said board etc."

---

*Hening's Statutes at Large, Vol. X, 278.
†It was not long before the Governor learned that the two Eastern Shore Galleys had been deserted by officers and men, ard had been despoiled of "their furniture." A plan to bring the two ships over to the western shore, for the protection of Gloucester, was never effected. In 1781 the two derelicts were sold.

CHAPTER XII

PICAROONS AND PUNCTILIO

The bold privateers, now to be the capital object of action following legislation, found adversaries to test their mettle. "The ship Adventure, Captain Reeves, 16 guns and 60 men," reported the *Virginia Gazette* of June 28, 1780, "in 17 days from St. Croix, with a cargo of rum, sugar, salt etc. is safe arrived in James river. About 40 leagues east of Cape Hatteras, fell in with the brig Hammond of 18 guns and the sloop Randal of 10 guns, two privateers from Bermuda with which he engaged near three hours within pistol shot, and obliged the Hammond to strike; but being so much disabled in his sails and rigging, and the wind light, he could not get possession of the Brig before the sloop towed her off, and got clear. What is something remarkable, Captain Reeves had not a man hurt during the engagement. Between the capes he saw eleven sail of privateers, in a chain from cape Henry to cape Charles, but not one of them attempted to come near him. The brig general Warren, Captain Nicholson, and the schooner Grand Tiger, Captain Smith, parted from him the 9th instant in latitude 22."

This chain of privateers was doubtless the same "fleet supposed to be hostile off the capes", news of which Col. Mallory of Elizabeth City communicated to Jefferson, who in turn wrote to Samuel Huntington, President of Congress, promising that if he could find some means of clearing the Bay supplies would go forward to the Continental troops by the end of the month, and a hint to the same effect was given to the Committee of Congress at Headquarters, with detailed data as to the enemy: "These have been from six to eleven in number the largest carrying twenty guns. To them are added at present eight frigates: though I can scarcely believe these mean to continue. In this situation nothing can venture out of our rivers."

On Monday, July 3, the day following the dispatch of letters to the northward, Captain James Barron, recommended by his prestige and experience, was appointed commodore of the armed vessels of the Commonwealth, and three days later Captain James Maxwell was intrusted with the post of Commissioner of the Navy, created by the recent Assembly.

The new era was inaugurated by orders that the brig Thetis, returned to service by Act of Assembly, the Tempest, the Dragon and the Jefferson should be put in a state of efficiency for the defense of the Chesapeake and of Hampton Roads against the hostile small vessels so augmented as to constitute a perpetual menace to the State commerce and the dwellers along the shores, "insulted", as Jefferson expressed it, by this harassing species of warfare. And one of the Virginia armed vessels, the brigantine Northampton*, had been taken, but the prize was promptly re-captured by the brigantine Wilkes (doubtless named after John Wilkes, noted or notorious, according to viewpoint) and the schooner Betsey and Peggy.

The end of August saw Jefferson making conditions plain to the French Envoy: "Were it possible for this state to have an interest distinct from its confederates it would be the Bay of Chesapeake. Our attempts to establish a force on the water have been very unsuccessful; and our trade has been almost annihilated by the most contemptible part of the enemy's force on that element." In view of the fact that the cares of Congress had not been equally extended in that particular the Governor felt justified in counting upon the ally's willing and immediate support against the common enemy, the more speedily to consummate the common design.

Meanwhile the picaroons must receive instant attention. This same day, the Governor instructed Maxwell, newly appointed Commissioner of the Navy, to prepare the brig and such of the boats as could be equipped and also the Eastern

---

*The Virginia Gazette of November 5 of this year advertised the Northampton for sale, the purchase money to indemnify those who re-captured her. In the same issue the fast-sailing Brigantine Rattlesnake was also offered for sale.

During Arnold's invasion the Wilkes was sunk, and the Rattlesnake "taken up the river and burned."

Shore galleys, with the object of joining a force from Maryland. Discretionary powers were placed in the hands of Commodore Barron as to the direction the intended expedition should take.

A few days later the brig Jefferson was reported in tolerable readiness and prepared to act with the two swift armed vessels, Liberty and Patriot, for the undoing of pirates. The Thetis was "getting into Readiness." And presently the Governor was able to report offensive operations. With a crew drawn by the promise of ten dollars a day, a congregation so nondescript and unskilled that Barron gave expression to the fear that with such navigators the brig was in danger of being taken by very inferior vessels, a cruise was undertaken up to Tangier Island and as many prizes netted as the Commodore could furnish men to man; namely, five schooners and row boats employed in the inimical business of supplying with provisions the enemy's cruisers in the Bay.*

The next mission of the same little squadron, sailing from York, was to convoy provision ships to the northward. In the event, however, that the commander met the expected vessels from Maryland he was to turn aside and join forces with them. Signals were prearranged to ensure recognition: "He who first makes the signal is to take in his force (fore) gallant sail, and hoist the continental ensign at the fore top gallant mast head; the other to let fly this main top gallant sheets and hoist a Continental jack at the main top gallant mast head."

At this juncture, when fresh plans, in succession to Barron's promising beginning, were ripe for execution Jefferson was sorely tried by the exasperations of the Chevalier D'Anmours, the consul whose advent in the train of Gérard's treaty the Virginia Executive had hailed with a New Year's adjuration to "all good citizens of this Commonwealth and all subjects of his Most Christian Majesty, and others within the same, duly to respect the prerogatives and jurisdiction of the said Consul established by law, as they will answer the contrary at their peril."

---

*It was probably in reference to this cruise that Pascow Herbert testified (U. S. pension claim papers) that seven or eight prizes were taken in an enterprise in which he, along with Lt. John V. Kautzman, took part.

The Chevalier, with an exceedingly high sense of his importance and correspondingly testy, exploded, under the aggravation of an affair on the Eastern Shore whereby, as was alleged, one Captain Lacraie had been deprived of his crew, into a group of animated demands, the last of which, touching migrations, is of an ingenuousness that passes all comprehension: "If I demand that the Government of Virginia would make all possible and proper regulations to stop all desertions and prevent emigrations from France and her possessions it is not only because I think it an act of justice, but because I think it to be one of prudence. By the nature of things every man that will emigrate from every other country but France will diminish the number of the enemies of America; from France it will lessen the number of her friends and such friends that will always be ready to take up arms in her defence."

Withal, as a tonic to amity, he extended the most flattering assurances of the high consideration in which his Most Christian Majesty, champion of a people struggling for liberty, held the Commonwealth of Virginia. To the consul's boasting, toasting and conventional blandishments Jefferson wrote a reply that has not been preserved, but, in view of his prevailing desire, he doubtless handled the situation with that serenity which he recommended to his fellow-citizens plagued by adventurers pressing for favors and privileged places.

This prevailing desire was the advent of the French fleet from Rhode Island, an event that was anticipated as likely soon to take place. To meet this anticipation D'Anmours, successor of the departed "look-out," Major Galvan, requested an escort, presumably the accepted usage, and in addition a convoy.

In his answer of September 9 Jefferson expressed himself somewhat after this fashion: In consequence of the sailing of the brig Jefferson and two other State vessels that very day he lacked a ship sufficiently august to bear his Most Christian Majesty's representative. He feared in consequence that the vice-consul would have to content himself with the little boat Nicholson, which, in a week's time, after needed alterations in her sails and cleaning, would be at the vice-consular bidding.

Due instructions were therefore transmitted to James Maxwell Esq., who in turn charged Lieutenant Steele to proceed with his vessel to Cape Henry, wait on the French consul there, and follow his orders implicitly. And that D'Anmours might cut the courtlier figure, the Governor enjoined Major Wishart, County Lieutenant of Princess Anne, to detail twelve of his militia (the number of Galvan's suite) along with a ranging company of six or eight horse, carefully selected, as a setting, or perhaps as a foil, to the faultless port of the consul.

With all the frills of ceremonious welcome provided D'Anmours had the stage to himself. The fleet still rendezvoused elsewhere.

By a curious irony of fate the Nicholson, after service under Lieut. Ham in transporting provisions during the siege of York, fell a victim to a British frigate with woodwork cunningly painted French style and masthead flying French colors.

With no French fleet in the offing the Virginia Assembly in October determined on liberal measures for gathering seamen and for effecting the defense of the seacoast. Officers and crew were to share the whole of their prizes. A hospital for the marine was to be established. And the navy was to furnish an asylum for the fatherless: the county courts were "imposed and required to cause half of such [specified] male orphans at least, who may live below the falls of the respective rivers in the eastern parts of this commonwealth, to be bound to the sea under the most prudent captains that can be procured to take them."* Two new galleys of a large type were projected, and five vessels of the State fleet ordered made ready for service at once.

But this same month the presentiment of an imminent incursion became a reality. "On the 20th instant," announced the *Virginia Gazette* "arrived in Chesapeake Bay a British fleet of 54 ships, 25 of which are large, the residue small. On the 23rd they landed 1000 infantry and 100 horse at Newport News, who immediately proceeded to Hampton, of which they

---
Hening's "Statutes at Large," Vol. X, 385.

took possession. Part of them are gone into Elizabeth river, but whether they have effected a landing is not certainly known. It is supposed the whole land force is 5000 men commanded by Leslie, and the fleet is said to be commanded by Commodore Rodney, son of the admiral of that name. The people in the neighboourhood of the invasion turn out with great alacrity and spirit, and trust they will be immediately supported by their upper brethren."

Seized with fresh misgivings and torn by uncertainty, the worst of ills, Jefferson sounded the tocsin. The lower, even more than the "upper brethren", were exhorted to action, while the little fleet scuttled off to the recesses of the rivers and of the Bay.

A party of 800, debarked from the hostile ships in the environs of Hampton, committed, in Jefferson's words, "horrid depredations." On October 28 the Governor, in his perplexity, turned towards General Gates in the South: "The enemy have retired to their ships, which on the evening of the 26th, were strung along the road from New-ports-news, to the mouth of Nansemond, which seems to indicate an intention of coming up James River**Would it not be worth while to send out a swift boat from some of the Inlets of Carolina, to notify the French Admiral that his enemies are in a net, if he has leisure to close the mouth of it?"

Unluckily the French admiral's marine arm was beyond the compass of or the leisure for net closing even could he have been notified that the great moment had come. Within the net the invading forces proceeded to occupy Portsmouth and strengthen the defenses, but, on receipt of a communication from Charles Town, other enterprises beckoned. Four weeks after arriving they re-embarked, and on the evening of the twenty-second of November weighed and emerged unmolested from the mouth of the net and stood out to sea.

Jefferson, along with the Commonwealth, now breathed with more freedom. The hidden ships came forth into the open in the event that men and funds were forthcoming. The Northampton, Safeguard, Page, Lewis and Hero were pronounced to be in tolerable order. To the command of the brig Jefferson Capt. Willis Wilson, of the decayed Caswell galley, succeeded Capt. Markham, transferred to the Tempest, and received orders to set out on a cruise with weather eye open for persons who came under the description of pirates that, on apprehension, they might be submitted to court-martial and receive their desserts.

The Assembly in December was again much concerned with the Navy. The brig Jefferson and the armed boats Liberty and Patriot were to be forthwith armed for suppressing the hostile cruisers in the Chesapeake. The Lewis galley was to be put into condition with all possible dispatch. Seamen were to be impressed. A generous scale of wages was agreed upon. Vessels were to have all prizes they took, division to be made according to the regulations for the distribution of prizes.

But the legislators had expended most of their energy in vain. Just before Christmas, General Nelson expedited by courier to the Governor tidings of sinister import: twenty-seven vessels, eight of them square-rigged, had entered the Roads. The memorable year of the surrender at Yorktown was about to open with the most dismal of prospects: the destroyer of the Virginia Navy was within the gates.

CHAPTER XIII

ARNOLD THE DESTROYER AND THE SEQUEL TRIUMPHANT

For a few days the hostile fleet of nineteen ships, two brigs and ten sloops continued at anchor, but with the first favorable wind they weighed and proceeded up the James into the heart of the country. Whether Richmond or Petersburg was their objective was a question that exercised the Executive. On the evening of January 3 the invaders advanced to Kennon's, and when they reached Westover with the next favorable tide all doubts were resolved as to the destination intended, and Jefferson took hastily the discreet step of crossing over to Manchester on the southern shore of the James. Ravaging the country in their passage, a regiment of the enemy's forces marched upon the village capital and entered it on the afternoon of the fifth. A company of about thirty horse pushed on to Westham, but, finding there little to demolish, they returned to Richmond the next morning, burned some public and some private buildings, and about noon withdrew towards Westover, and, within the neck of land, encamped the next day.

On the approach of Baron von Steuben towards Hood's, the enemy, after "their very extraordinary and successful attempt on Richmond", made no move against Fredericksburg, as Jefferson had apprehended, but re-embarked, hoisted sail, and "with the assistance of a very fine Gale, which sprung up on the instant, fell down the river in a very short time", and shortly afterwards retired to Portsmouth, and there settled as if for an indefinite stay, shutting up the Chesapeake to commerce by means of their vessels and cutting off the provisions for the Southern Army which the State was "in a fair way of supplying."

On January 5 the President of the Maryland Council, yet unapprised of the new turn of affairs in Virginia, wrote a suggestion to his southern neighbor that, in view of the certainty that the enemy would take post in the vicinity of Portsmouth during the coming summer, it would be the part of wisdom to urge the French to forestall them, and to the projected stronghold Maryland engaged to contribute twenty 18 and six 9 pounders. For fear of giving umbrage (Jenifer inferred) the ally would hesitate to take such a step without formal invitation on the part of Virginia. As a postlude the correspondent expressed the sense which was entertained of his Most Christian Majesty's sincere attachment and of the magnanimous attitude he had taken in favor of the United States.

No sooner had Arnold encamped within the defenses of Portsmouth, shielded by his cordon of ships, than the Virginia Executive plunged into plans for his dislodging and capture. And, to further this programme, Capt. B. Edgar Joel, "animated by a spirit more enterprising than is the natural portion of his fellow creatures", came forward with a bold though by no means novel expedient—the destruction of the hostile fleet by means of a fire-ship. This happy inspiration Jefferson found worth sponsoring and so advised General Nelson. Joel then went at once to the Chickahominy shipyard, received permission to make use of the only ship there, the decrepit Dragon*, long under water and marketable at no more than 50 pounds, old money, at the Governor's estimate.

Despite the adventurer's urgencies it was only after a delay of five or six days, "the usual fatality attending our service," that he was put in a position to act. The Dragon was brought to the surface, things came to a state of much forwardness, and when a bungling pilot ran the hulk on a bar Joel "condescended even to the meanest employments of a common sailor" for the purpose of getting her off. Then, at this promising juncture, his hands were unexpectedly tied by a message from Nelson. The undertaking had been given such generous publicity that, as the Governor explained, the enemy were undoubtedly apprised of it, and when the essential

---

*In March 1780 the Dragon had been put in the service of the Board of Trade: her former officers either became supernumerary or were put on other vessels.

element of surprise flew to the winds there was nothing more to be done. This conclusion the sedulous Joel received in no agreeable temper, and in a bristling retort gave expression to the hope that he at least "would not be included in the enemys laugh at the abortion of the scheme."

Now not all the British vessels were keeping their stations. In February George Sisson of Richmond County was a participant, under duress, in an engagement in Virginia waters. He was captured on the fifteenth of the month in Corotoman River by the Cornwallis brig, Capt. Downey, acting in conjunction with the sloop Hybernia, Capt. John Disney, the Trimmer schooner, Capt. Phillips, and another schooner commanded by Capt. Thomas. The next day the Hybernia and the Trimmer attacked a Baltimore brig of fourteen or sixteen guns off the mouth of Rappahannock. The action continued for a considerable time with a number of casualties resulting on the British ships, which, finding they had more than met their match, sheered off and ran for it, pursued almost into Hampton Roads by the triumphant American. Sisson and other prisoners on board had been formed upon the quarter-deck and forced to take up arms against their compatriots.

Lieut. Joseph Saunders has left his reminiscence of another daring effort of this time that did not end with pursuit: "Some British ships came up James River as high as Chickahominy. Lt. Chandler and myself obtained permission of the Commissioner Capt. James Maxwell to take a galley and Man her and go and attack a British ship that lay off the mouth of the River. We accordingly went down and made the attack. The ship was a letter of marque, and the action continued. Our ammunition failed and we had to bare away, no lives lost on our side but shot Langraze and round shot flew thick around and through our sales & rigging until we got out of reach."†
And now came aid from New England.

"Two days ago," wrote Jefferson on February 17, "I received notice of the arrival of a 64 gun ship & two frigates of

---

*Declaration of George Sisson, published in the "Virginia Calendar of State Papers," Vol. II, pp. 83-84.
†Statement of Joseph Saunders in his pension application papers, Revolutionary Records, Washington, D. C.

36 each, part of the French fleet at Rhode Island**they are equal to the destruction of the British vessels, could they get at them, but these are drawn up into Elizabeth river into which the 64 cannot enter."

These ships, anchored for the time being in Lynnhaven Bay between the Horse Shoe and Cape Henry, would be attended by great service to the American cause (the Governor informed Baron von Steuben) consequent on their cruising off the Capes and intercepting communication between New York and Charles Town. To Capt. Maxwell instructions were sent to wait on the French commanding officer and receive from him the arms which, Jefferson was confident, had been consigned for transportation to Virginia, and Maxwell was further instructed to render at once "the armed vessels of this state subservient to the performing necessary offices for the French fleet". The brig Jefferson, the Executive conceived, would at this time prove useful in preventing the escape of small vessels from Elizabeth river.

The French commander, however, gave no sign of delivering arms, which, as a matter of fact, were not in his hands, and, without exchanging courtesies with Jefferson, set out on a cruise of the Bay, in the course of which eight prizes, including the before-mentioned Cornwallis, were taken, and then the visitor vanished from sight. The Governor, firm in the conviction that the Admiral was lying in wait off the Capes, informed Lafayette on March 1 that the enemy in Portsmouth, "environed by the Militia of this state and of North Carolina are afraid to venture forth to maraud for fear of the French fleet." Maxwell, however, on March 5 made report of an occurrence that proved that the Governor's reasoning admitted of argument.

The Commissioner of the Navy, bearing dispatches from the Marquis de la Fayette to the French Naval Commander, had embarked on a boat from Annapolis. When the haze lifted on the morning succeeding, the occupants of the American boat, discovering that they were the object of pursuit by three large sloops, were forced to withdraw at their best speed up Back River into shallower water, and in that situation awaited developments. From their retreat they had a clear view of British lookout boats, some cruising up the Bay and others, the General Monk and the sloop Hope included, making sail down towards the Capes. On Sunday the Boat Liberty put in an appearance and was ordered to lie by. On the night of March 6 Maxwell planned to brave the perils of the Capes the next day and "stretch out to sea" in quest of the French squadron. The morning was productive, however, of a disconcerting surprise. About seven o'clock there suddenly emerged from the heavy mists eight flat boats returning from a plundering expedition up Back River. The Liberty, aground, was immediately boarded and seized. The captors then stripped her of sails and military stores, and finally left her, carrying off the sailing-master Gibson and eight other men, who had "offered all the resistance that their situation would permit."

While this was going on, Maxwell's boat had been hastily got up a creek and sunk. Her crew, on the shore, stood determined to resist to the death any attempt to capture her. But the British went off without making any movement in this direction; whereupon, the sunken craft was raised and sailed safely to York, where it was hoped that the Liberty might soon be able to join her.

The British marauders, three hundred in number, found determined opposition from some forty militia, collected at a place called Race Path about three miles from Hampton, who fired upon them, killing Lieut. Salisburg of the Charon and two others. Col. Dundas, the British leader, had his horse shot under him. The enemy afterwards killed a few cattle and returned to their shipping the next morning.

The Virginians' loss was Col. Mallory and five others killed, and William and Robert Armistead taken prisoners.

Capt. Maxwell, thus lucklessly checked and diverted, was in confidence informed by the Governor several days later that from the Marquis Lafayette had come the intelligence that "the French Commodore is returned to Rhode Island," and he then enjoined, "No attempt must be made to carry my Letter out till a French naval force is known to be in the Bay."

About this time Joel, whose fire-ship ambition had foundered, reported on his most recent activities, from the Chickahominy shipyard, whither he had recently gone in the Lewis galley to replace a foresail. For three weeks, he assured the Executive, he had been cruising from Newport News to Warrisqueake Bay, with a crew without clothes or necessities of life. Yet, thus handicapped, he had hindered many slaves from running away to the enemy, and claimed in reward of his services a commission as captain of the galley. This wish was not gratified, and Joel, disgruntled, was soon demanding his pay in arrears, the time he had spent with the Dragon included.

Amid cares, small and great, Jefferson applied his ingenuity to developing plans for discomfiting Arnold. "We have set every instrument in motion that can possibly avail," he assured the Marquis, whom he had supplied with maps of the vicinities of York, of Hampton, and of Portsmouth, and exhorted his ally to make the most of an unprepared people tasting the fruits of war for the first time, "that have all those habits to acquire that their Northern brethren had in the year 1776 and which they have purchased at so great an expence."

Jefferson's "instruments" included the procurement of ten pilots, the requisitioning of saddle-horses for officers, a scheme for enlistment general and special, devices for impressing men in the Navy, the establishment of a line of communication at Hood's and an endeavor to supply artificers, "exceedingly scarce in this Country."

While the Executive acted and continued to act, report came that a fleet flying the flag of France, "who will not leave to us alone the honor of taking Arnold," had entered the Bay. With joyous anticipations Capt. Buckner, bearing dispatches from the Marquis and accompanied by other pilots, was sent out by von Steuben with orders to meet the visitors and steer them directly to York. But unhappily Buckner and his companions were rowed into a camouflaged trap and consequent captivity—to use his own words, he "joined the said fleet and to his great mortification found them to be British and commanded by Admiral Arbuthnot."

The grievous truth of the arrival of a powerful fleet (later learned to consist of seven ships of the line, two 50's and other smaller ones under Graves and Arbuthnot) was officially reported to the President of Congress, to General Washington, and to the Governors of North Carolina and of Maryland. Unaware that the French fleet was already, by actual contact, apprised of the movements of the enemy, Jefferson hurried a dispatch to Col. Avery, County Lieutenant of Accomac County, conjuring him to procure lookout boats with the object of warning the French Naval Commander. "I am very apprehensive," he explained, "that the French fleet expected here, not apprized of this circumstance, may run into the mouths of the enemy."

The hostile fleet soon took on an air of permanency, and the Governor was brought to a realization that, as he informed Lafayette, their presence and "the lack of ammunition and clothing abridge our intentions against Portsmouth," and to the Governor of North Carolina he stated with finality, "our plans against Portsmouth will fall to the ground."

While his plans were still brewing, however, Jefferson had been assembling, to supplement the State's armed vessels, a flotilla of vessels impressed. This auxiliary group, rendezvoused at Turkey Island, comprised the ship Renown, 16 six-pounders and 20 men, with Capt. William Lewis, of the State troops, in command; the ship Willing Lass, Capt. Williams, 12 four-pounders and 20 men; brig Mars, Capt. Thomas, eight four-pounders and 13 men; sloop Eminence, 1 howitzer and 8 men; brig Wilkes, Capt. Cunningham, and some still smaller craft. And within these inadequate crews of Lewis and his aide Mitchell a ferment had arisen owing to the total absence of grog. On March 15, after Lewis had joined the State vessels at Hood's, he wrote from his "flagship," the Renown: "We have never had a drop of spirits on Board since we have been in the State service and Seamen are creatures that must have it especially when an Expedition of this kind is on foot." And Mitchell wrote in the same strain with less elegant phrasing.

But officers of the "public vessels" were undergoing vestiary afflictions as well. Capt. Edward Travis, of the Tempest, revealed the distressing state of his naval colleagues with some very plain speaking: "These injured gentlemen have not cloaths of any kind to defend them from the inclemency of the weather and to my knowledge frequently shun company by not being able to appear as an officer**The Partiality of the Assembly in advancing four months pay to the land officers" he deprecated as "the greatest injury offered to the navy and in my opinion ought to be resented by the resignation of the whole line, and I make no doubt would have been the case, had not the noble spirit of serving their country got the better of their resentment."

The Governor's answer was soothing, with the assurance that "the supply of cloathing is in considerable forwardness." He suggested that the aggrieved men lay their case for redress before the approaching Assembly.

In this anxious time Jefferson, on March 31, presented Virginia's plight in a letter to the President of Congress: "The Affliction of the people for Want of Arms is great, That of Ammunition is not yet known to them**An enemy 3,000 strong not a regular in the State nor Arms to put into the Hands of the Militia are indeed discouraging Circumstances." The Governor urged the rushing of the State's arms from Rhode Island, stressed the pressing need of lead, and, on April 6, made a highly rational forecast: "Should this Army from Portsmouth come forth and become active (and we have no reason to believe they came here to sleep) our Affairs will assume a very difficult Aspect."

A week later he was even more explicit to the Chevalier de la Luzerne: "I believe it may therefore with truth be said, that the opposition to the two hostile Armies in North Carolina and Virginia falls at present on Virginia only aided with about 500 Men from Maryland: While our Northern Brethren, infinitely superior in numbers, in compactness, in Strength of Situation, in Access to foreign Supplies, of necessaries, possessed of all the Arms and military Stores of the Continent, opposed by an Enemy not superior to ours, have the protection of almost the whole of the Continental Army, with the important Addition of the Army and fleet of our Allies."

And in Virginia retrenchment went on. On March 28, two days after General Phillips took command of the British land forces in Virginia, Jefferson informed Lafayette that, for reasons of economy, it was imperative to discharge all but the three largest vessels, which should be retained to bring stores and provisions to Richmond. To the problem of manning the boats continued in service, he supplied the solution: he knew of no better way than draughting from the lower militia such men as were used to the water.

Three weeks later there was ominous news concerning the enemy. "We have received advice this morning," announced Jefferson in Council on April 19, "that the enemy were in motion up James River in eleven vessels most of them square rigged, the foremost of which was in the afternoon of yesterday within sight from Burwells Ferry." To the President of Congress and to General Washington he reported, on April 23, their further advances: "On the 18th the Enemy came from Portsmouth up James River in considerable force**They landed at Burwells ferry below Williamsburg and near the Mouth of Chickahominy above it." Of these "cowardly plunderers" one body entered Williamsburg on the 20th and the other proceeded to "a Shipyard we had on Chickahominy**I take for granted they have burnt an unfinished 20 Gun Ship we had there."

But the crushing blow to the Virginia Navy was delivered at Hood's, and this achievement Arnold duly reported to Sir Henry Clinton: "Finding the enemy had a very considerable force in ships four miles above Osborn's drawn up in a line to oppose us, I sent a flag to the Commodore proposing to treat with him for the surrender of his fleet, which he refused, with the answer that he was determined to defend it to the last extremity**I immediately ordered down two 6 and two 3-pounders, brass field peices to a bank of the river, nearly level with the water, and within one hundred yards of the Tempest†, a twenty-gun State ship, which began immediately to fire upon us, as did the Renown, of 26 guns, the Jefferson, a State-brigantine of 14 guns, and several other armed ships and brigantines; about two or three hundred militia on the opposite shore, at the same time kept up a heavy fire of musketry upon us. Notwithstanding which, the fire of the artillery under the direction of Captain Fage and Lieutenant Rogers, took such place that the ships were soon obliged to strike their colors and the militia drove from the opposite shore*. Want of boats and the wind blowing hard, prevented our capturing many of the seamen who took to their boats and escaped on shore, but not without first scuttling and setting fire to some of their ships which could not be saved. Two ships, three brigantines, five sloops and two schooners loaded with tobacco, cordage, flour, etc. fell into our hands. Four ships, five brigantines, and a number of small vessels were sunk and burnt—we had not a man killed or wounded."

After waiting for the return of scouting and foraging parties dispatched to various points about Richmond, one division of which at Manchester is said to have scampered, on an attack by the Marquis de la Fayette, for their boats in a *sauve qui peut*, Arnold returned down the river to the neighborhood of Chickahominy and on the 27th fell in with Lieutenant Colonel Abercrombie, who had successfully destroyed the public property at the shipyard.

The Chickahominy shipyard had not been seized without at least a spark of resistance. At the threat of the enemy's approach Lieut. Saunders of the Lewis galley filled the galleys under his charge with naval stores and planned to save both ships and cargoes by concealing them further up the river, but

---

†Capt. Markham of the Tempest was taken prisoner; his parole was dated April 28, 1781. Lieut. William Harwar Parker, who set off from the Tempest in the same small boat with Markham, escaped by swimming ashore under fire of the enemy. Lieut. Steele of the same vessel was captured.

*According to an American eye-witness the Virginia vessels were not drawn up in line of battle, and the statement is also made that Arnold's cannon were planted on a bluff from which he was able to rake the flotilla while the ships' guns could not be sufficiently elevated to reach their assailants.

wind and tide being against him, he was compelled to "come to." He then put a spring on his cable and waited for the invaders, who were not long in coming in sight. On their closer approach he discharged his cannon at them, then sank his vessel, and he and his men made their escape to the shore, with bare life.

British land operations likewise swept onward. A body of over 2000 soldiers under General Phillips put ashore at City Point and turned their arms southward in a march upon Petersburg, which goal they attained after their progress had been retarded by the obstinate defense of less than a thousand militia under Baron von Steuben, who behaved "very handsomely", with a loss of between sixty and seventy in killed and wounded, and who, before they were forced to give way, inflicted even greater loss upon the invader.

The British General, established in Petersburg in expectation of contact with Lord Cornwallis, dispatched by a flag a protest against threats of retaliation on the crews of prizes to "Thomas Jefferson Esq. American Governor of Virginia." Jefferson, piqued at the studied discourtesy, refrained for a time from breaking the seal, but considering the matter more coolly and dwelling upon "the miserable condition of our brethren in Charles Town, while a punctilio would be discussing," he mastered his first impulse. Yet he determined to have his revenge and his answer went back "To William Phillips Esq., commanding the British forces in the Commonwealth of Virginia." However, convinced that the Briton would be so hotly incensed that he would never open the message, Jefferson embodied its purport in a letter to Gerlach, captain of the flag, who would not fail to bring it to the attention of his superior. Jefferson reckoned without a swifter accountant. "William Phillips Esq., the proudest man of the proudest nation on earth", was soon beyond the power of displaying arrogance, indignation, or any other human passion or emotion. At Bollingbrook, his headquarters in Petersburg, the British commander passed away "of a fever" on the thirteenth of May, and Benedict Arnold ruled, for a space, in his stead.

The Governor, the day before he sought to pay Phillips in his own coin, conveyed to the Chevalier de la Luzerne his obligations for his Excellency's readiness to "secure us against the malice of our prisoners taken on the Romulus," singling out as markedly capable of mischief the merchant Jonathan Eelbeck (Eilbeck), whose ashes now repose undisturbed in Norfolk, Virginia, at the north door of St. Paul's. The Romulus, a 44-gun man-of-war, successively used as a transport for American prisoners to England and as an asylum for Loyalists, had fallen into the hands of Captain de Tilly during his February cruise of the Bay.

An event that probably befell in May was the seizure of a hostile boat off the eastern shore of Accomac, by a party of volunteers. The Americans had detected in the distance a barge making her way close under the coast. The alarm was given. Speedily a small rowboat and four canoes were manned, and chase given to the lurking intruders, who, observing that they had been detected, attempted to effect their escape. The fugitives were overtaken, however, some four or five leagues from the shore. The boat was found to be equipped with swivels and the men armed with muskets; yet only feeble resistance had been offered. On the person of one of the prisoners was discovered a letter from Lord Cornwallis directed to Sir Henry Clinton.

And about the same time a Mr. or Captain McLane succeeded in securing a prize off the mouth of Rappahannock, after firing but a single shot. On board the captured vessel were ex-prisoners, who had escaped, possessed themselves of this ship, procured weapons, and were on their way to join the British. Among them were a noted Tory of Delaware and members of the crew of Capt. Cane's Hero's Revenge, one of the Chesapeake's most destructive marauders.

This spring, in faraway waters, saw Captain John Cox, veteran of many West Indian voyages, engaged in his Sally Norton with the British Brig Eagle of twenty guns. The American, with her ten guns, put up a courageous resistance, and when forced to give way, only surrendered after she had made every effort to outdistance her adversary. Cox and his crew were taken to the Island of Tortola, but he promptly made his escape to St. Eustatius and returned to Virginia in the Renown, Capt. Elliott, which soon afterwards, in the James, under Capt. Lewis fell a victim to Arnold.

The loss of the Sally Norton was followed by that of the Scorpion. Capt. Wright Westcott, bound for Martinique, made out early one morning, as the mists broke away before the sun, a sail bearing towards him with clearly hostile intent. As the distance between them diminished, the stranger revealed herself as a powerful frigate, subsequently learned to be the Cerberus under command of Sir Jacob Wheat. To engage with any prospect of victory was for the Scorpion out of the question. No valor could avail against so formidable an adversary. Crowding on all her canvas, the Scorpion bore away with all the speed of which she was capable. The pursuit continued in earnest, with early chances favoring the Virginian's escape. But, with the rising of the wind as the day advanced, the larger vessel gained an advantage. Yet the Scorpion held her way for hours, and it was not until the same sun that had betrayed her presence in the early morning was dipping beneath the horizon that the American was overhauled and captured. Officers and crew were carried to Bermuda, and there held in prison-ships until the declaration of peace.*

General Nelson, to whom the guidance of the Commonwealth had been committed in the emergency succeeding Jefferson's withdrawal from Richmond in May and his subsequent hurried ride, in the nick of time, from Monticello to the shelter of Staunton, had immediate occasion to bewail a Navy annihilated by the enemy, who with a ship or two moving everywhere on the water at their pleasure, "will effectually keep possession of this River and Fort" and cut off supplies from our troops, while in the Eastern and Northern States trade is free, extensive and busy.

The General had nevertheless solid ground for elation. Cornwallis, he declared, for all his ostentatious running up and

---

*Among prisoners returned to Virginia on January 7, 1783 on the Bermudan boat Dolphin were Lieut. John Crew, Peter Fiveash, sailing-master, and Laban Goffigan, pilot, all of the Scorpion.

down the country, retreats with precipitation when even a small force is mustered to meet him. He is further from the conquest of Virginia than when he entered it. Withal the spirit of the people is higher than it has been for some months past.

And just now they had before them an example of notable daring. Capt. John Cox, undismayed by his recent experience, obtained a new boat, the Game Cock, and associated himself with St. George Tucker in a descent upon Bermuda, as a result of which all the powder on the islands was seized, landed safely in Virginia, and transported to the Williamsburg Magazine.

In August there were renewed movements by the British in Virginia waters. A fleet of transports fell down the Bay and moved into York "where they will make themselves so strong that it will be difficult to get them out," prophesied the commander who was to take a signal part in achieving their ultimate reverse. To face the new situation, all available shipping was ordered impressed. Sir John Peyton was charged with the commission of getting a swift-sailing vessel to effect the crossing of the Bay, and Commodore Barron, "a Gentleman in whom we can place the highest confidence," was designated to furnish the Executive with information as to the movements on the ocean and the Bay, at the earliest possible moment.

On September 2 came the long wished for and expected tidings that the Count de Grasse with a powerful armament of 28 ships of the line, six frigates, and 3000 land forces, after pushing aside an attempt to engage him at sea, had cast anchor close to Cape Henry. And this time pilots launched out withour fear of deception. William Jennings, under instructions from Capt. Richard Barron, took charge of the Northumberland, which, along with the other French vessels numbering thirty sail (according to Capt. Pasteur), all capably piloted, was conducted in safety from the Cape to York Spit about twenty miles below York Town.

No sooner had the visitors arrived than the Virginia "Mosquito fleet," supervised by Colonel Pickering, Commissary of the Continental Army, and Commodore Barron, stationed at Trebel's landing near Burwell's Ferry, became industriously active. Lookout boats were impressed. Capt. Callender, with numerous barges and small boats in the upper James, bestirred himself to procure and forward provisions for the use of the troops concentrated in and about Williamsburg and York. Capt. Thomas Herbert, in command of a flotilla of small craft that even included canoes, transported provisions. The Nicholson, which as well as the Boat Liberty had been sunk for concealment from the enemy, was floated and put to similar service. General Nelson, much concerned over the insufficiency of supplies despite all these exertions, took steps to see that a French brig's rum-laden prize, cast away on Little Wicomico, might discharge its cargo through the proper channels to the Army and Navy in dire straits for the lack of this article. The strange spectacle of seamen strolling about the countryside while militiamen were called upon to man boats, gave place to the more seemly one of seamen treading the decks in the way of their calling

Finally, when announcement of the surrender of Cornwallis came through a signal from the French Admiral, Lieut. Joseph Saunders, lying in his galley off the mouth of York river, sailed straight through the British fleet to deliver his cargo. This done, he was presently directed by Capt. Edward Travis to take a sergeant and guard and go aboard a British ship "about to sail unrestricted as to load" and make search for slaves held contrary to stipulation. The fruit of this mission was a single female slave, whom he brought to shore and turned over to the proper authorities.

In Virginia the struggle on land had ended triumphantly, but for more than a year and a half a preditory foe was to hold more than his own on the waters.

CHAPTER XIV

THE LAST OF THE PATRIOT AND THE MARQUIS LAFAYETTE, PRIVATEER

The period of the British occupation in the year 1781 saw the end of the Patriot, that swift, daring vessel, companion of the Boat Liberty in service dating from the inauguration of the Navy of Virginia. The Patriot's final engagement was recounted by Commodore James Barron, the younger, in the *Virginia Historical Register*:

"In the spring and summer of the year 1781, a large fleet of British men-of-war and transports were assembled in Hampton Roads, for the purpose of protecting and transporting Lord Cornwallis's army from Portsmouth to Yorktown. This fleet remained in that position for some time, and during that period caused the most annoying interruption to the intercourse of the inhabitants of the surrounding country. For the boats and small craft belonging to it, were always on the look-out, day and night, and rambling far and wide from the shipping, going up the river as high as Jamestown, and looking into all the smaller streams, Nansemond, Pagan Creek, &c., for supplies and plunder. At this time neither the Government of the State nor that of the country could afford any effectual relief to the citizens suffering from these predatory excursions. At length, however, it was resolved that an effort should be made, with the only vessel then afloat belonging to the State Navy, to check this evil as far as possible, and afford some small relief to the people—that is, more particularly, to the women—for the men generally were either gone to sea, or to the army, or were prisoners of war; and indeed they were so thinned off about this time that soon after the investment of York Town it was said that there were not more than five old men in the county of Elizabeth City, except a few that had paroles; but there were but *few* who would accept such protection.

"An order was accordingly sent to Lieut. James Watkins commanding the Schooner Patriot, then lying high up the James River for safety, to proceed down to the waters most annoyed by the British cruisers, and use his best endeavours to give the inhabitants such protection as his small vessel could afford, for the Patriot was but a small thing mounting only eight two-pounders, on swivels; but these were so judiciously arranged that she had more than once captured vessels of twice her number and weight of metal. In the action too, that she had with a heavy British Government Schooner when she was commanded by Captain Richard Taylor, afterwards Commodore Taylor, she made a most gallant defence, and would in all probability have captured this vessel of double her force, had not Capt. Taylor and many of his men received such dangerous and painful wounds, as obliged him to allow the British cruiser to go off. Captain Watkins, then, with his first Lieutenant, whose name was Umphlet, and a small crew, hastened down the river in this sharp little schooner, to do his duty. At this time, the British had, for some weeks, caused a sloop, apparently a common craft, of about 60 or 80 tons, to run far up the river on petty plundering expeditions; and this sloop soon attracted the attention of Capt. Watkins, who watched all her movements and readily concluded from them that she was only a freebooter making the most of her opportunities, and quite as anxious to avoid a meeting with the Patriot as he was to effect it. And now for the closing scene of the affair, which the writer of this article happened to witness himself, as follows:

"I had gone out some short time before with my elder brother and a very singular and meritorious character in the person of an African, who had been brought over to this country when he was young, and soon evinced a remarkable attachment to it; he was brought up a pilot, and proved a skilful one, and a devoted patriot. Our little party had taken shelter in a small house in the great gust wood, in Elizabeth City county, with a view to cross over, on the first opportunity we could find, to the South side of the James river, where we expected to meet some friends who had preceded us, and with whom we hoped to enjoy a degree of safety not then to be found on the North side where we were. With this object in view we made daily excursions to the river side about three miles off in hopes to find some craft or boat to take us over to the opposite shore. At length, on one Sunday forenoon, about 11 o'clock, as we stood on the bank of the river on a spot belonging to the respectable family of Massenburgs, in Warwick county, we saw the schooner Patriot in chase of the suspicious sloop, and, as we supposed, fast coming up with her. Here Capt. Starlins (for so our African called himself) allowed his patriotism to get the better of his judgment, and gave free utterance to the most extravagant expressions of joy—at the same time hopping about with uplifted and clapping hands,—in the hope, which indeed we all indulged, that we should soon see both vessels changing their course and going up the river, instead of down to the Roads.

"But now for the end. The sloop was purposely delayed in her downward progress by a drag thrown out over her starboard bow, which enabled the Patriot to come alongside of her, when, all at once, up jumped fifty Marines with their officers, who had hitherto not been seen;—and the capture of the Patriot was but the work of a minute. And what now was the dismay of our thunder-struck group at this sudden disappointment of all our hopes. . . . Poor Captain Starlins was struck dumb and motionless. . . . My brother had more command over his feelings. He was indeed exceedingly grieved, but although young, being only fifteen years of age, he was already remarkable for that dignity of character which afterwards became so conspicuous in him, and restrained himself. . . .

"Our countrymen, as we heard, were immediately sent off to Charleston, South Carolina, and locked up in the Prevost prison, where Lieut. Watkins died. Lieut. Umphlet survived, and returned to his friends after the British evacuated that city.

"The Patriot was afterwards taken round to Yorktown with the British fleet that attended Lord Cornwallis's army when he established his headquarters in that place, and when he afterwards surrendered to the combined armies, she fell into the hands of the French, according to the terms of the capitulation, and the last that we heard of her was that she was carried to Cape Francois, and there employed as a government packet.

"But to return to Captain Starlins, the noble African. He lived and died a slave soon after the peace, and just before a law was passed that gave freedom to all those devoted men of colour who had so zealously volunteered their services in the patriotic cause. It is, however, an agreeable part of my duty, as the historian of this little affair, to assure my readers that the Captain never felt any degree of restraint that could serve to remind him that he was not absolutely a free man; for his master was as proud of his character and deeds as he himself was of the estimation in which he knew that he was held by all worthy citizens, and more particularly, by all the navy officers of the State.

Norfolk.   J. B. [James Barron.]"

In the account above the writer failed to mention Lieutenant Thomas Chandler, who fell into the hands of the enemy and died in a prison ship off Norfolk on July 25 of this year.

"Immediately on receipt of your Letter of the 9th by Capt. Travis informing me of the loss of the Boat Patriot," Jefferson notified General Weedon, on April 14, "we engaged Captain Travis to go over to Appomattox, where he procured another Boat (the Washington) said to be a better sailor (*sic*) than the Patriot; Being ready manned and equipped for sailing she receives orders today to fall down and take your Commands."

In the following month occurred the successful exploit of Capt. Meredith, of the ship Marquis LaFayette, recounted by the vessel's lieutenant John Cowper, who also related her further career, in a letter of April 6, 1833, to Commodore Barron:*

"I have often promised you that I would put on paper the circumstances attending the remarkable escape of the private armed ship Marquis Lafayette, from Nansemond river, through

---

*Published in the *Virginia Historical Register and Literary Advertiser*, July, 1849.

Hampton Roads, during the revolutionary war. This promise I shall now redeem, as far as some memoranda, which, by accident, I recently found, and memory will permit. The circumstances are yet very strongly impressed on my mind, having occurred at a period of my life, when very strong impressions are made; besides which, I was deeply interested in many ways, in the result of an attempt deemed so very difficult, if not impossible, at the time it was undertaken.

"The ship Marquis Lafayette was owned by my father and his two brothers, trading as merchants, under the firm of Wills Cowper & Co., and residing near Suffolk, that town having been destroyed by the enemy in the year 1779. The ship was commanded by Captain Joseph Meredith, and calculated to carry 26 guns, including 6 quarter deck guns; but at the time alluded to, mounted only 12 guns, six pounders, and was manned with only 40 persons of all descriptions.

"There was something so extraordinary in the fortunes of this ship, that although not connected with her escape, they may not be deemed without interest. She was built within half a mile of Suffolk, and every preparation for launching her was made, to be carried into execution the next day, when an express arrived, stating the arrival in Hampton Roads of a British fleet. This was about the middle or latter part of October, 1780. It proved to be a fleet of ships of war and transports, having on board an army under the command of Major General Leslie. The main army landed without a moment's delay, and took possession of Portsmouth, while two detachments were sent up Nansemond river, one landing on the south side of the river, the other on the north side, intending to unite (as they afterwards did) at Suffolk. The owners of the ship, apprized of the approach of the enemy, hastened their preparations for launching, to prevent her being burned on the stocks. They completed their operations of launching, and had her scuttled and sunk in about eighteen feet water, only about half an hour before the detachment that landed on the south side of Nansemond river arrived at Suffolk. Whether from the haste in sinking it was imperfectly done, is not known; but in a very few hours she was raised, and subsequently taken down to Portsmouth. Fortunately, her sails and rigging had been removed to about seven miles from Suffolk. On the night of the same day on which she was removed, the detachment that landed on the north side, came to the place where the sails, rigging, &c. were stored, and remained nearly half a day, but did not open the house where they were stored.

"On the arrival of the ship at Portsmouth, preparations were made to fit her out and send her to New York; but at this moment, General Leslie received orders to evacuate Virginia without delay, which he did; and the ship was again sunk at Gosport. The owners lost no time in raising her, and taking her up the Nansemond river. They had nearly prepared for the sea, when about the latter end of December, or early in January, Arnold arrived in Virginia, and was subsequently followed by General Phillips, and the State permanently invaded; in addition to which, Lord Cornwallis was expected in Virginia.

"It was at this juncture that Captain Meredith took command, and prepared for the enterprise in which he afterwards succeeded. Those who know what situation the country was in at that time will appreciate the difficulties which presented themselves to such an undertaking. The cavalry and infantry of the enemy were daily, and the artillery, occasionally, on the shores of the Nansemond, as high up as the head waters. It was most dangerous to remain a moment in the narrow waters, and accordingly the ship was moved near the mouth of the river, where it is wide; but this movement brought her in full view of the enemy's ships. The entrance of Nansemond river is extremely difficult, and it was believed the enemy had not a pilot who could bring a ship of sufficient force to attack this ship in that river. They did not attempt it, but sent some boats in the night, which were discovered, and retreated without making the attempt.

"In this situation the ship remained a long time, until about the 1st of May, 1781. This delay arose from the difficulty to procure seamen to navigate her, should we succeed in putting her to sea. At length, however, they were procured, and about this time, the movements of the enemy indicated that the delay of one night might render all further attempts abortive. To my best recollection, it was on the second or third of May that it was decided that on that night the attempt should be made, although the moon was advanced in her second quarter. In the morning Captain Meredith, with one of the owners, accompanied by a skilful Hampton pilot, named Ross Mitchell, went down in the ship's barge to reconnoitre the position of the enemy's ships. They were distributed nearly as follows: One ship of the line, a frigate, and a sloop of war lay under Newport Noose (*sic*); two frigates and two sloops lay off Hampton bar, about half a mile from each other; three vessels of war were at the entrance of Elizabeth river, near Seawell's point; and several vessels of war, of what description or number I do not now remember, were near Old Point Comfort. The transports and merchant vessels, about eighty to one hundred, were distributed in different parts of the road, and from whom nothing was to be apprehended, unless those higher up should give notice of our approach; which was also to be apprehended from the ships under Newport Noose. It ought to have been stated, that the orders were issued by Captain Meredith in the morning before he went down to the Roads. All spirits were forbidden to be used on that day. After entering Hampton Roads, the duty of the ship was to be carried on in a tone so low as not to be heard out of the ship. The guns to be loaded, but not to be fired without special order, even if we were fired into. Captain Meredith stated to his officers, that by not returning the fire of the enemy, we might pass for one of their own ships, and it might cease; but if we fired, our character could not be mistaken. He further stated, that upon entering the Roads, almost a dead silence must be observed. His plan was to get among the transports, as near to them as possible, and to keep one or more of them between him and the ships of war.

"All things being ready at dark, we got under way, with the ebb tide, and a moderate breeze at about w. n. w. and proceeded down. Having cleared the river the road pilot took charge, and a boat was ready to take off the river pilot, when the wind became light, and in a short time it was calm. This was an awful moment—to return was impossible, on account of the tide—nothing remained but to anchor. Captain Meredith was pacing the quarter deck, and with much anxiety looking to the northwest, when an officer came and said that all was ready to let go, and that the pilot notified that it must be done immediately, as the ship could not be commanded. Orders were given to let go the anchor, when Captain Meredith called out 'stop.' I was near to him and heard him exclaim, 'I see the cloud from whence we shall have a wind.' At this moment the higher sails began to swell, the top-sails bent, and immediately spread themselves to the breeze. Those who know how a north-wester comes on, will know what was the effect.

"We now entered fully into the roads. The first ships we passed were those under Newport Noose; we saw them very distinctly when the clouds did not obscure the moon. They probably did not see us, as they gave no signal to the ships below. We now approached the frigate that was highest up, and passed her at a distance of a quarter of a mile. We soon got among the transports, passing them most rapidly, and often so near as to hear the conversation on board. We were never hailed by one. It may be well imagined that with a strong ebb tide—wind sufficient—a fast sailing ship—a press of sail—and a smooth water—there was little time for observation; and I am certain that, by the time a gun could have been brought to bear, we should have been out of sight. The great danger was from notice being given by the ships above to those below.

"At length we passed the ships near Old Point Comfort, and began to feel easy, when we approached a very large ship at anchor, near Willoughby's Point. She hailed us, but no answer was given; and what she was we never knew—probably some ship that had come in that afternoon, and anchored upon the making of the ebb tide.

"A very short time elapsed before we cleared Cape Henry, and after a sound sleep I found myself on blue water; and I was as much rejoiced as I had ever been on my return to port after a long voyage. Escaped from an enemy that was gathering round us every day, and by whose grasp we must have been shortly seized, the ocean was hailed as our deliverer.

"These are the material facts of an escape that was thought miraculous at the time, but to me it appears to have been less so than I could have supposed. The rapidity of the ship's movement when under way was such that it was impossible to have stopped her unless it was known that she was on the way down; and it is surprising that the enemy's ships did not keep a better look out. My father, who was a prisoner in Norfolk at the time, told me the enemy had not supposed the attempt would be made on a moonlight night—nor would it have been made but from pressing necessity. The boldness of the enterprize made the enemy less vigilant.

"This narrative may show to those in difficulty that success is one-half secured when we are determined on a bold enterprize. Placed in the circumstances in which Captain Meredith and the owners were, from the situation of the country, many persons would have saved the materials and equipment, and abandoned the hull.

"After getting to sea Captain Meredith decided to get into the first port, and accordingly he made for the Delaware, and early in the morning made land a little to the south of Cape Henlopen. Upon coming up with that Cape we saw a large British frigate (as supposed) at anchor, who was soon under way in chase of us. By four o'clock P. M. she gave up the chase, and we pursued our way for Rhode Island, where we arrived without accident.

"At Rhode Island the ship was completely armed and fitted with 18 guns—6 pounders—on the battery, and 6 fours on the quarter deck, and 140 men, with which she proceeded on a cruise off the port of Charlestown (as then called), S. C., which was occupied by the British. Within four miles of the bar we captured a British brig of 400 tons, with a cargo of dry goods, worth at that time in the United States 350,000 dollars; and on the same day captured two other vessels of no great value, burned one, and with the brig and the other proceeded for Rhode Island.

"Our movements had not passed without notice by the enemy. We boarded a Flag the next morning, from which we learned that two frigates and two sloops passed the bar in the afternoon of the same day we disappeared. On the second morning, some time before day, saw a large ship under the lee; Captain Meredith hailed the prizes, and ordered them to haul to the eastward, and proceed according to their instructions in case of separation.

"For the safety of his own ship Captain Meredith had no fear, from her superior sailing; but feared for his rich prize, a very dull sailor. He practiced a manoeuvre which, I think, succeeded in preventing the enemy from knowing our size; for, had we presented the broadside, it would have shewn the distance between the masts; but we bore down upon him. There is reason to believe that we saw this vessel before we were seen, as it was nearly three quarters of an hour after we parted with our prizes before any movement was discovered by the enemy. Day was now breaking. The vessel was a large frigate, and was preparing for action. In the meantime, everything on board our ship was prepared to haul on a wind for running. As the morning advanced, we could no longer practice the imposition, and hauled our wind. The chase then commenced; our prizes were three or four miles to the eastward; the enemy did not notice them, or did not care for them. Our enemy proved to be a better sailor than we expected, for, after getting into our wake—which Captain Meredith permitted, our ship, to do her best required the wind a little free—she kept even with us, or pretty nearly so, which induced us to go more large; but at that moment we made another ship to leeward, which it would be difficult to pass as we were then standing. The ship astern kept way with us and it was thought would have come up with us, if we hauled up a wind to avoid the ship to leeward. Captain Meredith was always prompt in his decisions, and determined to pass the ship to leeward, even if exposed to a broadside or two. This ship proved a very inferior sailer to her consort, and though she was almost in our path, she only gave us one fire from her broadside, and at the same time her consort opened upon us astern. Their fire did us little damage, and we were soon relieved from the ship last seen, who bore away, leaving us to her consort, who kept up the chase until four o'clock P. M. when, for the first time, we began to feel confident of our superior sailing. At sundown she gave up the chase. Next morning, we boarded another cartel, and from the prisoners we learned that the ships that had chased us were the Blonde and the Carysfort; the former a very fast ship.

"After returning to Rhode Island, Captain Meredith proceeded on another cruise, which was cut very short by the following circumstances. Captain M. determined to look into the Chesapeake, and then proceed to Charleston and Savannah. On the 5th of September, 1781, being off Hogg Island, stood in to the south, and about meridian saw a fleet ahead, and to leeward; upon standing on, perceived it was a fleet of British ships of war, formed into a line of battle. Presently we saw a French fleet beating out of the Capes of Virginia. About 3 or 4 o'clock an action commenced. These were the fleets of De Grasse and Graves. About sundown, the French bore away for the Capes. It was this naval action, and the arrival of the Rhode Island squadron, which we also saw going in, that put an end to the hopes of Lord Cornwallis at York. The French, by the junction of Du Barras, from Rhode Island, with DeGrasse gave them a superiority which the British, in those seas, dared not face. All this time the British were between us and our friends.

"About dark we hauled off to the eastward, wind light, and so continued until daylight; when we saw two frigates, about two miles to leeward and abreast of us. Captain Meredith immediately tacked ship to the westward. It may be proper here to state that after our return to Rhode Island, under the impression that our ship required more sail, a change took place in sparring her. The foremast was sprung at the head in the early part of last cruise in chase; it was well fished, and answered very well; but it was taken out, the mainmast put in for a foremast, and a new mainmast procured. It is astonishing how these changes affected the sailing of the ship; and the very day we made the fleets, Captain M. had decided to return to Rhode Island, and take his old Virginia mast again. It is said that sharp vessels are easily put out of trim; and therefore, when they are found to sail well, beating everything they meet, it is not wise to *try* to make them sail better.

"Captain Meredith was afraid of a long chase, and tacked to the westward, being about twelve leagues from the land. The chase commenced, and we were in great danger, and must have been taken, if the headmost frigate had not so frequently rounded to, in order to give her broadside. This she was induced to do by our nearing the land. Captain M. now consulted his pilot, Ross Mitchell of Hampton, upon the soundings, and to know if he could anchor him, so as to be out of close gunshot of the frigate. He said he could. The necessary preparations were made, and the chase continued, until we got in three fathoms water, and an order was issued to let go the anchor, when the frigate hauled off, and made for the fleet. It was understood that they were the Iris and Richmond. We returned to Rhode Island, where Captain M. and the writer left her.

"The old Virginia foremast was again taken in, and the mainmast replaced, and the ship sailed as at first; which should be a caution to innovators.

"She made another successful cruise under Captain Munroe, and had a severe engagement with a Liverpool Letter of Marque, of 16 nine pounders and 87 men, which she captured. Captain Munroe received a wound which obliged him to leave the ship, and from which he never recovered, though he lived several years after.

"The Marquis returned to Rhode Island, and was ordered to Virginia (to take a cargo of tobacco, for France,) to be coppered, which in those days could not be well done here. She was now drawing to a premature death. Under an indiscreet commander, a little to the southward of Cape Henry, she was chased by a frigate, from whom she was getting away fast, when another frigate was discovered, shaping her course to cut the Marquis off from Cape Henry. The Virginia officers that remained assured the commander that they could round the Cape without the danger of more than one or two broadsides at most, and perhaps without one. He was not a Meredith, but ordered the helm to be put up, and ran this gallant, enterprising little ship ashore; and thus, after so many hair-breadth escapes from danger, she was lost, when the danger existed only in apprehension."

CHAPTER XV

FRENCH OVERLORDSHIP

The French fleet sailed for the West Indies, leaving a small force to safeguard French interests in and contacts with Virginia. Presumably relying on the ally's vessels that lingered, the Virginia Assembly, in November, 1781, resolved, in view of the necessity of husbanding the scant funds of the State with the utmost economy, "That the officers of the navy of every denomination, be, and they are hereby reduced; also that all and every person of the naval staff establishment, including the commissioner of the navy, chaplains,* surgeons, paymasters, or others, shall be, and they are hereby dismissed * * Provided that such officers as shall be thought necessary for the command of the look-out boat Liberty shall be retained in the public service."

Still, in the face of the French protectorate, the privateers continued to harry. Capt. James Maxwell in his Cormorant and Capt. Harris in the Oliver Cromwell were unequal to the task of subduing them. As the naval department was financially on the rocks the Loyalist was sacrificed to meet the expense of purchasing new ships or reconditioning old ones. The winter brought little relief. Aggression on the water was to continue for another year unabated.

On March 1, 1782, Commodore Barron, stationed at Hampton, wrote in modest terms to Governor Harrison concerning what was actually an exploit of conspicuous gallantry. On the Sunday preceding, a small privateer and whale boat from New York had entered the Bay, captured close to Point Comfort a schooner with forage from Baltimore, and chased another schooner into the harbor of Hampton. This audacity excited the bitter indignation of Barron, who sprang into action at

---

*The writer has been unable to find record of a single chaplain in the service of the Virginia Navy.

once. His application to the officers commanding the French troops for twenty men was readily granted, and, adding to these some sailors who volunteered from the town, the Commodore manned the refugee schooner, armed his men, and hurried off in pursuit of the privateer making off with her prize under convoy. The prize, deserted by the captor in her flight, was promptly re-taken, and then the chase of the privateer continued, and was only abandoned when the closing-in of night caused the American to lose sight of his quarry.

This incident and the circumstance that, within ten days preceding, several other vessels had been seized in the Bay by the British, Barron held up as a warning of the necessity of putting vessels into service before the coming summer, and men must be provided; he had not then one seaman in service. Otherwise the British would infest the Bay with impunity and craft would be unable to pass from one river to another. Mr. Hope was just at this time repairing the boat Liberty and the building of a galley was planning.

In this same month of March the Governor was drawn into an unpleasantness with one of Virginia's "contiguous sister states". On the ground of illicit commerce Capt. Schemerhorn of the Virginia privateer Grand Turk had taken out of Edenton harbor a "Flag" addressed to the State of North Carolina, and conveyed his capture to Virginia for condemnation proceedings before the Court of Admiralty* in Richmond. The North Carolina Executive remonstrated in the most forthright and resolute manner at this violation of the rights of a State, vowing to retrieve the Flag by armed power if necessary. There followed awkward attempts at explanation, communications to Congress, and finally the way was paved for adjustments.

The other "contiguous sister state" proved an offender. Captain Maxwell's Cormorant and Capt. Harris's Oliver Cromwell, after having transported a portion of Washington's returning troops to the head of Elk, were subjected to an assessment by the Maryland authorities, "contrary to the law

---

*The members of the Admiralty Court at this time were Benjamin Waller, Richard Carrington, and James Henry.

of nations", and the Governor of Virginia furthermore propounded, "A Vessel in pursuit of the enemy would have to stop at the state line, for fear of being treated in so degrading a manner."

In May, the month when Paul Loyall, M. O. Brown and Thomas Newton, Jr., were designated Commissioners, with the task of superintending the protection of the Bay, Gouverneur Morris submitted a report to Congress suggesting that in view of the fact that Great Britain, foiled in her plan of conquest, was now making it her object to annihilate American commerce, the Chesapeake should be protected by two ships of the line and two frigates, to cruise when occasion required.

But in this direction nothing was done. Virginia fell back on her Cormorant, which Captain Hardyman, with his aides Clark, Webb and Selden, endeavored to supply with marines, in consideration of a commission of five dollars for every able-bodied soldier who entered the company and ten dollars for each recruit who had made one or more voyages to the West Indies or Europe.

The summer brought, in increasing numbers, ships under flags of truce—some on equivocal missions—over which Barron was directed to "keep a watchful Eye." The advent of a visitor from Jamaica is thus recorded in the Journal of an observer on board:

"7th July 1782—About seven o'clock we came off Cape Henry. Four miles up the Chesapeak the French frigate, "Sybil", was at anchor; she carried twenty-eight twelve pounders on her main deck—in all, forty-two guns. The officers boarded us, and we came to anchor close by her. She had been on this station seven months, to guard the entrance of the Capes from English privateers molesting the trade from Virginia. N. B.—The heat, this day and the last six or seven days, was more disagreeably oppressive than in Jamaica.

"On the 8th of July, 1782—Arrived off Hampton and anchored in the Road—James River.

"The occasion of our going to America was this:—Mr. Ross wanted to see his brother David, who had large possessions in Virginia and who went hand in hand with the American

Revolution * * * We had been sailing from Jamaica under a flag of truce, granted to us by Governor Campbell, and as a salvo, we carried eleven American prisoners to exchange. Mr. Ross had rendered himself very obnoxious to the Americans, by his violence against their cause, and by the depredations he had committed on their trade by his numerous privateers. He wrote to his brother to get us leave to land from Governor Benjamin Harrison. This leave did not arrive until the 15th, and limited us to time, and district of country about Hampton. Our Captain, whose name was Fish, and I went on shore in the afternoon of that day, and waited on Commodore James Barron, who treated us very politely; and said he would receive our prisoners, but had none to exchange, and that we must depart the next morning. We then waited on the French officer commanding on shore, who had an interview with the Commodore. * * * * We remained in Virginia, in the neighborhood of Hampton, from the 15th until the 22nd of July, when we again returned on board our vessel, and sailed from Hampton Road on our way to England.

"When we came down to the mouth of the Chesapeak, off Cape Henry, the French Frigate, 'Sybil', was there, with fourteen sail of ships, brigs, and schooners under her convoy, bound for Cape Francois, in Hispaniola, laden with flour. She fired a shot at us, brought us to, and ordered us to return to Hampton and wait for further orders from the Commodore, as his fleet was going out, that we might convey no intelligence to the English cruisers on the coast. We went back as far as Linhaven Bay only, where we came to an anchor and lay all night. The next day we saw, by the aid of our glasses, the 'Sybil' and her fleet under way; and as soon as they were out of sight, we weighed anchor and sailed out of the Capes. We passed Cape Henry at three, p. m., with a strong south wind, and pushed out to sea in a violent storm that greatly favoured our escape from the 'Sybil', whose orders we had disobeyed. * * We were in great peril about an hour—the storm then suddenly subsided—the sun again shone in full splendour—the sky was serene and beautiful. But the 'Sybil' and her fleet were scattered at great distances; several of them, as we supposed, foundered as they were not to be seen after the storm, the 'Sybil' herself was just in sight; and night coming on, we were in hopes of seeing her no more.

"24th July—At day break we saw the 'Sybil' and her fleet astern at a great distance. The 'Sybil' chased us for some time, but as we steered directly opposite to her course, she did not deem it prudent to leave her convoy, and so pursued us no further.

"27 July.—At two o'clock, discovered two large ships to leeward. They chased and gained on us; but night coming on, we saw no more of them."*

Capt. Fish and his "Lively", whose movements are thus revealed, had been causing an unhappy quarter of an hour to the Chevalier de la Valette, who, in petulant mood, upbraided the Governor for permitting the ship to make sail. Harrison, on July 29, justified his procedure: "I am sorry the Flag from Jamaca has sail'd as you wished the contrary tho' I know of nothing that can be communicated but what all the world knows. I gave orders to Capt. Barron who superintends the Flags to send her off as soon as possible lest any circumstance should take place that might be material during her longer stay."

In compliance with the wishes of the French commander, however, the Governor required that from that time other Flags should be detained and "blinded" by removal up the River to Burwell's Ferry, with the assurance to their captains, through Commodore Barron, that they would be permitted to sail "as soon as I can do it with propriety", for, as he informed Colonel Charles Dabney, "Colo. Lavalette certainly had no just right to give orders for the detention of the Flags, nor do I suppose he would have done it without application to me, if the Case would have admitted of Delay."

And to cap this difference of viewpoint came an order from General Benjamin Lincoln directing the French to demolish

---

*From the diary of Dr. Benjamin Moseley, a passenger on the "Lively" brig, of one hundred and thirty tons burthern, from Port Royal, Jamaica, to England via America. Included in the "Family Memoirs," by Sir Oswald Mosley, Baronet.

the forts and fortifications at Yorktown. When intelligence of this singular proposal reached the Virginia Executive he protested, with dignity and fervor, to the Virginia Delegates in Congress, "Your Secretary at War (General Lincoln) has I think insulted the sovereignty of the State exceedingly by giving orders (without even writing to me on the subject) to Lavalette the French Officer commanding here", to effect this destruction of works all built by the State, and necessary for the defense of the York and its trade. "We shall never be right or respectable," Harrison wrote to General Washington the same day, "till the Executive are left to do the business of an Executive without the interference of any other Power * * * The rod of correction has been applied in vain, and fatal experience changes not measures."

On later representations, however, Governor Harrison tempered his feelings towards "my good friend the General Lincoln", and laid the blame at de la Valette's door.

The Governor was meanwhile anxious to see the French commander's energies exerted in another direction. "A Banditti of Pirates," as he somewhat singularly phrased it, was, or were, plundering the Bay and its shores, distressing the trade of Virginia and of Maryland. If the French in the West Indies looked for an uninterrupted supply of flour it was imperative that Capt. Villebrun, with his captured Romulus and his three other small vessels riding in Hampton Roads, should set out to sweep the Bay of its terrors at once.

In September Richard Henry Lee, stirred by the continued depredations on the Rappahannock and the Potomac, gave expression to a comment that incensed the Executive: "It is greatly unfortunate for this Country that no exertions are made to defend its Honor and Interest upon the Water within the very Bowels of the State".

"Where you intended this answer to fall I know not," retorted the Governor, "if you meant it for the Executive it is injurious and more particularly so from a Gentleman who had so great a share in taking this Business out of their Hands." And he furthermore explained that the defense of the Chesapeake was in the hands of Commissioners with Executive power to correspond and consult with the Executive of Maryland on the best means of proceeding. In reality neither Commissioner nor Governor was to blame; "the fund appropriated to the use of the Navy has not yet brought in more money than will pay the expenses of the Commissioners travelling backwards and forwards to the Ships."

One of the ships that doubtless required commissioners' journeyings was that under construction at the price of 7 pounds per ton, as contracted for with John Nash, on October 7, "John Nash Ship Carpenter agrees to build see & deliver to Paul Royall & Thomas Brown on or before the fourth day of December next, a certain Vessel he is now building***demensions; vizt fifty five & a half feet Keel, Twenty one and a half feet beam and ten feet four inches hold, measuring part of the waist, as agreed; the waist to be near foot high, and a roundhouse about fourteen feet long; the whole of the waist to be filled in with the heart of poplar timber, lined with Inch & quarter, or Inch & half plank, & caulked inside and out, with fourteen ports at least for Guns, and to fit her compleat with Masts & other Sparrs for a Schooner."

The autumn Assembly, after directing the sale of the Cormorant, expressed substantial appreciation to the Navy for services rendered: "And all officers, seamen and marines, or their representatives shall be entitled to the same bounty in lands and other emoluments as the officers and soldiers of the Virginia line on continental establishment."

Early in the year 1783 a hostile visitor fell, by dispensation of the elements, into the hands of the patriots. The Prince William, fitted out by New York Loyalists, swept into the Bay with its twenty-two guns, six and nine pounders, and approached close to Elizabeth River. At this point a heavy wind, by no means ill for the Virginians, drove the invader ashore. The captain and crew of one hundred were secured by a hastily assembled force of militia. "A number of prisoners that were taken yesterday and sent to York Town," wrote Governor Harrison to Commodore Barron, on January 21, "are ordered down to be sent to Bermuda in the Flag Ship".

A welcome "flag" was that from the Lyon man-of-war with tidings in the guise of a copy of "the King of Britains speech" that pointed to an early end of hostilities. Yet the Commissioners, who forwarded this intelligence, were wary. They were exceedingly at a loss to know how, in the event of continuance of warfare, the small efforts of the little Navy of Virginia could avail against the great power of the enemy. "We shall have in a very short time," they added, "a Vessel of Twelve Guns ready for cruizing in the Bay; with her, we intended to have two Gallies and Two Barges."

There were other signs of the times. On February 25 Barron was able to report that British ships had sailed out of the Capes on the 15th and, cruising southwards, were seen every day. The Commodore inferred that they were on the lookout for French ships expected from Baltimore.

Finally came the announcement of peace. The barges Richmond and York, the schooner Harrison and the Cormorant were disposed of. The Liberty, sole survivor of the Navy, and the new Patriot *were retained, for a period, to carry out the directions of the port officials (the "Naval Officers"), to apprehend smugglers, and to warn those suspected of contraband tendencies of the penalties that followed misdeeds.

---

*Commodore Barron's "Journal of the Patriot", for parts of the years **1784, 1785, 1786**, and **1787**, are included in "Papers Concerning the State Navy, Vol. II", Virginia State Archives.

CHAPTER XVI

THE BATTLE OF THE BARGES

The persisting picaroons were victors in what was probably the last engagement of the Revolution in Virginia waters: this was the "Battle of the Barges", or, as it has also been termed, "The Battle of Kedge's, or Cagey's Strait", from a locality off Tangier Island, just within the Virginia border, where the action took place on November 30, 1782, the very day of the signing in Paris of the preliminaries of peace. The story belongs more properly to the history of the Maryland marine: the flotilla of American barges was, for the most part, manned by Marylanders, and was under the command of Commodore Whaley of Maryland.

The circumstances were these. A detail of barges *had been dispatched by the Maryland authorities with a view to putting an end to incursions of hostile craft, manned partly by British seaman but largely by Tories and by renegades of the most abandoned character, upon the defenseless inhabitants of Somerset County. Whaley, thus commissioned, was cruising in that region of the Chesapeake known as "The Sound" when to the westward he descried the flotilla of that Commodore Kidd of whose exploits two have already been related. As the hostile force, consisting of six large barges filled with well-armed men and served by cannon of considerable calibre, was too formidable an adversary for the Marylander's equipment he judged it the part of wisdom to proceed to Onancock Creek, Virginia, and in that neighborhood appeal for added support to enable him, with some prospect of success, to hunt down and endeavor to destroy the marauding flotilla.

Fortune favored the Maryland commander. He landed on a court-day when the men of the countryside were gathered,

---

*The barges, both American and British, had oars to supplement sails as driving power, mounted sixteen-pound guns, and carried a complement of seventy-five men each.

according to custom, for bargaining and discussion of the dramatic events of the time, not too far from the solacing tavern. Colonel Cropper, head of the militia, gave a ready ear to Whaley's appeal. The colonel had merely to proclaim on the courthouse green the visitor's mission to be besieged by a considerable body of volunteers, including several Continental and militia officers ready and eager for action. Without taking time to bid farewell to their respective families the men of the auxiliary force crowded the Maryland boats, and, when these were filled to capacity, a Virginia barge was pressed into service to carry the overflow.

Feeling himself now in a condition to strike, Whaley directed the course of his flotilla towards Tangier Island. After a few hours' sail the Americans got sight of the hostile barges drawn up in line of battle off Cagey's Strait, twenty miles north of Onancock. The Commodore acted in accordance with the reputation he had long borne. He was wholly fearless, but governed by his own initiative alone. His barge, the swift-moving Protector, had left the remainder of the force too far in her wake to admit of a concerted assault on the enemy, and from this circumstance Col. Cropper and other officers aboard besought the commander not to imperil needlessly his men and the issue of the engagement by rushing into action; rather, to "lay to" until the slower boats had time to come up. Whaley, not to be turned from his purpose, answered by giving orders to bear down on the enemy and rush the attack. If followed then as a matter of course that the lone barge, as she swiftly shortened the distance between herself and her adversaries, drew the concentrated fire of the whole opposing flotilla. Yet stoutly the American sustained and fiercely returned the volleys, inflicting grave damage and brilliantly standing off the enemy's superior force. The conflict continued sanguinary and obstinately maintained on both sides, and, had the remainder of the American flotilla been close at hand, the result would not have been doubtful. But, at a critical juncture, the Protector's magazine exploded, killing and maiming a number of the crew and forcing several others to leap overboard in order to escape with their lives.

Even now a steadfast remnant of the Americans held to the part of the deck that still furnished footing and defended themselves with enfeebled but heroic resistance, and these survivors might have protracted the struggle for many minutes if their nerves could have been steeled by assurance that aid was presently at hand. But such was far from the case. At this agonizing moment the lagging barges were seen to turn tail, without firing a single shot, and flee to the southward. The barge Victory, manned by Accomac volunteers who had not been able to find place in the Maryland barges, was not on the scene; she had gone aground before gaining the mouth of Onancock Creek.

In the thick of the conflict the rash and ill-fated Whaley fell mortally wounded; most of his officers were already either killed or disabled. And Cropper, now left in command of the shattered craft and the pitiful remnant of the crew, was soon wounded himself, and, with succor out of the question, was forced to yield at discretion to avert the distruction of all. And he too would have been counted among the slain if it had not been for the interposition of a former family servant, a negro who had been carried off on one of Kidd's raids. The colonel, bearing several severe wounds including a sabre cut on his scalp, was defending himself with musket and bayonet when he was set upon by a brawny black and two white men. One of the last-mentioned, in the act of dealing Cropper a terrible blow with a gun-rammer, had his lower jaw carried away by a shot. And yet, as if through a last convulsive effort, his last blow descended upon Cropper's already lacerated head and felled him to the bottom of the barge. Then advanced the negro, cutlass in hand, prepared to ensure the victim's death by a final thrust when, suddenly recognizing the familiar features, he dropped his weapon and broke forth into exclamations of surprise and attachment. He besought his companions that his master's life might be spared, and the petition was granted.

The Colonel's official report of the engagement, in a communication to William Davies, under date of December 6, 1782, runs as follows:

"Dear Sir:

"On the 28th ultimo, I received a letter from Commodore Whaley, requesting a number of militia to full man his fleet, in consequence of his intention to attack the enemy's barges then off Onancock. In compliance with which request, on the 29th I went on board his fleet myself, with twenty-five volunteers of the Accomac militia. On the 30th, at the head of Cagey's Straits (or Kedge's) we fell in with and engaged the enemy. When we approached them, within about three hundred yards, and the fire began to be serious, our barges all ran away except the Commodore's, the "Protector," in which were Major Smith Snead, Capt. Thomas Parker, Capt. William Snead, myself and five other volunteers. This dastardly conduct of our comrades brought on our barge the whole fire of the enemy, which was very severe, and it was as severely answered by the Protector, until the enemy's six barges were within fifty yards, when most unfortunately the cartridges of our short eighteen-pounders caught fire amidships; the explosion of which burned three or four people to death, and caused five or six more, all afire, to leap overboard, and the alarm of the barge's blowing up made several others swim for their lives. The enemy, almost determined to retreat from our fire, as they told us afterwards, took new spirit at this disaster, and pushed up with redoubled fury. On the other hand, our people opposed them with the most daring resolution. There was one continued shower of musket balls, boarding pikes, cutlass, cold shot and iron stay-sails, for eight or ten minutes, till greatly overpowered by numbers, and having all the officers of the barge killed and wounded, we struck to them, after having wounded their Commodore, killed one captain, wounded another, killed and wounded several of their inferior officers, and killed and wounded fifteen of the Kidnapper's crew, the barge which first boarded us. Commodore Whaley was shot down a little before the enemy boarded, acting the part of a cool, intrepid, gallant officer; Captain Joseph Handy fell nigh the same time, nobly fighting with one arm after the loss of the other—Captain Levin Handy was badly wounded. There went into action in the Protector sixty-five men; twenty-five of them were killed and drowned, twenty-nine were wounded, some of whom are since dead and eleven only escaped being wounded, most of whom leaped into the water to save themselves from the explosion. At the foot you have a particular account of the loss sustained by the volunteers on board the Protector. After the surrender, I entered into an agreement with Commodore Kidd to take ashore such of his wounded as chose to go and to have them nursed and attended at the public expense, upon condition that he would parole all our prisoners, as well the unhurt as the wounded; which agreement I hope will meet the approbation of his Excellency in Council and the Assembly. Being very much disordered with my wounds, I am scarcely able to write, therefore I beg leave to subscribe myself,

"Your most respected servant,

"John Cropper, Jnr.

"*Major Smith Snead* was wounded with a cutlass in the head, and boarding pike in the arm, and a contusion of a cold shot in his body.

"*Captain William Snead* was wounded in the head with a cutlass, and had his arm broken with a musket ball.

"*Captain George Christian* was killed with a musket ball.

"*Mr. John Reville* was wounded in the arm with a musket ball, and on the head with a cutlass.

"*Captain Thomas Parker*, Mr. William Gibb, and Mr. Evans, escaped being wounded, probably by leaping overboard at the alarm of the barge blowing up.

"*Myself* was wounded by a cutlass on the head, slightly by a pike on the face and thigh, slightly by a cutlass on the shoulders, and after the surrender was knocked down by a four-pound rammer, the blow of which was unfortunately near upon the same place where the cutlass hit.

"You will do me a most singular favor *to excuse the sally* I took in the barge, and have me exchanged as soon as possible.

Yours affectionately,

J. Cropper, Jnr."

Among those who sprang, for salvation, from the Protector into the waters of the Bay "at the alarm of the barge blowing up" was a young Scot, William Gibb, who, though "Naval Officer" of Accomac County, was unable to swim, and was in consequence on his way to Davy Jones's locker when his companion-at-arms, Capt. Thomas Parker, who had also sprung, grasped the helpless man by the hair and kept him afloat until both were picked up by their foes. In commemoration of his rescue Gibb, who became deputy clerk of the court of Accomac County, held on each recurring thirtieth of November a celebration to which were invited all his fellow-survivors of the "Battle of the Barges". At this "Feast of the Swimswimnati", as he called his dinner with a jocular play on the name of the "Society of the Cincinnati", the host always regarded Parker (in due course, Colonel Parker) as the guest of honor, and the chicken pie, the *pièce de résistence*, was never cut until "Tommy", no matter how belated, had turned up and taken his place. Gibb continued these dinners until his death forty-five years after his dip in the Bay. *

To Parker, Gibb was probably endebted a second time for preservation from death in another shape and in a lighter element. Kidd, loyal Scot-Briton, had looked on Gibb as a renegade of the deepest dye, and when his dripping fellow-countryman was dragged aboard and thrust into the bottom of the barge, the Commodore swore, with appropriate oaths, that the damnable rebel should swing from the first limb that presented itself after they had touched ground. On hearing his sentence Gibb, limp and exhausted, feared to show the faintest spark of vitality. A contrivance of his friend, however, succeeded in restoring to him both hope and ambition at once.

The imperturbable Parker, hail fellow with everybody, soon on friendly terms with his conquerors, bore in mind that his fallen comrade had a far keener relish for firewater than for seawater, and, assuming that the poor fellow could hardly survive without an incentive for living, managed to secure an extra ration of spirits on the pretext that he needed it as a

---

*Episodes recounted by Thomas R. Joynes, Sr., who had the facts from the lips of participants.

sedative for his own damaged state. Well aware of the wizardry of suggestion, he took a position where he could both be seen and heard by the sufferer. He then poured out half the contents of the container in such manner that a delectable rippling and babbling would strike the Scot's ear, and then deliberately and with relish swallowed his draught. The effect was amazing. Gibb not only opened covetous eyes, but by the time Parker had emptied his glass a parched tongue was extended in mute but fervent supplication for even a "wee drap" of the elixir of life. The pantomime had a witness of influence, whose organ of compassion was melted. Kidd not only ministered spirituously to his ex-compatriot, but also, when Parker put in a word for his friend, renounced the design of playing the hangman.

Another incident with a flavor of humor had to do with dress as a factor of fate. It will be recalled that Cropper's volunteers did not give themselves time to visit their homes before joining the flotilla; hence more than one officer was not garbed as befitted his rank. Captain Parker was dressed in his uniform; Major Snead was caught in civilian dress. When the survivors came into the hands of the enemy Snead begged his comrades to refrain from using his title in order that with the appearance of a private he might more readily contrive his exchange. The plea was respected, with humiliating results.

Now the popular Parker was invited to dine with the Commodore when anything more savory than usual appeared on the mess for the day. On several of these occasions, when host and guest were whetting their appetites by pacing the quarter-deck, Snead happened to loom in the way. Whereupon, to the secret delight of the uniformed Parker, Kidd would bellow at the intruder: "Out of the way, you damned rebel, and let the *Captain* pass."

Holding fast to his purpose, Snead swallowed his gall, no doubt swearing inwardly to have his innings as soon as the tables were turned.

AFTERWORD

The Virginia Navy of the Revolution, largest of all the State navies, included, in addition to the vessels already mentioned, the following: Brig American Fabius, the Hampton, the Morning Star, the Schooner Experiment (under command of Lieut. Ham in October, 1778—*Navy Board Journal*), Sloop Eminence, the Apollo, Industry, Pocahontas, and the Pilot Boat Fly. Most of these were, doubtless, vessels "impressed" at the time of the projected campaign against Arnold. On the authority of Dr. Palmer, there was also the Dasher Galley, Capt. Wilson in command. This ship is said to have been driven ashore on Lynnhaven Bay, and her captain and crew, captured by a detachment of British soldiers, were marched, according to the account, to Portsmouth, and there submitted to severe treatment in prison.

In May, 1776, the Virginia Convention ordained the appointment of a Board of Naval Commissioners to superintend and direct the navy that was coming into being. The Commissioners Thomas Whiting (styled First Commissioner), John Hutchings, Champion Travis, Thomas Newton, Jr., and George Webb held their first meeting in Williamsburg on July 8, 1776, and this Board (with some changes in its personnel) continued, until its abolition by legislation in May, 1780, to control the affairs of the Navy.

In April, 1777, the Naval Board acquired, for five hundred and ninety-five pounds, a tract of one hundred and nineteen acres in Charles City County, on the Chickahominy River, about twelve miles from its mouth, for the establishment of a shipyard—a site chosen partly for its sheltered location and partly on account of the superior timber that grew on the neighboring shores.

But there was also the Gosport shipyard, in the State's service during the earlier years of the conflict, and at Fredericksburg, South Quay, Frazer's Ferry, and at points on the James river and the Appomattox, shipyards of private ownership furnished numerous vessels to the Navy.

Of the public rope-walks and manufactories of ducking, sail-cloth, etc., the most important was that at Warwick on the James, about five miles below Richmond.* Skilled sail-makers were probably drawn from the Ulster settlement in the Valley of Virginia, some of whose members had doubtless served an apprenticeship in Ireland. The assignment of Col. Sampson Mathews, of Augusta County, to a committee on the supervision of naval equipment is not without significance.

Naval equipment was important, but nautical knowledge was vital, and in this matter the infant Navy was dependent on the veterans of the merchant marine. From this service came Richard Barron, Eleazer Callender, John Calvert, John Cowper, James Markham, Richard Taylor, Edward Travis, Celey Saunders, Isaac Younghusband, and John Catesby Cocke, who brought with them into the Navy many sailors seasoned by West Indian voyages. Most of the vessels commissioned at the outset were merchant-men transformed.

The navy thus created played its part heroically. Its vesssels, with the added service of the merchant marine, transported to Europe and to the West Indies great quantities of tobacco, whereby the credit of the States with friendly nations was largely sustained. And, without the supplies convoyed safely to the Head of Elk, the Continental Army would have suffered, in trying days, even more acutely, perhaps with resultant disaster.

*"No other state owned as much land, property, and manufactories devoted to naval purposes, as Virginia,"—Paullin's "The Navy of the Revolution", p. 400.

ROSTER

OF THE

Virginia Navy of the Revolution

The following Roster of officers and men of the Virginia Navy of the Revolution aims to be as complete as extant records admit. The sources of information include MS ship lists, county order books, pension claim papers, bounty warrants, military certificates, rejected claims, and the Journals of the House of Delegates of Virginia.

Unhappily, many documents dealing with the naval service were destroyed or have disappeared, and, in consequence, the name and service of hundreds of patriotic seamen and marines must remain in oblivion. That the list of officers, however, approaches completeness is reasonably assured.

After each name of a man in service follow data, wherever such were discoverable, concerning rank of officer or status of enlisted man, name of vessel or vessels served upon, length of service, native county, reference to sources of information as to heirs, and, in certain instances, a partial list of descendants.

When reference to authority for service is not set down in the Roster, it is to be understood that, in most instances, the record may be found in the MS collection entitled Navy 8, deposited in the Virginia State Archives. Record of service other than that designated below may, in many cases, be ascertained through the medium of the printed lists of the "Revolutionary Soldiers of Virginia" (Bulletins of the Virginia State Library). Material catalogued in these Bulletins is available in the State Archives.

A date following the name of a ship in the Roster indicates that the list or item in which the individual's name occurs was recorded on that day. The full period of service is often specified, but there are numerous instances where this cannot be determined, from records now in existence.

The native county of many members of the Virginia Navy is indicated, but that of many more has eluded research. It may safely be surmised, however, that the crew of a ship immediately after its commission was largely drawn from the locality where the vessel was constructed or first put into service.

KEY TO ABBREVIATIONS

Aud. Acct.—Auditor's Account Books numbered with Roman numeral.
B. (followed by a page reference)—To Lewis A. Burgess's "Virginia Soldiers of 1776," without mention of heirs.
BH.—A reference to the same work, containing record of heirs.
BW (LBP).—Bounty Warrant Papers—applications for grants of bounty land. MS Index to a collection of MS in the Virginia State Archives.
CS.—Journals of the Council of Safety, 1775–1776.
E. (followed by a numeral)—A collection of loose papers, MS and printed, for the most part pension lists, in the Virginia State Archive Department.
Ex. Coms. (followed by date)—Executive papers; loose papers (MS).
HD.—Journals of the House of Delegates, extending from 1776 to 1835 (MS and printed).
LBNB.—Letter Book and Minutes of the Naval Board. MS in the Virginia State Archives (bound in Vol. 1; Papers concerning the State Navy.)
LBP.—Land Bounty Claim Papers, Virginia State Archives.
NAB.—Naval Account Book, Virginia State Archives.
NBJ.—Journal of the Navy Board. MS, Virginia State Archives.
N's Accomack.—"Revolutionary Soldiers and Sailors from Accomack County," by Stratton Nottingham.
N's Lancaster.—"Revolutionary Soldiers and Sailors from Lancaster County," by Stratton Nottingham.
N's Northampton.—"Revolutionary Soldiers and Sailors from Northampton County," by Stratton Nottingham.
Maxwell.—Journal of James Maxwell, Commissioner of the Navy, 1780.
MC, I, II and III.—Three volumes, MS of Military Certificates, in the Virginia Land Office, Capitol Building.
RC.—Rejected Claims: a MS index to a collection of loose manuscript applications for land bounty grants rejected by the Governor frequently containing data concerning heirs and relatives of the Revolutionary soldier or seaman.
USP.—Documents submitted to the Pension Bureau in Washington in connection with pension claims for service. Archives Building, Washington, D. C.
VSR.—Magazine of the Virginia Sons of the Revolution.
War (followed by a numeral).—A collection of MS volumes bearing on the military establishment of the State during and after the Revolution.

A

ABRAM. A Negro. War 5, 31.

ACHESON, WM. Tempest, Dec. 7, 1779.

ADAMS, JOHN, of Fairfax Co. Corporal; capt. marines, Ship Congress. Living in Oct., 1831, aged 82. LBP Wm. Skinner.

AJORNING (Agoing), PETER. Dragon, 1778. Deserted.

ALEXANDER, GEORGE. Aud. Acct. XVIII, 619.

ALLEN, THOMAS, of Norfolk. Boatswain; gunner. Dragon, April 22, 1777 to Sept. 2, 1779; also Oct. 7, 1779. LBP James Jennings.

ALLEN, THOMAS. Lt. H. D. 1835–6, Doc. 6, 76.

ALLISON, JOHN, of Alexandria, Captain, marines; lt. col. land forces from April 18, 1776 to Feb. 6, 1778. Md. Rebecca McCrea, April 24, 1788. Capt. Allison died in Wilkes Co., Ga., April 16, 1803. Issue: Robert (s. p.), James (s. p.), John (s. p.), and William, heir in 1832. USP. LBP.

ALLMAN, WM., of Elizabeth City Co. Gunner. Boat Liberty, NBJ, Aug. 17, 1777. LBP Dr. David Brown.

ALMOND (Almand), WM., of Northumberland County. Entered service Jan. 13, 1777, as an able seaman; served three years; turned over to Capt. John Pasteur of the schooner Molly. On Vessel Patriot Aug. 16, 1777, NBJ.

AMIS, LEVI. Diligence Galley. LBP Solomon Powell.

ANDERSON, DAVID, of Louisa County. Dragon. Surviving heir in 1835, Elizabeth Evans.

ANDERSON, JOHN, of Gloucester County. On board of the Raleigh Privateer of sixteen guns in the capacity of a private; died while in the hands of the British. Heirs in 1832, Archibald Anderson, of Lancaster County, and sisters Anne E., Mary, and Lettice L.

ANDERSON, LUKE. Brig Jefferson. Dec., 1779 to Jan. 20, 1780. In his LBP occurs the following from one of the affiants: "I have understood that a Gunner, a Mate and a Boatswain, received higher pay and were of equal rank with midshipmen. They are called 'officers' by a Resolution of Congress. On reference to those Resolutions (see I Vol.

Journal of Congress, p. 549), I find they did receive higher pay than midshipmen."

ANDREWS, ELCANY (Elkanah), of Accomac County (born 1761). Enlisted on Accomac as "Cabbin Boy." Andrews was living in 1840, aged 77. N's Accomack, 35, 68.

ANDREWS, ISHMAEL, 2d lt. Accomac Galley, Oct. 16, 1777. Discharged Feb. 10, 1779. N's Accomack, 20.

ANDREWS, WM. Accomac Galley. LBP. N's Accomack, 35.

ANGEL, BAKER. Tempest, Dec. 7, 1779. Voucher, 1783.

ANGEL, JOSEPH. Dragon, Deserted, Va. Gazette, July 3, 1779. LBP James Jennings.

ANGEL, WM., of Northumberland or of Lancaster Co. Deserted from Dragon, Va. Gazette, July 3, 1779.

ANTHONY, JAMES. NBJ, Aug. 25, 1778.

APPLEWHITE (Applewhaite), DR. JOHN, of Isle of Wight Co. Surgeon's mate, along with Jonathan Calvert and John Orr, to Dr. John Ramsay. Also in naval service. One of the two surgeons retained after close of the war. USP. In 1834, only heir, his daughter, Judith Cary Applewhite, of Norfolk.

ARBADO, FRANCIS, "a black Frenchman." Deserted from Manley Galley, Va. Gazette, May 16, 1777.

ARCHER, JOHN. Recom. Jan. 2, 1777, lt. Sloop Scorpion; rec. 2d lt. Gloucester. NBJ, Aug. 27, 1777. Lt. on Liberty; captured and confined in N. Y.; returned to Virginia about the time of the surrender at York. Married, in the Borough of Norfolk, May 12, 1792, by the Rev. James Whitehead, to Elizabeth Calvert, dau. of Mrs. Mary Calvert. He died Oct. 18, 1793. His will mentions his wife, his brother Edward, his nephew John, and a niece Anna Maria. His widow in 1799 md. Alexander Martin, USP.

ARCHER, ROBERT (?). BH, 191.

ARCHER, WM. MC III, 179. Heir in 1831, Bartlett Archer.

ARCHIBALD, BARTHOLOMEW. Safeguard Galley, June 16, 1777.

ARELL, JOHN, of Fairfax Co. Capt. marines, succeeded Peers, resigned.

ARELL, SAMUEL, of Fairfax Co. Lt. marines, Nov. 13, 1776. NBJ.

ARMISTEAD, THOS. Lt. marines. C. S., 1776, p. 97. In the USP there is the record of a Thomas Armistead, Va. State troops, who was at one time of Richmond: will, King William Co., June 19, 1809: wife Jane. Possibly this is the Thomas Armistead who was a marine lt. in 1776.

ARMANDO (Armondo), AMBROSE. Gunner, Henry Galley, May 1776: three years service. B. W.

ARNOLD, ELMER. Hero Galley LBNB, Feb. 13, 1778.

ASHBURN (Ashbourn), LOTT, of Lancaster Co. Dragon, Sept. 2, 1779. N's Lancaster, 32.

ASHBURN, LUKE. Page Galley. N's Lancaster, 34, 35, 37.

ASHBURN, THOS. War 5, 31.

ASHBY, BENJ. H. D. 1833-4, Doc. 33, 3.

ASHBY, WARREN. Midshipman, Brig Liberty, LBP George Rodgers.

ASHLEY, WM. Master's mate. War 5, 29.

ASKEW, THOS. Tempest, Dec. 7, 1779.

ASKINS, JOHN. H. D. 1833-4, Doc. 33, 10.

B

BACHUS (negro). H. D. 1833-4, Doc. 33, 15.

BACKHOUSE, JOSEPH. H. D. 1833-4, Doc. 33.

BACKUS (Bachus), CHAS. Hero Galley, LBNB, Feb. 13, 1778.

BACKUS, JOHN. Hero Galley.

BADGER, JESSE. War 5, 38.

BAGBY, EDWARD. War 5, 38.

BAILEY, JAMES. War 5, 44.

BAILEY, JESSE, Certificate Rich. Taylor, LBP.

BAILEY, JOHN. Steward. H. D. 1834-5, Doc. 48, 5.

BAILEY (Bayly), LABAN, of Accomac Co. Quartermaster and Sailing Master, Diligence Galley. He md. May 25, 1790 Mary, who, after Laban Bailey's death at sea, md. West, and was living in 1836. USP. MC III, 175, Peggy Bayly. In 1836 John Bayly Sr., one of the heirs, and John I. Bayly, administrator.

BAILEY, PETER. War 5, 36.

BAILEY, ROBT. R. C. War 5, 42.

BAILEY (Bayly), SOUTHEY. Diligence Galley. N's Accomack, 62, 63. BH, 1341.
BAILEY, THOS. N 8, 20.
BAILIFF, PETER. Dragon, Sept. 2, 1781.
BAKEHOUSE, JOSEPH. Safeguard Galley, March 1 to June 16, 1777.
BAKER, DAVIS (negro). H. D. Oct. 1794, 44 (petition for promised freedom).
BAKER, THOS. Aud. Acct, XVIII, 371.
BALL, JOHN. Dragon. **to Jan. 20, 1779.
BALL, JOHN. Safeguard Galley, LBNB, Feb. 13, 1778.
BALLARD, EDWARD. Pilot and Lt. R. C. LBP, testimony of James Barron, July 27, 1832: "Rendered important services during the whole war, as did also Edward Cooper, Wm. Roe Cunningham, Wm. Watkins, and James Lattimer, Pilots. Mr. Ballard was promoted to a lieutenancy for his patriotism, shortly before the close of the war** The rank of a Pilot, in those days, corresponded to that of a Junr. Lt."
BALLARD, WM. Pilot, 1783. LBP John Flynt.
BALLENTINE, ANDREW. Surgeon, Brig Raleigh, 29 July, 1776, NBJ.
BALLENTINE, CHURCH. Manley Galley—Ex. Coms., 1776.
BALSON, THOMAS. N 8, 14. Dragon. Enlisted Sept. 2, 1779.
BANDER, JOHN. H. D. 1883-4. Doc. 33.
BANEYWELL, THOMAS. Manley Galley, 11 Sept., 1779.
BANKHEAD, JAMES. 2d lt. Capt. Dick's marines vice Thompson resigned.
Lt. James Bankhead was the son of Dr. James Bankhead, of Westmoreland County, and his wife, Eleanor Monroe. Lt. James Bankhead md. Christian Miller, and had issue: (1) Gen. James Bankhead, U. S. A., U. S. attaché in France and in England. He md. Anne Pyne, of Charleston, S. C., and had issue: James Monroe Bankhead; Honora Smith md. George Guest, of Pennsylvania; Capt. John Pyne Bankhead, U. S. N. and C. S. N., commander of the Monitor; Capt. Smith Pyne Bankhead, C. S. A.; Elizabeth I. md. Lt. Wm. Henry Ball, U. S. A.; Gen. Henry Cary Bankhead, U. S. A. (2) Elizabeth Bankhead md. Thomas Magruder. (3) Jane md.

Robert Dunlop, of Glasgow, Scotland. Elizabeth Bankhead and Thomas Magruder had among issue: (1) Elizabeth Magruder md. John Pendleton; (2) Capt. George Allan Magruder, U. S. A., who had issue: Commodore George Allan Magruder, whose daughter Helen md. Wm. Frederick Scarlett, 3rd Baron Abinger, whose son James Yorke Macgregor, 4th Baron, died unmarried in 1903; (3) Major-General John Bankhead Magruder, C. S. A., and Major-General under Maximilian.

BANKHEAD, JOSEPH. Capt. marines. Died in prison in New York after twelve months' confinement. Captured on Brig Raleigh. LBP.

BANKS (Bankes), JAMES. Sailing Master. LBP. John Flynt and of James Gray. USP, Marriage Bond to Mary Smith, March 30, 1789. Banks died about 1795 in Elizabeth City Co. Mary Banks, who was aged 75 in 1845, died in Hampton May 19, 1848. Her will, probated August 26, mentions daughter Mary A. Willis**"child of my granddaughter Caroline Godwin."

Thomas Lattimer was her son-in-law.

BANKS (Bankes), WM. B. W.

BARKER, JOHN. War 5, 42.

BARNES, SAM. Brig Jefferson, Dec. 2, 1779 to Jan. 20, 1780.

BARNETT, ARTAX. H. D. Dec. 1801, 60.

BARNS, GRIFFIN. Dragon, NBJ, Sept. 10, 1778.

BARR, JOHN. War 5, 37.

BARRETT, JAMES. Boatswain, Hero Galley. "A short time he was in command of the Liberty, not, however, the larger vessel of that name." LBP.

BARRET (Barrot), JOHN. July 1776, 1st lt. Brig Raleigh. Capt. Hero, NBJ, Feb. 26, 1778; resigned, Sept. 3.

BARRETT, JONATHAN, of Princess Anne Co. In 1778 lt. (?) Brig Raleigh, Capt. Travis; taken prisoner and died, after a year's imprisonment in New York. Left two children. Petition of Amy Barrett: H. D. Nov. 5, 1778, BH, 1328.

BARRON, JAMES. Commodore, Virginia State Navy.

The father of Commodore Barron was Samuel Barron, commander of Fort George, destroyed by the great hurricane of

1749. After this, Samuel Barron moved to Mill Creek, Elizabeth City Co. He had the following children: James, Samuel, Mary, Richard, William, Robert, David, and Ann. Samuel, Jr., moved to N. C. Richard married three times, By his first wife he had two children: Elizabeth and Mary; by his second marriage, one son, Thomas, lost at sea as captain of a schooner out of Norfolk. William Barron, a zealous patriot from the very commencement of the Revolution, was killed by the bursting of a gun on board the Boston Frigate on her passage to France. Samuel was lost on board a merchant ship. James died on a return voyage of the ship Ules from Holland. Robert married a Miss Loyall, of Norfolk, and had issue: Mary, Elizabeth, Robert, Susan, David, and Ann. The sons died young, and one of the daughters married a Mr. Locke.

David, the only one of the brothers who did not go to sea, settled in Newbern, North Carolina, and had issue: Samuel and Ann. Mary Barron married twice; first, a Mr. Servant, by whom she had issue: Capt. Samuel Servant, lost at sea during the Revolution, and Lieut. Richard Servant, killed in an action off Cape Henry.

This Lieut. Servant had one son, Richard, born about three months after his death.

Ann Barron married three times; first, a Mr. Cunningham, brother of her sister's husband, and had issue: William Cunningham, lost at sea in 1795 on a pilot boat schooner on which he served as pilot; Samuel, who died in Newbern, North Carolina, in 1795, and James Cunningham, lost at sea during the Revolution while he was serving as a mate. Mrs. Cunningham married, secondly, a Capt. Johnston, and had issue: James and Mary Johnston. She married, thirdly, a Mr. Noden, and had two sons, both of whom died young— one lost at sea at the age of 16.

James Barron, Commodore of the Virginia State Navy, was senior officer in 1779, and in 1780 appointed commodore of all the armed vessels of the Commonwealth—a position that he held till his death. According to the testimony of his son, Capt. James Barron, Jr.:"My father, the late Commodore

James Barron, entered the naval service in December [25th], 1775, as captain and was commissioned commodore of the armed vessels of this commonwealth in July, 1780 (after I had entered the service as a midshipman), and to my certain knowledge continued in the Naval Service until the close of the war, and afterwards commanding the armed vessels of the Commonwealth until his death which occurred on the 14th of May, 1787."

Commodore Barron left two sons, Samuel and James. Samuel, after service in the Revolution, entered the United States Navy. In 1798 he saw service as a captain in the Mediterranean; was held a prisoner in Tripoli for three years, and in 1810 became commandant of the navy-yard. He died when about to make a toast at a dinner in Hampton, October 29, 1810.

James, son of Commodore Barron of the Virginia navy, was later a commodore himself. He was wounded when in command of the Chesapeake in 1812. He was one of the principals in the celebrated duel with Commodore Decatur in 1820. He was inventor of the first dry dock and iron clad. He served until his death in 1851, when he was the senior officer in the United States Navy. He left a widow and three daughters. His daughter Jane married Mr. Hope and was the mother of the poet and publicist James Barron Hope, whose daughter is Mrs. Janie Hope Marr. Sarah Virginia Barron married Mr. Prendergrast. Mary married Francis Blake, afterwards a Lieutenant-Commander U. S. N.

Samuel Barron, eldest son of Commodore Samuel Barron, was born at Hampton, November 28, 1808. He was the youngest commissioned officer ever connected with the Navy of the United States, for he was appointed by act of Congress a midshipman in January, 1812, at the age of three years, with full pay, in recognition of the distinguished services of his father, and he made his first cruise to the Mediterranean in his eighth year. At twenty he was lieutenant and executive officer of his vessel and served continuously till the breaking out of the War Between the States, when he cast his fortunes with his native Virginia. At one period he was sent to London and Paris to look after the purchase of cruisers for the Confederate Navy. After the war he settled in Essex County, on the Rappahannock, and there remained till his death.

Captain Barron married Imogen, daughter of Mathew P. and Mary Taylor Wright, of Norfolk, by whom he had six children: Imogen (never married), Samuel, Elizabeth (died young), Virginia, James and Thompson. Of these children, Samuel (born August 20, 1835) first went to sea as captain's clerk on the U. S. Ship John Adams, commanded by his father. On the return trip from the East Indies on a merchant ship he was commissioned first mate of the vessel. His life was filled with adventure; he made cruises to all parts of the world; he operated a coffee farm in Brazil for several years; conducted a ranch in California; went to Oregon and Washington Territories, and was first officer on a Government transport in Puget Sound. On the outbreak of the Civil War he managed with great difficulty and peril to reach his native State, where he entered the Confederate Navy. He was on the Jamestown during the Merrimac-Monitor engagement, and, after the capture of the Florida, he served on the Shenandoah to the end of the war. After Appomattox he was one of a number of exiled Confederates who entered the service of the Emperor Maximilian in Mexico. In 1868 he returned to Virginia and made his home with his father in Richmond Co. He married Agnes, daughter of Col. Smith, of "Mantua", Northumberland Co., and had issue: Sallie Hagner, Imogen Wright, Samuel, James (now of Norfolk), Agnes Newton (Mrs. Segar), and Armistead Wellford.

Of the children of Capt. Samuel Barron, Virginia married Capt. Edward R. Baird, C. S. A., and had issue: Benjamin, Edward, Virginia, Imogen Sarah Elizabeth, Julia, Mary, and Samuel Barron, James married Kate Ashton, and died at "Malvern," Essex Co., Va. The youngest son, Thompson, married, first, Helen, daughter of Capt. Bontelle, U. S. A., and had issue: two children; he married, secondly, Charlotte

Long, and had issue: Samuel Richard Barron and Wm. Thompson Barron.

BARRON, JAMES JR. Midshipman. Later Captain. B. W. B, 473. USP.

BARRON, RICHARD, of Elizabeth City Co. Captain, Brig Jefferson, 1778–80. Given leave Oct. 11, 1780, to go to the West Indies for the recovery of his health, LBNB. Will proved April 28, 1791: wife Rebecca; sons Thomas Cary, Miles Selden, and Richard Barron; dau. Elizabeth Jones; dau. Mary Graves. USP. BH, 1329.

BARRON, RICHARD JR. (son of above). In 1818 Mrs. Ann Barron, widow. She md. in 1824 James B. Balfour, and after his death md. James Hubbard, whom she survived, and was living in Gloucester Co. in 1858.

BARRON, SAMUEL, of Elizabeth City Co. Born in Hampton Sept. 5, 1765. Left William and Mary College to enter Navy on Frigate Dragon. Was Lt. Commander on lookout boat on cruises. Barron was engaged in an action that was fought off the mouth of Hampton Creek, between one of the vessels of war and a British tender, in which engagement Samuel Barron bore a conspicuous part, though not more than seventeen at the time. It was regarded by all as a most brilliant achievement, as more of the British were taken or destroyed than there were men on board the Virginia vessel. He was later Commodore U. S. N.

BARRON, WM. Captain. B. W. USP. On June 8, 1837 a power of attorney from Miss Ann M. Barron, daughter and only heir of Wm. Barron, first Lt. on the U. S. Frigate Boston, on which he was wounded and died. BH, 1326-7.

BARTEE, JAMES JR. Caswell and Washington Galleys, Feb. 15 to Nov. 15, 1778. Norfolk Co. Petition, Oct., 1794.

BARTEE, SAMUEL, of Norfolk Co. Carpenter's mate, Caswell Galley. Petition, Oct., 1794.

BARTEE, WM. Carpenter's mate. War 5, 38.

BARTLETT, JOHN. N, 8, 35. Marine, enlisted Jan. 20, 1783.

BARTLETT, PHILIP, of Hampton (died 1809), Surgeon. Came from New York. Boat Liberty. On Patriot at end of war. LBP. See also VSR, July, 1930, p. 29. BH, 1386.

BARTLEY, RAFE. Aud. Acct, XXII, 80.

BASCO, JAMES. B. W.

BASS, JOHN, of Middlesex Co. Deserted from Dragon, Va. Gazette, Sept. 11, 1779.

BASSFORD, JOHN. Hero Galley. NBJ, Nov. 4, 1777.

BASSIL (Bassill), JOHN. Ship Gloucester. H. D. 1833–4, Doc. 33, 11.

BASSIT, JOHN. Northampton. NBJ, Sept. 10, 1778.

BATEMAN, JAMES. Ship Gloucester. NBJ, Nov. 4, 1777.

BATSON, THOS. Entered sailor under Capt. Thomas, 1779, B, 244.

BAXTER, ANDREW. Gunner's mate, Brig Liberty, May 18 to July 30, 1776, LBP George Rodgers.

BAXTER, ———, of Northumberland Co. Accts. C. S. 1775–6, 62.

BAYLIE (Bayley), PETER. Aud. Acct. XXIX, 78. B. W.

BAYLIE (Bayly), ROBT. N's Accomack, 35, 62.

BAYNE (Baynes), CAPT. JOHN, of Norfolk Co. Sloop Liberty. Appt. capt. June 9, 1777. Col. Stephen Wright attested that Bayne was lost at sea.

BEACH, BENJAMIN. Diligence Galley. Northampton. Master's mate. LBP Elkanah Andrews.

BEALLY, WM. Voucher, 1786.

BEAN (Been), JOHN. Aud. Acct. XXIX, 10.

BEASLEY, WM. Enlisted on the Patriot in 1778. See R. C., John Christian.

BEATLEY, RALPH. MC II, 13.

BEATLEY, WM. Sailor; served three years. MC II, 10.

BEATTY (Beatley?), RALPH. Dragon, Sept. 2, 1779. N 8, 14.

BECHAN, PRESLEY. Ship Dragon, March 16, 1777–May 13, 1779.

BECKETT (Becket), GEORGE. Accomac Galley. N's Accomack, 54.

BELL, JAMES. Brig Northampton. Died in New York c. 1832. Heirs, N's Accomack, 61.

BELL, WM. SMITH. Surgeon. Caswell, Sept. 21, 1776.

BENN, WHITTEN. H. D. 1833–4, Doc. 33, 10.

BENNETT, ARTEXES. Gunner.
BENNETT, CHARLES. Sailing Master. Dragon, March 17, 1777; Jan. 20, 1779; wounded, see NBJ, Feb. 19, 1779. LBP James Jennings.
BENNETT, ELIAS. War 5, 42.
BENNETT, WHITTIN. Safeguard Galley, March 1, ——, June 15, 1777.
BENNETT, WM., of Accomac Co. Sailing Master. "He was occasionally changed from Boat Liberty to Boat Patriot as the whole crew were." Left service May 19, 1781; died April 22, 1783. Covington Bennett, administrator. USP. See also N's Accomack, 61.
BESS, JOHN. War 5, 44.
BEST, MALACHI. Private. War 5, 44.
BETTRANGE (Bestgrange), JOHN. Dragon, March 17, 1777 to Jan. 29, 1779.
BEVELL, JOHN. Henry Galley, 1776.
BIGGS, THOS. Dragon, June 15, 1778–Jan. 20, 1779.
BINGHAM, HUGH, of Norfolk Co. Boatswain. NBJ, Nov. 1, 1777, Sept. 18, 1778, Henry Galley.
BINGHAM, PHILIP. Dragon. NBJ, Sept. 10, 1778. LBF James Jennings.
BIRCH, BENJ. Master's mate. Diligence Galley, Feb. 6, 1777; Oct., 1779. LBP Wm. White.
BIRD (Byrd), LEVIN (Leavin). Pilot. Heirs, N's Accomack, 22.
BISCOE (Biscowe), JAMES. Seaman and Boatswain. Boat Liberty, Nov., 1779. Voucher, 1783.
BISCO, JOHN. Marine. Certificate, Lt. Jos. Saunders.
BISCOE, JOHN. B. W.
BISHOP, JOSHUA. H. D. 1834–5, Doc. 48, 4.
BLANDON, LEVIN. B. W.
BLANKINSHIP, WM. War 5, 34.
BLASSFORD, JOHN. H. D. 1833–4, Doc. 33, 10.
BLAWS, JAMES. Midshipman, March 27, 1776. Recom. 2d lt. Sept. 8, 1777. NBJ Manley Galley, vice Chamberlayne resigned.
BLAWS, ROBT. Appt. 2d lt. Caswell Galley, March 26, 1776.
BLEAUFORD [Buford (?)], JOHN. Henry Galley, 1777.

BLICK, JAMES, of Brunswick Co. Stated by Col. R. Y. Bland, to have been a Cabin Boy in Robt. Bolling's vessel. See USP Robt. Bolling.

BLOXSOM (Bloxom), GEORGE. Accomac Galley. N's Accomack, 25, 48.

BLOXSOM, J. of Capt. R. Taylor's vessel (not named), 1778. LBP John Flynt.

BLOXSOM, SCARBOROUGH. (born 1754, Accomac Co.; living at the age of 79, in Norfolk Co; died Oct., 1836). Accomac Galley. Midshipman. USP Leah Bloxam, heir. See also N's Accomack, 35, 71.

BLOXSOM, STEPHEN. Accomac Galley. N's Accomack, 35.

BLUNDELL (Blandell), WM. Brig Jefferson, Dec. 20, 1779 to Jan. 20, 1780. LBP.

BLUNDEN, SAMUEL. LBP Wm. Blundon.

BLUNDLE (Blundell-Blundow-Blundon), SETH. Midshipman. Dragon. LBP John Flynt.

BLUNDON (Blunden-Blundow), SWAN. Protector Galley.

BLUNDOW, SAMUEL. Aud. Acct. XVIII, 689.

BLUNDON, WM. Enlisted June 16, 1776. Protector Galley.

BOLLING, ROBERT, of Dinwiddie Co. (Will proved Feb. 24, 1791). Prior to Oct. 16, 1776 he was commander of the vessel "Peace and Plenty", (employed in trade). March 21, 1776 1st lt. Manley, vice Sturdivant promoted. Married (bond, Dec. 18, 1779), Mrs. Clara (Yates) Bland, the mother of R. Y. Bland (later Col. Bland). In his will he names his wife Clara, his two children Robert and Susanna, and mentions lots at Broadway in Prince George Co. and five acres of land joining that of Theodorick Bland and Wm. Gilliam. USP. The witnesses (Sept. 7, 1789) were Susanna Meriton, Alex Bolling, and Robt. Walker, Jr. Mrs. Bolling died intestate in August, 1832. Susanna Bolling md. Samuel Gilliam, of Brunswick Co., and left issue. (See "Gilliam Family" in V. S. R., Vol. VI). Robert Bolling, Jr. lived in Brunswick Co., where his will was proved in 1867. Of his children, Maria E. md. Mr. Kennedy; Wm. H. L. Bolling, his executor, was living in 1878; Clara A. Yates Bolling (b. Dec. 8, 1823) md. Napoleon S. Mathews (b. April 15,

1832; d. May 21, 1875.) (Mrs. Mathews, b. Dec. 8, 1823, of "Oak Hill", made her will in 1878, Will Book 20, p. 310, Brunswick Co.); Susan G. Bolling md. a Mr. Stewart; John R. Bolling, in Dinwiddie Co. at the time of his death, made his will on Sept. 2, 1847; probated 1849, Brunswick Will Book 15, p. 249.

BOLTON, JAMES. Serg. marines. On Congress. LBP Wm. Skinner.

BOND, HANCE. Capt. marines on Caswell galley in N. C. Aud. Acct. XXV, 306.

BOND, JAMES. War 5, 43

BONNEWELL, GEORGE. NBJ, Sept. 8, 1777.

BONNEWELL, THOS. Sailing Master. Dilligence. Manley. Northampton, NBJ, Sept. 8, 1777. Went to Kentucky. BH, 541-545. N's Accomack, 32. USP.

BONWELL (Bonnewell), WM. Master. See USP Thos. Bonnewell.

BOOTH, THOS. Aud. Acct. XVIII, 537.

BOOTH, WM. Pilot, Dragon, Oct. 7, 1779; Jan. 19, 1783.

BOOTH, WM., of Elizabeth City Co. Enlisted and served three years as pilot and sailing master. Protector Galley, USP. In LBP James Burke stated he knew Booth twenty five or thirty years after the war. Brother and heir, Thos. Booth, of Princess Anne, Somerset Co., Md.

BOSTON. Negro. H. D. 1834-5, Doc. 33, 15.

BOSTON (Booton (?)), ADAM. Marine, Jan. 10, 1783.

BOSTON, THOS. H. D. 1834-5, Doc. 43, 4.

BOSWORTH, OBADIAH. Gloucester. NBJ, Aug. 26, 1778. Dragon.

BOTTON (Button), JAMES. Serg. marines, Sloop Congress, 1776. LBP James Jennings.

BOTTOM, JOHN. H. D. 1834-5, Doc. 48, 5.

BOUCHER (Bowcher), JOHN THOMAS. Lt. Defense, Md. Navy; First Commodore of the Va. Navy. On Congress. Resigned Nov. 26, 1776. LBP Wm Skinner.

BOUSH, CHARLES SAYER (pronounced Sawyer). Lt. marines. Recom. 2d lt. Norfolk Revenge, Aug. 29, 1777; turned over to the Caswell, Aug. 30, 1777. See "The Researcher" (magazine), I, 123. Norfolk Petitions, Nov. 16, 1789.

Charles Sayer Boush md. at Sewell's Point (bond dated May 23, 1774), Martha Sweeny, dau. of Charles Sweeny and niece of George Wythe, signer of the Declaration of Independence. They had issue: Anne Wythe Boush, born Feb. 16, 1775, and Martha S. F. S. Boush, born Nov. 23, 1787.

Anne Wythe Boush md. John Mallory (bond dated July 13, 1779), and had issue: Anne Wythe Mallory, who md. Kennon Whiting, and had issue (1) Thomas Beverley, md. Hannah Bassett Starke, of Norfolk; (2) Anne Beverley md. Capt. James Barron Hope, of Norfolk; (3) Elizabeth Kennon md. Judge John Critcher, of Westmoreland Co.; (4) Martha Kennon md. Samuel Read Chisman, of York Co.; (5) Henry Clay md. Mary Simkins Segar, of Elizabeth City, N. C.; (6) Louisa Frances md. Jacob Heffelfinger, of Penn.; (7) William Perrin md. Ross Edgerton, of Maryland; (8) Julian Wythe md. Ida, dau. of Gen. Lawler, of Mobile, Ala.

Martha Boush, the second dau. of Charles S. Boush, md. Marshall Parks.

Charles S. Boush died in 1809.

BOUSH, DANIEL. War 5, 43.

BOUSH, GEORGE. War 5, 43.

BOUSH, GOODRICH. Recommended Jan. 31, 1777, to command Washington Galley. Recruiting men for Ship Washington, Feb. 3, 1777; Congress in Feb., 1777. "Died in service." Will pro. in York County in 1782. Notice of the death of Capt. Boush, Virginia Gazette, May 22, 1779. Capt. Boush md. Jan. 25, 1759, Mary Wilson, and in his will he mentions children Wilson, Samuel, James, Ann, Mary and Elizabeth. His daughter Ann md. Brough, and in 1831 was one of the claimants to bounty land, BH, 1353. Only heirs in 1860 Ella R. and Ligan H. Robinson, of Essex Co., children of Henry Robinson.

BOUSH, JACK. War, 5, 43.

BOUSH, JAMES. Brig Jefferson, Dec. 1779; Jan. 20, 1780, Brig Adventure (Maxwell).

BOUSH, ROBERT. Claim was made before the Court, July 25, 1835, by Ann N., wife of Dr. George Kennon and Catherine B., wife of Dr. James Cornick, sole heirs of Robert Boush, formerly of the Borough of Norfolk, for bounty land on the ground that he was a midshipman; rejected in view of failure to present positive facts. Robert Boush was appointed Feb. 8, 1779, Commander of Naval Stores and superintendent of all naval rigging. He was also Paymaster in the Virginia State Line.

Robert Boush was a son of Samuel Boush III, and a nephew of Capt. Goodrich Boush. He died c. 1809, leaving issue: (1) Betsey, wife of Burwell B. Moseley, who left an only daughter, Catherine (Cornick); (2) Kate, d. s. p., and (3) Ann, md. Dr. Kennon.

BOUSH, WILLIAM. Negro. HD, Oct. 1789.

BOUSH, WILSON. Midshipman, Ship Washington, Feb. 1, 1777. In 1831 (LBP), Anne Brough, daughter of Capt. Goodrich Boush and sister of Wilson Boush, made affidavit that the latter entered the State Navy very early with her father and was afterwards midshipman and continued with her father till her father's death.

BOWEN, JOHN. Dragon, March 3, 1777, to Nov. 27, 1778. Died in service.

BOWING (Boweing), JOSHUA. Ship Gloucester.

BOYD, AUGUSTINE, of Wicomico Parish, Northumberland Co. Deserted. Va. Gazette, Sept. 11, 1779.

BOYD, GIST. Brig Jefferson.

BOYD, GUSTAVUS. H. D. 1833-4, Doc. 33.

BOYLE, WALLER (Walter?). Aud. Acct. XXV, 83.

BOYLE, WALTER. Voucher, 1784. Cert. Capt. George Elliott.

BRANAN, SETH. Cadet, Protector Galley. NBJ, March 21, 1778.

BRANBOW, JAMES. Sloop Liberty, Aug., 1777.

BRANDFORD, JOHN. Mosquito, 1776. N 8, 30.

BRANNON, JOHN. Aud. Acct. 1780, 6.

BRAWFORD, HENRY. H. D. 1834-5, Doc. 48, 8.

BRENT, RICHARD. N's Lancaster, 22.

BRIAN, HENRY. B. W.

BRICKHOUSE, JOSEPH, of Princess Anne Co. Lewis Galley. LBNB, Feb. 13, 1778.

BRIESON, ANDREW. Northampton. NBJ, Sept. 10, 1778.

BRIGHAM, JOHN. Midshipman, Brig Liberty, May 18, July 30, 1778.

BRIGHT, CAPT. FRANCIS, of York Co. Appt. by the Council of Safety, April 1776, Brig Northampton, first cruiser fitted out on Eastern Shore, Jan., 1776. Resigned May 11, 1778, NBJ. After the war Capt. Bright was sent to England in the State Vessel Perseverence with a cargo of tobacco. LBP. He died Dec. 10, 1811, leaving three children: Elizabeth, Susan Hannah, and Margaret Mary. Elizabeth left five children: Susan H. Moore, Elizabeth (wife of Henry Edloe), Virginia F., Catherine M., and Julia S. Travers. Susan H. Bright left one child, a minor in 1831. USP. See also BH, 1357.

BRINSLEY (Brumley), JOHN. Ship Carpenter, Henry Galley, Sept., 1778.

BRISCOE (Bisco?) JAMES. Aud. Acct. XVIII, 635.

BRITTON (Brittain), JOHN. Sailing Master. LBP. B, 1041.

BROADUS, WM. In Culpeper Petition, 1824. Broadus, then aged 76, affirmed that he entered marines at age of 15.

BROADWATER, CHARLES LEWIS, of Fairfax Co. (living in 1836, aged 84). Midshipman, Sloop Congress, April, 1776. In spring of 1777 he entered land service at Petersburg. USP. LBP Wm. Skinner.

BROADWATER, COVINGTON (Covinton). Accomac Galley. N's Accomack, 25.

BROADWATER, GAVIN. Accomac Galley. Midshipman. BH, 1930.

BROADWATER, JAMES. Quartermaster, Accomac Galley. LBP Dr. Wm. White.

BROADWATER, JOHN. Gunner's mate. Accomac Galley. MC III, 171. Heirs in 1831 Sally Beverly, and Eliz., Wm., and Rebecca Broadwater.

BROCKENBROUGH, DR. JOHN. Born at Hobbs Hole (Tappahannock), Essex Co., in 1744, son of Col. Wm. Brockenbrough, of Richmond Co. Signer Westmoreland protest

against the Stamp Act, in 1764; J. P., Essex Co. Mentioned
in NBJ for service in connection with the Navy.
He md. Sarah Roane, and had issue: Dr. John, of Richmond,
President of the Bank of Virginia, William, Arthur, Austin,
Thomas and Lucy (md. James Cox).

BRODUT, JACQUES and FRANCIS, sailors on Brig Liberty, June,
1778.

BROMLEY, PHILIP, of Kingston Parish, Gloucester Co. Henry
Galley, 1776–1779. LBP.

BROMLEY, WM. War 5, 44.

BROOK, JOHN. Minor officer, Brig Mosquito. LBP Chas.
DeKay.

BROOKE (Brookes), REUBEN. On Mosquito. H. D., Oct.,
1794, 77.

BROOKE, CAPT. WALTER, son of Major Walter Brooke, of
Chickamun, Charles County, Maryland; died, in 1798, at
"Retirement," Fairfax County, Virginia. Was serving on
the Sloop "Liberty" in August, 1776. Afterwards Commodore.

In 1831 the heirs at law of Commodore Brooke were Mrs.
Ann Graeff, (who had married John Graeff, of Washington,
D. C.), Walter Darrel Brooke (married October, 1799, Lucy
Triplett), B. E. Brooke, Lucy A. Brooke, Virginia Brooke,
Jabez Rooker and Mary C. Rooker (nee Mary Brooke, who
had long had in her possession her father's commission).

In the LBP is a statement from Hening, Vol. 10, p. 375, That
a provision was made for the General Officers of Virginia in
the Continental service, allowing a Major General 15000
acres of Land and a Brigadier General 10000 acres of Land.
Also a provision was made for all the officers, Seamen &
Marines of the State Navy or their representatives (Hening,
Vol. 11, p. 165), allowing them the same bounty in lands and
other emoluments as the officers and soldiers of the Virginia
line on continental establishment. LBP Walter Brooke.
BH, 1037. USP.

BROOKE, LAWRENCE. Surgeon, Continental Navy. On Alliance
and Bonhomme Richard, with John Paul Jones. USP.

BROUNLEY, WM. (See also Bromley and Brumley). Isaac Brounley attested that two Wm. Brounleys enlisted in the State Navy: one, the father of Eliz. and Polly and Wm., who left an only son, Columbus. The other Wm. was a brother of the affiant, and died in service, unmarried: James B. was his oldest brother.

BROWN, BERRYMAN. War 5, 41.

BROWN, DAVID, of Elizabeth City Co. Surgeon, Dragon, from July 21 to May 3, 1778: then transferred to Tartar. Died in New York c. 1784. LBP.

BROWN, FRANCIS, of Matthews Co. Henry Galley, 1776. Capt. Doughity, and was then removed to Lookout Boat Liberty. Capt. Robt. Hall. LBP Philip Brumley. BH, 588.

BROWN, GEORGE, of Culpeper Co. Entered first as soldier, then on Henry Galley, in 1776, as midshipman. Returned in winter of 1779-1780, and served in the militia. Children: Wm., James, Nancy, Elizabeth, and George. LBP.

BROWN, HARRY. Dragon. Enlisted Sept. 12, 1779.

BROWN, JOHN. Dragon, March 30, 1778, to Jan. 28, 1779.

BROWN, JOHN. Able Seaman.

BROWN, JONATHAN. Cert. and discharge by Markham.

BROWN (or Browne), JOSEPH. Hero Galley. NBJ, Nov. 4, 1777.

BROWN, THOMAS. Tempest, Dec. 7, 1779.

BROWN, WILLIAM, of Kingston Parish, Gloucester. Midshipman, Tempest, 1776 or 1777; Dragon, Sept. 2, 1779; frequently in Pepper Creek and East River. LBP. BH, 202.

BROWN, WILLIAM, of Northampton County. Midshipman. See N's Accomack, 27.

BROWN, WINDSOR. Midshipman. BH, 202. There was a Windsor Brown, Capt. in State Line, from Mar., '76, to 3d Nov., '83. See BH, 200, 201. Heitman, 104.

BROWN, ROBERT WINDSOR. Lt. Marines, Sanders' Cruiser, 16 June, 1776. Capt. Marines, 1st lt. Sloop Congress, LBP Robt. Skinner. USP. Said to have been an Irishman by birth. Entered at Alexandria, Va. Capt. and paymaster 1st regt. Died 1785. Nephew and only heir Robt. Dougherty. In 1822 Mary King stated that she was an heir. Same as Windsor Brown above?

BROWNE, JONATHAN. N 8, 14. Dragon.

BROWNE, RICHARD. Manley Galley, 11 Sept., '79.

BROWNLEY, PHILIP (see also Bromley). Henry Galley, Nov. 1, 1777.

BRUMLEY, WM., of Kingston Parish. LBNB, Nov. 1, '77. LBP.

BRYAN, FRED. Henry Galley. LBNB, Nov. 1, 1777.

BRYANT, DANIEL. Marine, Jan. 30, 1783. N 8, 35.

BRYANT, HENRY. Northampton. NBJ, Sept. 10, 1778.

BRYANT, JOHN. Aud. Acct. XXVII, 20.

BUCKNER, CAPT. WM., of Kingston Parish (later Matthews Co.). Master of a ship before the Revolution. Attended frequently to having the galleys and other vessels rigged. Commanded both in land and naval services. Made a prisoner March 19, 1781, sent to England; returned March 7, 1782. Died last of February, 1804. He married an aunt of Wm. Armistead. Children: Mary md. Thos. M. Norman, of Baltimore; Elizabeth, wife of Francis Armistead, Esq., of Matthews Co.; Dorothy, wife of Dr. Bartlett Gayle, of Matthews Co.; Susan, wife of Ephraim Beazley; and Martha, first wife of Dr. Gayle (children: Alex., Wm., Math., and Joshua). BH, 1400.

BUDD, THOS. Diligence Galley. LBP. N's Accomack, 25.

BUFFIN, JOHN. Sergeant and Adj. marines. Congress. LBP Wm. Skinner.

BUFORD, JOHN. NBJ, Aug. 8, 1778.

BULLEY (Bully), JOHN, of Elizabeth City Co. Patriot. Liberty, Nov., 1779. Boatswain. LBP. BH, 1225.

BULLY, EDWARD, of Elizabeth City Co. Liberty, Nov., 1779. Boatswain. USP Dr. P. Bartlett. BH, 1225, 1392.

BULLY, THOS., of Elizabeth City Co. Enlisted in 1778. Schooner Patriot. Capt. Richard Barron. Liberty, 1779.

BUN, MATHEW. N 8, 9.

BUNDICK, LEVIN. N's Accomack, 35. B, 245.

BUNKS, WM. Aud. Acct. XVIII, 436.

BURDERS, ANDREW. Tempest, Dec. 7, 1777.

BURDERS, ANTHONY. H. D. 1833-4, Doc. 33, 10.
BURK, JOHN. Carpenter. R C.
BURK, JOHN. Gunner. LBP Thomes Flynt.
BURK, JOHN SMITH. Carpenter. LBP.
BURKE (Burk), JAMES, of Elizabeth City Co. Gunner on Patriot, that generally cruised in James and York Rivers and Chesapeake Bay. Was in several skirmishes and one regular engagement. Aged 73, July 21, 1832. USP. Had a large family. MC III, 180, James Burk, heir.
BURKE, JOHN. Brother of James. LBP Dr. David Brown.
BURNE, JOSEPH. Died in service. N's Lancaster, 25.
BURNLEY, CHRISTOPHER. H. D. 1833-4, Doc. 33, 10.
BURNLEY, WM. H. D. 1833-4, Doc. 33, 11.
BURNS, CHRISTOPHER. H. D. 1834-5, Doc. 48, 5.
BURNS, GEORGE. E, 1.
BURR, EDMUND, of Stafford Co. U. S. Navy. Died Jan. 16, 1834, aged 77. USP.
BURRUS, CHRIS. LBP Wm. Forrest.
BURTON, JOHN. Manley Galley, Nov. 7, 1777.
BUSH, SAMUEL. War 5, 38. Doc. 43, 45.
BUSH, WM. Public Negro. Boat Liberty. LBP Dr. P. Bartlett.
BUTLER, EDMUND. N 8, 35
BUTLER, EDWARD. Marine, Jan. 18, 1783.
BUTLER, EDWARD. Pilot. Entered early and continued to end. LBP.
BUTLER, WM. War 5, 41.
BUTTON, MICHAEL. Pilot. B, 196.
BYBEE, JOSEPH. H. D. Dec. 1801, 60.
BYBY, EDWARD. Aud. Acct. XXV, 155.
BYRD (Bird), FREDERICK. Henry Galley, 1776.
BYRD (Bird), LEVIN. Pilot. Diligence Galley, Oct., 1777, LBNB. MC III, 171. Heirs, Sally W., wife of Thos. Ames; Betsey W. Hornsby; Anna, wife of Levin Ames; Washington H. and Anthony Ames, infant children of Elizabeth Ames (1831).

C

CABELL, ABSALOM. 1st lt. Sloop Congress, vice Skinner promoted, May 7, 1777. Served till ship was laid up. USP Wm. Skinner.

CAESAR, TARRANT. Aud. Acct. XXIX, 391.

CAIN, ABEDNEGO. R. C.

CAIN, ELIEZER.

CAIN, JOSHUA. Pilot. Boat Liberty. LBP George Rodgers, and testimony of Cain's son Jeremiah, who was a "sucking baby" when his father came from St. Mary's, Maryland, to Elizabeth City Co., Va. In 1781 Joshua Cain was captured on a lookout boat and died in Halifax, N. S.

CAIRONS, PETER. Dragon, Nov. 7, 1778, to Nov. 23. Deserted.

CALLENDER, CAPT. ELEAZER. Entered service in 1775. Commander of the Sloop Defiance and later of Dragon.

Living in Fredericksburg after the War, he petitioned the House of Delegates, on Nov. 12, 1791, for compensation for a valuable horse lost in service.

Capt. Callender was one of the original members of the Society of the Cincinnati, in Virginia.

CALVERT, CAPT. JOHN, of Norfolk. Sloop Defiance in Sept., 1776, Resigned, Sept. 8, 1777. Revenge Galley, Sept., 1778.

CALVERT, JOHN. Englishman. Deserted from Scorpion, Va. Gazette, Oct. 4, 1776.

CAMPBELL, JAMES. Ex. Coms. 1776.

CANADAY (Canady), DAVID, of Westmoreland Co. Enlisted along with his brother John, at Price's Old Tavern, under Midshipman Benj. Strother; went to Frazier's Ferry, where three months later he died and was buried. LBP John Canaday.

CANADAY, JOHN. Born Aug. 21, 1762, in Westmoreland Co. about two miles from Mattox Bridge. On Tempest, Dec. 7, 1777. After Tempest was deserted by her crew in 1781, he remained some time at or about New Castle, Hanover Co., and then marched to the siege of York. Lived five years in Fairfax Co.; fifteen years in Fauquier; followed a seafaring life till 1804. In 1832, he was keeper of the mill of Samuel

Marquess in Stafford Co. He was living in 1835. Interesting statement in USP. See also LBP.

CANE, TIMOTHY. Pilot. Captured on lookout boat in 1781, LBP, John Rodgers.

CANNON, JESSE (died Jan. 1, 1791, without issue). 2d lt. Diligence Galley; 1t, Oct. 16, 1777. N's Accomack, 34; BH, 930, 1464.

CANNON, LUKE (brother of Jesse). Midshipman (lt. ?). In 1834, Polly Buck, wife of Richard, of N. C., claimed to be only child. BH, 930, 1464.

CARMINES (Carmine, Carmins), LEBANON (Levin). Manley Galley, Sept. 11, 1779.

CARNEAL, PETER. N 8, 77.

CARNEY, PATRICK. E 1.

CARR, JOHN, Dragon. Sept. 7, 1779.

CARR, SAMUEL. Lt. marines. Capt. NBJ, Nov. 20, 1776. Died in service. B, 1244. C. S. 1776, 42.

CARRELL (Currell ?), GEORGE. Aud. Acct. XVIII, 646.

CARRELL, JAMES. Aud. Acct. XVIII, 646.

CARROLL, JOHN. Tempest, Dec. 7, 1779.

CARTER, ANTHONY. Dragon, from Oct. 28, 1777 to Dec. 16; deserted.

CARTER, FRANCIS. Dragon, Nov. 5, 1778 to Jan. 20, 1779.

CARTER, GEORGE. War 5, 51.

CARTER, JOHN. E 1. B. W.

CARTER, PHILLIP. E 1.

CARTER, THOS. NBJ, Oct. 3, 1778.

CARTER, WM. Brig Liberty, June 1778.

CARTER, DR. WM. NBJ, Nov. 26, 1776.

CARY, ROBT. Boatswain, Sloop Congress, 1776. LBP Wm. Skinner.

CASADY, WM. Pension.

CASS, JOHN. Manley Galley, Sept. 11, 1779.

CASEY, WM. Entered 1777 and served to 1783. LBP Thos. Humphlett.

CASIDY, JOHN. Aud. Acct. XXX, 5.

CASITY, JAMES. Enlisted, Jan. 6, 1777. Protector Galley, LBP.

Cassady, Wm. Aud. Acct. XVIII, 107.
Cassety, John. H. D. 1834–5, Doc. 48, 5.
Cassity, John. Aud. Acct. XXVII, 242.
Catherine, Joseph. Steward, Sloop Congress, 1776. LBP Wm. Skinner.
Catlett, George, of Port Royal, Caroline Co. Lt. Marines. On Pocahontas. Captured on Mosquito; escaped in spring of 1781, and was at siege of York. Married, May 11, 1798, by Rev. Abner Waugh, to Lucy Rucker (aged 22), who was living in 1848. In USP he was described by his wife as "a silent man", but would discuss his adventures with Commodore Richard Taylor, a frequent visitor. Catlett died Sept. 15, 1814. Heirs: Colin B., George T., Harriet H. and Ann Catlett. See also LBP, in VSR, July, 1930.
Causey, James. Dragon. LBP.
Cavernor (Cavener, Cavenga), Samuel. Henry Galley, 1776.
Cawson, John. Ex. Coms. 1776.
Chaldron, Francisway. Dragon, June, 1779.
Chamberlaine, George, of Warwick Co. (b. 1755). 2d lt. Henry Galley. Manley Galley. Appt. 2d lt. Brig Mosquito, Feb. 3, 1777. Captured and imprisoned in England. Escaped and returned to service in Va. Recommended 1st lt. Aug. 12, 1777. In 1778 commander of the Pilot Boat Molly. Lt. Boat Liberty, in 1779 and 1780. LBP. USP. Lt. Chamberlaine md. Ann Harlow Lucas of Warwick Co. and had issue: George Chamberlaine, of Norfolk, who md. Fannie Lowry Needham, of Hampton, issue: Richard Henry Chamberlaine (June 7, 1807–July 23, 1879) md. first, in 1831, Mary Eliza, dau. of Wm. Wilson, of New York, and, 2d, in 1851, Maria Elizabeth Loney, dau. of Wm. Loney, of Baltimore. Issue, 1st marriage: Samuel, George, Wm. Wilson, Agnes Wilson, Fanny, Richard, Henry; issue, 2d marriage: Rebecca L., Mary B., Charles Frederick, Robert Lucas.
George Chamberlaine (1834–1912) md. in 1857 Eliza Calvert Taylor, of Norfolk. Issue: Calvert Taylor, Richard Henry, Bessy Lucas, Eloise, Mary Maguire, Mabel B., Hildegarde. William Wilson Chamberlaine (1836–1923) md. Mattie

Dillard, of Rocky Mount, Va. Issue: Mary Wilson, Anne D., and William.

Fanny Chamberlaine md. Joseph Barker, of New York. Issue: Frank and Maria Elizabeth.

Rebecca L. Chamberlaine md. Benj. F. Fabeus, of Boston.

Charles Frederick Chamberlaine md. Emma Silsby Cogswell, of Mass. Issue: Wm. Cogswell, died in infancy.

Robert Lucas Chamberlaine md. Louise Madeira, of Baltimore. Issue: Charles Frederick Chamberlaine.

Calvert Taylor Chamberlaine (son of George, 1834–1912) md. Alberta Roberts, of Norfolk; Richard Henry md. Margaret Lee Garrett, of Baltimore: issue, Richard Henry Lee (1903–1933); Mabel Beatrice md. Charles Franklin Burroughs, of Norfolk, issue: Mabel Chamberlaine and Charles Franklin Burroughs, Jr.

Mary Wilson Chamberlayne (dau. of William Wilson Chamberlayne) md. Fergus Reid, of Norfolk, issue: Helen, Fergus, and Janet; Anne Dillard Chamberlaine md. Frank Coe, U. S. A., issue: Wm. Chamberlaine; Wm. Chamberlaine md. Margaret Smith, of Washington, D. C.

Maria Elizabeth Barker (dau. of Fanny Chamberlaine Barker) md. George Le Roy Irwin, issue: George Le Roy, Frances Josephine, and another son.

Charles Frederick Chamberlaine [son of Richard Henry Chamberlaine (1807–1879)] md. Jean Haynes, of Clarksburg, W. Va., issue: two daughters.

Lt. George Chamberlaine of the Virginia Navy of the Revolution is represented in the Society of the Cincinnati, by Mr. Charles Franklin Burroughs, Jr., of Norfolk, Va.

CHAMBERLAINE, PHILIP, of Elizabeth City Co. (brother of George, above). Appt. in 1776 first mate of the Hero Galley; later captain; personally resigned his command to the Board in Dec. 1777. Perished on the Dolphin, sunk in 1779. USP, he married Elizabeth Cooper, a cousin of James Barron, Jr., and had one child, died young. His widow became the wife of Nathaniel Powell Wilson, of Tenn. He had a sister, who married Capt. Wm. Finnie, and another sister Pamela, the wife of James Davis of Williamsburg. MC III, 175. BH, 1416.

CHAMBERLAYNE, BYRD (brother of Edward Pye Chamberlayne, below), of King William Co. Lt., Henry Galley. 1st lt. Mosquito. Escaped from Fortune Jail, England, and on his return to Virginia, ordered to take command of the Brig Jefferson, Sept. 10, 1779. LBP, Charles De Kay. MC III, 175. BH, 1416.

Lt. Byrd Chamberlayne md. Elizabeth, dau. of William Dandridge, Jr. and Agnes West, his wife. Only surviving children who left issue were two daughters:

1. Eleanor ("Ellen") md. John Camm Pollard; issue: Chamberlayne Pollard, who settled in Georgia, married, and left issue.

2. Evelyn Byrd md. Jan. 19, 1809, by Rev. John D. Blair, at "Greenwood", Henrico County, Virginia, to Robert Pollard, Jr., of "Zoar", King William County, and had ten children, of whom (1) Robert Byrd, b. Jan. 3, 1810, married. (2) William George, M. D., (Capt. Cavalry, King Wm. Co. Killed at the battle of Sharpsburg, Md., September, 1862) B. Apl. 2, 1818, md. March 4, 1845, Sarah Adams Smith, grandaughter of Governor Smith who lost his life in the burning of the Richmond Theatre in 1811. Only surviving child is Mrs. John Gascoine Moncure. (3) James Otway, b. May 6, 1820, md. February 3, 1842, George Anna (sister of Sarah). Has descendants living. (4) Eliza Dandridge, b. August 7, 1822, d. November 7, 1866, md. at "Zoar", April 6, 1847, Beverley Browne Douglas, issue: (a) Elizabeth Dandridge, md. Travers Daniel Moncure, no issue. (b) Evelyn Spotswood, md. James Colvin Causey, issue: Mary Douglas, md. Marion Kelly Kendrick, has two daus., one son: Beverley Douglas, md. Mary Katherine Paul, two daus. 3 sons. (c) Mary Ellen Douglas, md. William T. Weathers, has two daus: Elizabeth md. Tom Peet Cross, of the Univ. Chicago (two daus.); Willie True, unmarried. (5) Edward Spotswood, b. July 7, 1832, md. Mary Douglas, issue: Robert Spotswood, Walter Weir, William George,

Henry Douglas, James Hankins, John Beverley, M. D. Evelyn Byrd md. Albert H. Stoddard, Jr.

CHAMBERLAYNE, EDWARD PYE (1750-1806), of Prince William Co. Entered as midshipman in 1776; 2d Lt., 1777 and 1778; in 1781 bore a part in taking two of the enemy's vessels off the coast of S. C. and went with one of them as supercargo into some part of N. C. USP, Benj. Figg, who stated that he had lived for nearly two years in the same house with lt. Chamberlayne, remembered having seen him in uniform with other officers, at Frazer's Ferry subsequent to the siege of York. In USP is the petition of Wm. Byrd Chamberlayne, Lewis W. Chamberlayne, James Edward Ruffin, sole heir of Eliz. B. Ruffin, and Robert and Mary A. Williamson, only heirs of Lucy Parke Williamson.

Edward Pye Chamberlayne md. first, Agnes, daughter of Capt. William Dandridge and Agnes West, his wife; he married, secondly, Mary Bickerton, daughter of Lewis Webb and Mary Bickerton.

Issue by first marriage: Edward Pye, Wm. B., Robert, and Thomas (died young).

William B. Chamberlayne (1789–1858) md. Ann Williamson Mosby, and had issue: (1) Edwin Harvey md. Sarah Madison Scott; (2) Lucy W. md. Efford Bentley.

Issue by second marriage:

I. Dr. Lewis Webb Chamberlayne of "Windsor Shades", New Kent County (1798–1854), later of "Montrose", Henrico County md. April 11, 1820, Martha Burwell Dabney of "Elmington", Gloucester County, Va. (1802–1883), issue: (1) Edward Pye Chamberlayne (1821–1877), unmarried. (2) Hartwell Macon Chamberlayne (1836–1905), md. March 16, 1869, Elmina McDearmon, of Halifax County (1842–1894), and had issue: (a) William Nelson Chamberlayne. (b) Thomas Gallaudet Chamberlayne, died, 1894, unmarried. (c) Edward Pye Chamberlayne, of Roanoke, Va. md. Emma Frances Furbush, and had issue: Charles Hartwell; Edward Pye, Jr.; Ellen md. Earle Van Arsdale Conover; Ada Lee; A. Bentley; Frances. (d) Lewis Webb Chamberlayne (died 1906) md. in Oklahoma, and had issue:

Hartwell Macon and Mary Frances. (e) Sarah Dabney md. Thomas Walter Davis, of Staunton, Va., and had issue: Hartwell Chamberlayne md. in Texas, Vera Holden (and had issue: Virginia Louise and Hartwell Chamberlayne); Rebecca Cook md. Howard Cleo Burris of Calif.; Harrison Bolen; Parke Chamberlayne; Thomas Walter; Edward Dabney; Virginia; Dorothy McDearmon, the last two born in Calif. (f) John Stewart Chamberlayne, died young.

(3) John Hampden Chamberlayne (Aug. 22, 1840–Feb. 18, 1882) md. Oct. 15, 1873, Mary Walker Gibson, and had issue: (a) Martha Dabney Chamberlayne md. first, Edward Pleasants Valentine, and had issue: Martha Chamberlayne Valentine (md. John Hill Cronley, issue: John Hill Cronley, Jr.), and Ann Pasteur Valentine md. 1st, John Bartram Kelley, and, second, Oscar Edward Cesare (issue: Oscar Edward Valentine Cesare). Martha Dabney Chamberlayne md. secondly, Walter Scott McNeil, B. L., Ph. D. (b) Lucy Atkinson Chamberlayne, md. first, Richard Clarke Scott, Jr. (issue: John Hampden Chamberlayne Scott, died young, and Churchill Gibson Scott) md. second Clarence Maynard (issue: Lucy Chamberlayne, died infant). (c) Rev. Churchill Gibson Chamberlayne, Ph. D. md. Elizabeth Bolling (issue: Edward Pye and John Hampden, III). (d) John Hampden Chamberlayne, Jr. (died Oct. 3, 1925) md. Alice Doyle. (e) Lewis Parke Chamberlayne, Ph. D. (died 1917) md. Elizabeth Claiborne Mann (issue: Mary Gibson and Elizabeth Claiborne Mann Chamberlayne). (f) Bessie Gibson Chamberlayne.

(4) Lucy Parke Chamberlayne (1842–1927) md. Feb. 16, 1863, Dr. George William Bagby (1828–1883), issue: (a) Virginia Bagby, md. Henry Taylor, III, issue: Henry Taylor IV, md. Isabel De Leon Williams (issue: Alice Marshall and Henry Taylor, V); Lucy Parke Chamberlayne; Mary Minor Watson; Virginia md. Wilburn Birkenhead Sydnor; (b) Lewis Webb Chamberlayne, died in childhood; (c) John Hampden Chamberlayne Bagby; (d) Martha Burwell Dabney Bagby md. Hon. George Gordon Battle; (e) Woodville Latham Bagby, died infant; (f) Parke Chamberlayne Bagby md.

Charles E. Bolling; (g) and (h) George William and Robert Coleman, twins; (i) Ellen Matthews Bagby; (j) Philip Haxall Bagby (died, 1926) md. Mary Clarkson Allen, of Baltimore issue: Philip Haxall Bagby II and Virginia Allen Bagby.

II. Byrd Chamberlayne md. Mary Robertson Sully, issue: Mary Elizabeth, Lewis Webb, James Robertson, Richard Channing, and Spotswood Dandridge.

III. Elizabeth Mary md. Sterling Ruffin, issue: James E. Ruffin.

IV. Lucy Parke Chamberlayne md. in 1818, issue: 1. Robert Williamson. 2. Mary Amanda Williamson md. John Stewart, of Rothesay, Scotland and Brook Hill, Henrico Co., Va. issue: (a) Mary Amanda Stewart md. Thomas Pinckney, of Charleston, S. C., issue: Charles Cotesworth Pinckney; (b) Isobel Lamont Stewart md. Joseph Bryan (1845-1908), issue: John Stewart Bryan, md. Anne Eliza Tennant, issue: Dr. Robert Coalter Bryan md. Grace Hamilton, of Maryland, issue: Jonathan md. Mrs. Winifred (Duffy) Hayden; J. St. George Bryan md. Emily Kemp, issue: Thomas Pinckney Bryan md. Helen McGill Hamilton, issue: (c) Marion McIntosh md. the Rt. Rev. George Peterkin, issue: (d) Lucy; (e) Anne Carter; (f) Norma; (g) Elizabeth Hope.

CHAMBERS, HANCOCK (Hammock). Diligence Galley. LBP Solomon Powell, MC III, 180. Heirs in 1831 Harriet Savage (wife of George Savage) and Edmund W. Chambers.

CHANCE, SHADRACK, of Accomac Co. Seaman in 1779. Quartermaster, Accomac Galley. No issue. MC III, 306. Heirs in 1834: Charlotte Phillips, Louise N., Nancy Vernelson, Polly Hudson, Polly Thornton, and Wm. V. Thornton.

CHANDLER, THOMAS, JR. (son of Thomas and brother of Reuben), of Caroline Co. Marine: enlisted under Lt. Catlett. On Mosquito. Imprisoned in Barbadoes, and died in 1780 on a British ship. USP Charles De Kay. See petition, H. D. Oct. 28, 1780.

CHANDLER, THOS. Entered May, 1776; in July, appt. lt. Brig Northampton. NBJ, Sept. 10, 1778. Lt. of Patriot when she was taken, and died a prisoner July 25, 1781. USP.

In 1833, John B. Burton and Sarah, his wife, heirs. N's Accomack, 23, 50.

CHANNING, WM. War 5, 50.

CHAPIN, BENJ. Surgeon, Protector Galley, April 1776; Transferred to ship Tartar. In Nov. 1778 on sick leave in Alexandria and there continued till his death (will dated Aug. 13, 1781). MC II, 329. Warrant in 1792 to Hiram and Gordon Chapin, Richard W. Ashton and Elizabeth his wife, and Ann Chapin. According to Commodore Walter Brooke, Dr. Chapin had a son George Chapin and a daughter who md. Gratton. In 1838 James Gratton presented a petition on behalf of the heirs. BH, 1450.

CHAPIN, PLATO. N 8, 11.

CHAPMAN, JOHN. Master. LBP Thomas Flynt.

CHARLES, MOORE. Able Seaman. War 5, 54.

CHASE, JOHN. Manley Galley, Sept. 11, 1779.

CHASE, WM. Manley Galley, Sept. 11, 1779.

CHEESMAN, DR. THOMAS, of York Co. (died about 1799 at Hampton). Surgeon's mate in 1777, June 8, 1777 to Jan. 1779. On Tartar in engagement near Capes. At the siege of York. LBP.

CHESHIRE (Chesire), JOHN, of Prince William Co. Recommended lt. Sept. 2, 1778, USP. In 1848 Wm. C. Chesire, Sarah T. B., Olive, Margaret R. Chesire, Thomas I. Chesire, Geo. W. Chesire, lawful children of Wm. H. Chesire and Sarah his wife now deceased.

CHESIRE—. Sailing master of the Caswell. N. C. Archives XVII, 132.

CHEVIS, WM., of Warwick Co. Gunner. N, 8.

CHICK, JOHN. Gunner, Liberty, May 10—July 30, 1776. LBP George Rodgers.

CHILES, JOHN. Dragon, Boatswain. H. D. 1834-5. Doc. 48, 6.

CHILES, WM. Dragon, Sept. 1779.

CHILTON, JOHN. Brig Liberty, June 1778.

CHILTON, JOHN, of Westmoreland Co. In June, 1818, John Chilton, aged about 63, made affidavit that he entered service with Capt. John Thomas on the Fly in 1777, and continued on said boat until siege of York; then discharged. His Galley was burnt by the British in Great Wicomico, and after that he went to the South with Capt. Haney, and was wounded by a broad sword in the leg at the Battle of Savana; and from there he returned to York.

CHOWNING (Chuning), CHATION (Chatain). Enlisted Dec. 27, 1777. MC II, 340.

CHEWNING (Chowning), GEORGE. Enlisted Aug. 16, 1777. MC II, 349.

CHOWNING, WM. Surgeon's mate, of Middlesex Co. On Tartar, 1779–80. Died about the close of the War. R. C.

CHRISTIAN, GEORGE. Officer. For heirs, see N's Accomack, 26.

CHRISTIAN, JOHN. Enlisted on the Patriot in 1778. In the engagement with the "Lord Howe". Returned to the neighborhood of Carter's Creek on the Rappahannock. R. C.

CHRISTIAN, NICHOLAS, of Accomac Co. Steward. Boatswain, Lewis Galley, Feb. 13, 1778, LBNB, Feb. 13, 1778, Tempest, Oct. 7, Dec. 13, 1779. Killed in service in Chesapeake Bay in 1781. LBP.

CHRISTIAN, DR. THOMAS. Liberty, May 18—July 30, 1776. LBP George Rodgers.

CHRISTIAN, WM. Recommended 1st Lt. Brig Northampton, Jan. 16, 1778. LBNB. Resigned Feb. 2, 1779. LBP James Mitchell. MC III, 165. Heirs in 1830 Richard and Mary Ames, N's Northampton, 11, 12, 27.

CHRISTIE, WM. See "Cristie".

CHRIS. Mulatto, N. A. B.

CHYLDS, JOHN. E 1.

CLAIBORNE, Nathaniel. Ordinary Seaman. War 5, 53.

CLAIBORNE, THOS. Able seaman. War 5, 54.

CLARK (Clarke, Clerk), JOHN. Henry Galley, 1776, LBNB, Nov. 1, 1777; Safeguard Galley, March 1 to June 16, 1777.

CLARK, JOHN. Lt. marines. Cormorant.

CLARKE, WM. N 8, 30.

CLARKE, Z. N 8, 20.

CLARKSON, JESSE. Lad. N. A. B.

Claybrook, John. B. W.
Clements, John. Boatswain. War 5, 54.
Clements, Thos. War 5, 54.
Clemmons, John. War 5, 54.
Clendening (Clendenny), George. Dragon. LBP James Jennings.
Clerk, John. N 8, 11.
Cluverius, John. Henry Galley. NBJ, May 27, 1778.
Coats, Edwey (Edwy), of Lancaster or Northumberland Co. In service Sept. 2, 1779, but see Va. Gazette, July 31, 1779.
Coats (Coates), Jesse. Dragon, Oct. 8, 1777 to Jan. 20, 1779. Enlisted again Sept. 2, 1779.
Coats, John. Enlisted on Dragon Sept. 2, 1779. N 8, 14.
Coates (Coats), Raleigh (Rolly). Dragon. LBP James Jennings. From Oct. 8, 1777 to Jan. 20, 1779.
Coats, Samuel. Able Seaman. Page Galley, LBNB, Feb. 13, 1778. Dragon, March 30, 1778 to Jan. 20, 1779.
Coats, Sidney. Dragon. From May 17, 1777 to Jan. 20, 1779.
Coates (Coats), Thomas, of Lancaster or Northumberland County, LBP James Jennings. Dragon from Oct. 8, 1777 to Jan. 20, 1779. Advertised as deserted in the Virginia Gazette of July 3, 1779.
Coates, William. Dragon. N 8, 13.
Cocke, Capt. James. Brig Raleigh in Sept., 1776. Manley Galley in Dec. 1776.
Cocke, Captain John Catesby. According to RC he entered service as a captain in 1776; was a supernumerary captain on the discharge of the State Navy. Appointed capt. marines, Aug. 29, 1776. According to the affidavit of his son, John Presley Cocke, in 1834, Captain Cocke was near being shot by one of the Spring Guns fixed in the magazine, or arsenal, at Williamsburg; he was one of the company of minute men that marched with Patrick Henry, in April, 1775, to rescue the deposits of powder removed by Governor Dunmore; he was in the battle at the Long or Great Bridge near Norfolk. He had in 1781 a valuable estate in Chickahominy and in his absence the British burnt up his buildings, destroyed his flocks and stock and took off many valuable

Negroes. He was in service at the siege of York; commanded for some time a flotilla on York River; he was driven off with his little command by the enemy and afterwards came under the orders of Gen. Lafayette.

After the war Captain Cocke settled in Culpeper County, where he died in 1818. He had issue: Presley Thornton Cocke; Peter Presley Cocke, Catherine Tennison; Lucy Cocke (died without issue); Elizabeth Cocke, who married William Fitzhugh (issue: Presley, George S., Catherine, William C., Jane Lucy, Eliza, Louisa, and Maria Fitzhugh); Alice Cocke, who married Edmunds, and had issue: John, Alice, Peggy, and Helen Edmunds. Elizabeth Cocke Fitzhugh and Alice Cocke Edmunds both died before their father. BH, 1451.

COCKRELL, LITTLETON. NBJ, Sept. 4, 1778.

COCKERELL (Cockrell-Cockrill), LITTLETON. Protector Galley MC II, 10.

COCKRICAL, JOHN. Brig Jefferson, 20 Dec., 1779–June, 1780.

COFF, JOHN. N. A. B.

COLBERT, JOHN. Marine. Jan 16, 1783.

COLE, WALTER KING. H. D. May 30, 1783. Appointed surgeon in the Navy, and acted until June 1777 when he was appointed surgeon of the 1st State Regt. After the war settled on the lands in Henry Co. that remained of the estates of his father, Walter King, a native of Great Britain, and in this county he died in 1791. Resigned from army Nov. 1778 and entered Hospital under Dr. Rickman. Appointed surgeon on the State boat Fanny he was captured by the enemy.

COLE, WM. Jan. 20, 1783.

COLE, WM. Carpenter. NBJ, Aug. 25, 1778.

COLEMAN, JOHN. War 5, 51.

COLEMAN, THOMAS. Pilot. Brig Liberty, 18 May–30 July, 1776; July 30, 1777.

COLEMAN, WM., of Caroline Co. Enlisted in Dick's Marines at Fredericksburg, on Mosquito. Minor Officer. Living in 1837. LBP De Kay.

COLLIER, SAMUEL. Accomac Galley.

COLLINS, JAMES. Accomac Galley. LBP Wm. Travis. MC III, 246. Heirs in 1833: Skinner, Thomas, and Sophia Collins and Rachel Smullings. N's Accomack, 35, 49.

COLLINS, STEPHEN. Accomac Galley. Served also in State Line. MC III, 230. Heir in 1831, Stirling Collins.

CONNER, MICHAEL. Quartermaster, Brig Liberty, 8 May–30 July, 1776.

CONWAY, CAPT. ROBERT. Captain Schooner Adventure, Aug. 1776; Protector Galley; resigned from Protector in Nov. 1776. USP John Thomas.

CONWAY, ROBERT. N 8, 29.

COOK, DAWSON (Cooke). Midshipman, Brig Liberty, 18 May–30 July, 1776; acting midshipman, July 30, 1777. Ship Gloucester. USP. In 1850, Ann C. Brushwood, only living child of Dawson and Mildred Cooke, aged 60, stated that her father and mother married by "asking into church", previous to his entering into service, in Dec. 1775, and eldest child Mary born Oct. 15, 1776. Dawson Cooke died Nov. 14, 1828. His widow died Aug. 14, 1830. Will of Dawson Cooke in King and Queen County, probated Dec. 14, 1829 mentioned wife Mildred: daughter Anne C. Didlake (widow of John) **land on road leading to old Dragon Ordinary **son Dawson my mill, etc. **son Giles 100 acres Southeast of Tennessee river in Ky." part of land I purchased of Cary Wyatt **friend William Spencer **grandson Alexander Howlett** grandson Robert Didlake. Dawson Cooke's children were: Mary, Ann, Paschall, Mildred (md. Wm. Howlett), Henry, Dawson, and Giles.

Dawson Cooke, Jr. md. Ann (aged 48 in 1851). The widow of Giles Cooke md. in Jan. 28, 1847 the Rev. Cincinnatus Goodall (aged 42, in 1851), of Elizabeth City Co. In the USP is an interesting affidavit of George W. Brushwood (son of James) and of Ann Dillard, with references to "Parson Hughs", also several pages of the Newcomb Family Bible.

COOK, MATHEW. Boat Liberty. LBP Dr. P. Bartlett.

COOK (Cooke), CAPT. ROBT. (2d cruiser, Eastern Shore), 29 Feb., 1776. In merchant marine service before the war.

COOK, WM. Gunner. MC II, 269.

COOKE, JOHN. Ship Gloucester, Oct. 9, 1778, NBJ.
COOKE, J. N. Page Galley. N 8, 24.
COOKE, WM. Tartar. NBJ, Sept. 3, 1778.
COOKE, WM., JR. Able Seaman. H. D. 1834–5, Doc. 48.
COOLEY, THOS. Marine, Jan. 20, 1776.
COOPER, EDWARD. Pilot. "A man of large fortune **who performed many other services than those of pilot**. His home was burnt by the British in the very commencement of the War." LBP. MC III, 443. In 1838, Ann R. Cocke, sole heir at law of John Cooper decd, sole heir of Edward Cooper.
COOPER, HENRY. H. D. 1834–5, Doc. 48.
COOPER, JAMES. War 5, 54.
COOPER, PASS. E 1.
COOPER, WM. Aud. Acct. XVIII, 158.
COOPER, WM., JR. Able Seaman. War 5, 54.
COPES, BEVERLEY (died in 1811). Midshipman. Diligence Galley. "A very smart, active, and enterprising young man", testimony of Wm. Thornton, LBP John Flynt and of Wm. White. In 1831 heirs: Parker and Beverly Copes, Nancy Merrill, and Barbara Martin. N's Accomack, 28.
CORBELL, CLEMENT, of Northumberland Co. Protector Galley.
CORBELL, ELAM. Aud. Acct. XXX, 5.
CORBELL, FLEET. War 5, 47.
CORBELL, WM. War 5, 47.
CORBETT, CLEM. Aud. Acct. XXII, 434.
CORBETT, WM. Aud. Acct. XXVII, 242.
CORBIN, WM. Master at Arms. Accomac Galley. Died in Worcester Co., Md. LBP Wm. White. BH, 467.
CORNELIUS, WM., JR., of Lancaster Co. Gunner, Hero Galley, Nov. 4, 1777. N's Lancaster, 33.
CORNER, MICHAEL, Marine. Brig Northampton, LBNB, Feb. 12, 1778; Manley Galley, Sept. 11, 1779.
COSTO, SAMUEL. MC II, 244. In 1786, John Costo, heir.
COTTRELL (Cottorill), WM. Midshipman, LBP Wm. Flynt.
COTTRILL, THOS. Marine. Mosquito, LBP.
COURTNEY, SAMUEL, of Fauquier Co. Capt. Dick's marines; later in land service.

Covington, Samuel. Safeguard Galley, Jan. 16, 1777.
Cowper, James. Aud. Acct. XXVII, 434.
Cowper, Capt. John, of Nansemond Co., and of Hampton, Va. Perished in his Brig the Dolphin, in 1779. See statement in LBP, of his grandnephew, John C. Cohoon, of Suffolk. The loss of the Dolphin was the theme of a poem published in the "Christian Sun", Suffolk, Va., June 2, 1858. Capt. Cowper left issue: (1) John md. Mrs. Shepherd, widow, who had Betsey md. Wm. Darden (issue: Mary E. and Horatio, died s. p.); (2) Jane md. Edward Norfleet, issue: Nathaniel, Wm., Anne, and Jane; (3) Horatio Gates Cowper, Lt., U. S. N., never married.
Cowper, John, son of Wills Cowper, of Nansemond Co. Lt. Privateer "Marquis Lafayette". Editor of the Public Ledger and Mayor of Norfolk. For Cowper family see Va. His. Mag., Vol. II.
Cox, Anthony. Lewis Galley. LBNB, Feb. 13, 1778.
Cox, Edward. War 5, 55.
Cox, James. N 8, 11.
Cox, John, of King George Co. Carpenter, Safeguard Galley, March–June, 1777.
Cox, Capt. John, of Portsmouth. "I held a private command in the service of Virginia as a captain and commenced service in the year 1777, and commanded for several years thereafter many private armed vessels which were engaged in the transporting of munitions of war from the West Indies ** and in performing other duties for the State of Virginia." Dispatched as a special Agent to the West Indies to succeed Richard Harrison. On the Schooner Polly at St. Pierre in June, 1777. Equipped the Schooner Sally Norton. Cruising southward of St. Croix was captured after a gallant resistance by H. M. armed Brig the Eagle. Capt. McCauley; escaped from prison in Tortola to St. Eustatius, and then returned with Capt. R. Elliott in the Renown to Virginia. Formed one of the party organized by St. George Tucker to remove all the powder from Bermuda and transport it to the Magazine in Williamsburg. Commanded the Brig Augusta during the time of the French

depredations in 1798. Died in Gosport, Dec. 17, 1837, in his eighty-fifth year. An interesting article about him appeared in the Norfolk Beacon. USP. Ann P. Swift, administrator.

Cox, Thos. Seaman, Jan. 16, 1783.

Crabb, John, of Accomac Co. Gunner. Killed by bursting of a cannon on the Diligence.

Cracke (Crocka), Anthony. LBP James Jennings.

Craighill, Nathaniel. Midshipman. Dragon, June 6, 1777 to July 24.

Crain (Crane), James. Pilot. Master. Safeguard Galley.

Cranberry (Granberry), John. Sailing Master. Dragon. USP David Henderson.

Crandle (Crandolph), Wm. Hero Galley. N 8, 10.

Crawford, —. Sloop Congress. Wife Catherine. NBJ, Dec. 16, 1776.

Creed, Simon. Tempest, Oct. 7, 1779.

Crew (Crews), John, of Warwick Co. (died, unmarried, August, 1810). Lt. Sloop Defiance, Capt. Green. Captured on the Scorpion and held prisoner in Bermuda until April 1783. USP. Next of kin, nephews Walter Crew, of Brown Co., Ohio, and Wm. B. Crew, who died unmarried.

Cristie (Christie), Wm. Surgeon. MC III, 304. In 1834, John Rogers and his sister, only heirs of Mrs. John Rogers, sole heir of Wm. Christie.

Cropper, Jesse. Aud. Acct. XXIX, 8.

Cropper, John, Sr. Carpenter. Entered on board Accomac Galley, Aug. 20, 1777. LBP Wm. White. Col. John Cropper Jr. was his son. In 1830, Sally Cropper, only heir (Lilliston devisees). N's Accomack, 22.

Crow, Anthony. Dragon, June 20, 1777 to Aug. 20, 1779. Deserted.

Crowder, Joshua, of Lancaster Co. Dragon, June 20, 1777 to Aug. 20, 1779. LBP James Jennings.

Crowder, Robt. Dragon. LBP James Jennings.

Crump, Abner. Manley Galley, Aug. 30, 1776. In a letter written from Richmond, on June 29, 1785, to the Secretary of the Society of the Cincinnati, of which he became a member, Crump wrote: "In May, 1776, I was appointed Lieut. of Marines; in Nov. 1776 Capt. of Infantry, and the spring following was deranged to the 1st State Reg. commanded by Col. George Gibson; continued in service till the 22d April, 1783", ***Virginia State Archives.

CUFFY. Elenor Boury's negro slave, whom she caused to be enlisted on the Norfolk Revenge, Capt. Calvert, in Sept., 1777, as an able seaman. See H. D. Nov. 13, 1780, p. 47.

CUFFY (Cuffee). Pilot on Row Galley commanded by Capt. Richard Barron; died from injuries received in service. LBP Dr. Bartlett, testimony of Mary C. Ward, In USP Mrs. Mary C. Graves states that she was owner of Cuffee, died 1781. On the boat Wm. Graves was Lt. and Dr. Philip Bartlett, Surgeon.

CULLEY, ROBERT (brother of Armistead Culley), of Matthews Co. Carpenter on Brig Liberty, enlisted July 30, 1776. Taken prisoner. LBP Geo. Rodgers.

CULSON, JOHN. Henry Galley. LBNB, Nov. 1, 1777.

CUMMINGS, JOHN. Taken prisoner. USP Jesse George.

CUMMINS, THOMAS. Aud. Acct. 1779–80, 227.

CUNNINGHAM, JAMES. Lt. on Dolphin; perished with all hands on board. MC II, 503. Heirs at law in 1842: Helen Wilson, Wm. C. Gatewood, Eliz. Starke Williamson, and Eliz. Williamson. BH, 1453.

CUNNINGHAM, MICHAEL. Henry Galley, 1776. Tartar. NBJ, Sept. 3, 1778.

CUNNINGHAM, CAPT. SAMUEL BARRON. Merchant service.

CUNNINGHAM, WM., of the Borough of Norfolk. Lt. Later capt. of the Schooner Liberty, "Officer of great zeal and of the most distinguished courage as many of his exploits will testify," declared James Barron, Jr. Died in 1795. MC III, 170. Heirs in 1830: James B. Cunningham, Mary Weldon, Eliz. Gatewood, Philemon, Wm., and Eliz. E. Gatewood. LBP Wm. Jennings. USP. BH, 489.

CUNNINGHAM, WM. ROE, of Elizabeth City Co. Pilot. Entered in 1777; conducted French ships the whole time they remained in Virginia. LBP. B, 1413–14.

CURRELL, GEORGE. Midshipman, Page or Lewis Galley. LBP Hudnall. N's Lancaster, 33.
CURRELL, JACOB. Lewis Galley. MC II, 242.
CURRELL, JAMES. Page Galley, LBNB, Feb. 13, 1778. Midshipman (?). N's Lancaster, 36. BH, 1453. Died in Loudoun Co. c. 1830. USP. Heirs in 1845: James, Betsey, Polly, Alice, and Isaac Currell.
CURRELL, SPENCER. War 5, 55.
CURRELL, THOS. Lewis Galley. LBNB, Feb. 13, 1778.
CURTICE (Curtace), HENRY. Protector Galley. MC II, 12.
CURTIS, HENRY. Boat Liberty, Nov., 1779.
CURTIS, JAMES. Lt. N's Lancaster, 40.
CURTIS, JAMES, of Culpeper Co. Midshipman. BH, 486.
CURTIS, JAMES. NBJ, Sept. 10, 1778.
CURYONG, PETER. Dragon. LBP James Jennings.
CUTLER, WM. Brig Northampton. LBNB, Dec. 20, 1777.

D

DAGNELL, STEPHEN. Marine. Jan. 25, 1783.
DALBY, BRANSON, of Accomac County. For heirs, see N's Accomack, 21. BH, 1364.
DALE, LT. RICHARD, of Norfolk Co. Died in Philadelphia, Feb., 1826. B, 1084. In the autumn of 1775 he joined the state Navy under Capt. John Barrett; in March, 1776, the ship was captured by the British in James River. Distinguished himself in the Continental Navy. Heirs in 1832, John M. Dale, Edward Dale, and Elizabeth Reed. USP.
DAMERON, JOSHUA. Tempest. Dec. 7, 1779.
DAMERON, THOMAS, of Lancaster County. Protector Galley, BH, 1098. On the testimony of his son Dennis, it appears that Thos. Dameron entered the State Navy in 1776 or 1777 for three years and served most of the time on the Tempest (entered Dec., 1779). See VSR, July, 1930, p. 25.
DANE (?), DANIEL. Tempest, Oct. 7, 1779.
DANIEL. A Negro. H. D. 1834-5, Doc. 48, 7.
DANIEL, GEORGE, of Westmoreland County. Carpenter and Mate. Enlisted with Lewis Jones, 18, Feb., 1777, on Dragon,

Lieutenant Lurty. Discharged Oct. 12, 1780. LBP, 1784. R. C.

John Clarke and Washington Clarke stated that George Daniel was on the Defiance early in 1776.

DANIEL, JOHN. Brig Jefferson, 1779–80.

DANIEL, JOHN. N, 8, 15, 18.

DANIEL, THOMAS. Dragon, Sept. 12, 1779. LBP George Daniel.

DARBY, AYRES. Pilot. Accomac Galley, 1779; Henry Galley, 1776. LBP, 1834.

DARBY, DARMON, or Darmore, or Damon, of Accomac County. Pilot on Capt. Sanders' vessel. Entered service Jan. 1, 1777; served until Jan. 6, 1780. MC I, 653.

DARBY, WM., of Lancaster Co. Deserted from Tartar, Va. Gazette, Sept. 11, 1779.

DARMON, DARLEY. Pilot, Tartar, Sept. 28—Nov., 1779.

DAUGHERTY (Daughity, Daurity), JAMES, of Northumberland Co. Midshipman, Protector Galley, Jan. 19, 1777. Lt. Capt. Aug. 27, 1778. NBJ. In service after Sept. 10, 1779. USP. Went west, but returned, and died in March, 1830. His will names his wife Elizabeth; children James B., Susanna, S. A., Robert, Baladin, Aurelious Daugherty and Jane Wildy ** mentions land in Rutherford Co., Tenn. See also BH, 1098.

DAUGHERTY, JOHN. Aud. Acct. XXX, 5.

DAUGHTRY, TOLSON (Toulson). Aud. Acct. 1779–80, 319.

DAVENPORT, JOSEPH. Ship Washington. NBJ, Oct. 6, 1778.

DAVIES, JOHN. 3d lt. Marines, June 1, 1778, lately commanded by Capt. Marsden.

DAVIS, ALEXANDER. Dragon, Aug. 14, 1777 to ———.

DAVIS, ALEX. Manley Galley, Sept. 11, 1779.

DAVIS, AQUILA, of Culpeper County, March 19, 1781, Jan 20, 1783.

DAVIS, DANIEL. R. C. Certificate issued April 28, 1781.

DAVIS, GEORGE. Safeguard, 1st March to 16 June, 1777.

DAVIS, JAMES. Nov. 1, 1776, 3d lt. Marines, Capt. James Foster's Company.

DAVIS, JEDUTHAN. MC II, 244.

Davis, John (same as John Davies?). June 1, 1776, 3d lt. marines (lately commanded by Captain John Marsden). C. S.

Davis, John. Hero Galley. NBJ, Feb. 13, 1778.

Davis (Davise), John, of Westmoreland Co. Enlisted with Capt. Callender on the Dragon, and was on ship when she was attacked by the British ship of war Roebuck 4 days at sea from Capes of Virginia, and returned to Hampton Roads. He was discharged at the Chickahominy Shipyard after three years faithful service. He was married to Amy ——— by Parson Smith about middle of December, 1786. He died March 9, 1838. USP.

Davis, John, of Westmoreland Co. Dragon. Father red man, mother white. LBP James Jennings.

Davis, John. Norfolk Revenge Galley, 1776.

Davis, John R., of Elizabeth City Co. Lt. marines. Patriot. Followed the water a long time after the Revolution. Died in 1801 or 1802. USP. Heirs in 1849: Joseph H. Brough, of Norfolk (aged 40), John Davis, of Norfolk (45), Saml. Davis, of Norfolk (49), Ann E. Brough, of Norfolk (46), Hannah Hansford, of Elizabeth City Co. (44), grandchild Robt. Repeton (21), Helen Repeton (18), residence unknown, and Wm. Davis (21), residing in Williamsburg. MC III, 450 and 591.

Davis, Judithan. War 5, 62.

Davis, Zedick (Zadick). Hero Galley. NBJ, Nov. 4, 1777.

Dawsey (or Dorsey), Lawrence. Ship Gloucester, May 18, 1778. Sailing Master of the Nicholson (Maxwell, Sept. 2, 1780).

Dawson, Thomas. Tempest, Oct. 7, 1779. USNP.

Dawson, Thomas Bassett, of Williamsburg and of Matthews Co. Midshipman, NBJ, Sept. 12, 1778. LBP, 1834. Died 1798 or 1799, unmarried. "During the time of the invasion in 1781 he was employed to carry some public dispatches or a message for Gen. Nelson at Yorktown, and while in that service was pursued near Williamsburg by a party of British cavalry, overtaken, and severely wounded in the head and arms." He was a brother of William and of

Francis Dawson, and of Rebecca Dawson, who md. Col. Wilson Miles Cary. BH, 1086 and 1366.

DAY, GEORGE, of Wicomico Parish, Northumberland Co. Deserted from Tartar. See Va. Gazette, Sept. 11, 1779, but see also LBP, 1783.

DAY, THOMAS. Protector Galley. Jefferson, 1779 and 1780. Certificate, 1785, from Capt. John Thomas.

DEAN (Deane), CAPT. WILLIAM. Schooner Revenge, April 21, 1776.

DEANE, DANIEL. Tempest, Dec. 7, 1779.

DEARING, JAMES. Dragon, Sept. 16, 1777, to Nov. 21, Died in service.

DEBATTEASTER, JOHN. Dragon. LBP James Jennings.

DE KAY (Decay), CHARLES. Sailing Master. Mosquito, Imprisoned in England. USP. Died in Aug. or Sept., 1829. Son, John De Kay, of Vernon, Sussex Co., N. J. Thomas B. De Kay took letters of administration in 1859.

DEMOVILL (Demoville-Demovil), SAMUEL, of Lancaster Co. Armourer.

DENBY, WM. War 5, 62.

DENBY, WILLIS. War 5, 62.

DERHAM, WM. LBP James Jennings.

DICK, MAJOR ALEXANDER, of Fredericksburg. Known familiarly as "Sawny Dick". Appointed July 24, 1776, capt. Marines. On Mosquito. After return from imprisonment, major in land service. At siege of York. Will, probated July 3, 1786, mentions "my late father Charles Dick decd" *** friend Jas. Mercer, Esq. *** sister Mary Taliaferro ** nephew Charles Taliaferro ** nephew John Fenton Mercer". Mary Taliaferro afterwards married Sir John Peyton, and had by him one son, who died young. Charles G. Taliaferro died Feb., 1832, aged about 59, and devised his estate to Benj. F. Taliaferro and Theodore L. Garnett. USP.

Major Dick was a member of the Society of the Cincinnati. BH, 1100.

DICKES, ROBERT. War 5. 58.

DICKS, HENRY. War 5, 62.

DICKINSON, GEORGE. Dragon, Jan. 22, 1777, to Sept. 22, 1777.

DIGGS, WM. Tempest, NBJ, 19 June, 1778.
DISHMAN, JAMES, of Caroline Co. Marine. Entered in 1776 at Hobb's Hole, with Capt. Dick. On Mosquito. Captured. Made his way back to America from Jamaica, and entered land service with Capt. Waller. Married in Botetourt Co. Jane Green (bond, 25 July, 1788, Wm. Green, Sec.), by Parson Holt. He moved to Tenn. Was a minister. Died Oct. 10, 1820. After his death his widow md. a Mr. Gunn, and was living in Warren Co., Ky., in 1833. USP. His sister Sarah Beasley was living in Caroline Co., Va., in 1837. LBP James Dishman. BH, 217.
DISHMAN, JOHN. On Mosquito.
DISHMAN, WM. (born Essex Co., Va., Sept. 10. 1754). Marine on Mosquito. Married in Bedford Co., Feb. 15, 1782, Sally Salmons (b. Goochland Co., Va., Sept. 20, 1763). Moved to Ky. in 1810. Their son, Wm. Dishman, of Glasgow, Ky., stated that his mother Sally Dishman died July 7, 1839. Wm. Dishman, Sr. had died Dec. 4, 1833. He was a brother of John and James above, and also had a brother Jeremiah. USP.
DIXON, ANTHONY. Aud. Acct. XVIII, 257.
DIXON, NICHOLAS. Boat Liberty, 1784.
DOBSON, ROBT., of Elizabeth City Co. Sailing Master, Henry Galley, 1776. LBNB, Nov. 1, 1777. Died in Hampton Sept., 1819. USP.
DOBSON, ROBT. Seaman. H. D. 1834-5.
DOBY, ROBT. Safeguard. LBNB, Feb. 13, 1778. MC II, 473.
DOCKETT, EARL. Hero Galley. NBJ, Nov. 4, 1777.
DODD, ABLE. Boat Liberty, Nov., 1779.
DODD, JOHN. Drummer. Enlisted as marine at Fredericksburg. On Mosquito. LBP Thos. Chandler.
DODD, NEWCOMB. Henry Galley, 1776.
DOGGAT, GEORGE. Brig Liberty, June, 1778.
DOGGET, MATHEW. Hero Galley. LBNB, Feb. 13, 1778.
DOGGETT (Dougwood), CLEMENT, of Northumberland Co. Brig Northampton. NBJ, Sept. 10, 1778, MC II, 3.
DOGGETT, ELMORE (Elmer). Hero Galley, Feb. 13, 1778. NBJ. Tempest, Dec. 7, 1779.

DOGGETT, GEORGE. Carpenter, N's Lancaster, 39.
DOGGETT, GEORGE. Marine. USP. Lt. George Catlett.
DOGGETT, GEORGE, of Corotoman Neck, Lancaster Co. Entered service on a Galley; on Rattlesnake when the ship was captured. Left for the West. He had two sisters, Mary and Nancy. Affidavit of Wm. Doggett, of Portsmouth, ship captain, brother of Clement Doggett. LBP.
DOGHEAD, or Doggett, REUBEN. War 5, 61.
DOLBY (Dalby), BRANSON. N's Accomack, 36.
DONOHOW (Donohoe), HENRY. Henry Galley, 1776. LBNB, Nov. 1, 1777.
DONOVAN, MICHAEL. Henry Galley, 1776.
DONTON (Donnton), WM. NBJ, Sept. 10, 1777.
DORMAN, JOHN. Lad. N. A. B.
DOUGHERTY (Daughity), JAMES. Midshipman. Lt. On Protector when British chased and burnt her in Great Wicomico. USP. He died in March, 1830. James B. Daugherty, of Miss., and other heirs.
DOUGHERTY, JOHN. War 5, 59.
DOUGHERTY, JOHN. Clerk. War 5, 59.
DOUGHERTY, TOULSON. Marine. War 5, 59.
DOUGLAS (Douglass), JAMES. Master at Arms, Brig Liberty, 18 May to July 30, 1776. Also July 30, 1777. LBP George Rodgers.
DOUGLAS, WM. Dragon, Oct. 22, 1777, to Dec. 16. Deserted.
DOVE, JAMES. Ship Gloucester. Midshipman. NBJ, Oct. 29, 1778.
DOWDELL, JOHN. Ex. Coms., 1776.
DOWLING, JOHN. Ship Gloucester.
DOWLING (or Dollins), WM., of Caroline Co. Marine on Mosquito. LBP De Kay.
DOWNTON, WM. (died about 1808), of Lancaster Co. Gunner's Mate, Dragon to Jan. 20, 1777. MC I, 578. LBP, 1838. Heirs, William Downton, and Catherine md. Hammons.
DOWNTON, WILLIAM. Private. Dragon, Sept. 2, 1779.
DOYLE, THOMAS. N. A. B.
DRAKE, AUGUSTINE. Manley Galley, Sept. 11, 1779.
DREWRY, BENJ. Marine, Jan. 16, 1783. N 8, 35.

DRIVER, JOHN. H. D. 1834–5, Doc. 48, 7.
DRUMMOND, DAVID. Safeguard Galley, March 1 to June 15, 1777. LBNB, Dec. 15, 1778.
DUDLEY, JOHN (Jock). On Congress as lt. till she was laid up. Only daughter Ady, or Edy, was the mother of Eliza Dudley, wife of Harry Braddocks (Bruddicks?), of Baltimore. LBP John Dudley, and testimony of his acquaintance Amos Nicken in USP Wm. Skinner.
DUDLEY, JOHN. Seaman. NBJ, Sept. 10, 1778.
DUDLEY, ROBERT, of Gloucester County. On Dragon in 1779. Was on board when she was commanded by Capt. Callender, who took command in October, 1777, and Capt. Markham in 1778. Heirs, VSR, July 30, 1930. B, 234.
DUKE, AUGUSTINE. Manley Galley. NBJ, Sept. 1, 1778.
DUKE, GEORGE. LBP.
DUKE, JOHN. Tempest, 1779.
DUKOS, JOHN. Aud. Acct. XVIII, 394.
DUNFORD, WILLIAM, of Gloucester County (died July 13, 1798). Master Henry Galley; remained till after Henry was dismantled in Queen's Creek. Then transferred to the Northumberland. BH, 256.
DUNFORD, WILLIAM, of Nansemond County. Master. Entered in 1776 or 1777 and continued for four years, testimony of Solomon Whitfield. Died about twelve or eighteen months after he returned from his service. He was the uncle of David and William Dunford and Rolly Rogers, of South Quay, Nansemond County. R. C. 1835.
DUNLEAVEY (Dunlevy), JOHN. Clerk, Sloop Congress. LBP Wm. Skinner.
DUNTON, SEVERN. N's Northampton, 11.
DUNTON, STEPHEN. Boat Liberty, Jan. 1783. B. W.
DUNTON, WM. Gunner's Mate. N's Lancaster, 32, 42.
DURHAM, WM. Dragon. LBP Wm. Jennings.
DYHOUSE, EDWARD. Armourer, 16 Jan., 1783.
DYKE, JOHN. Tempest, 1779.
DYKES, HENRY. Boat Liberty, Nov., 1779. Protector Galley.

DYKES, JOHN, of Northumberland County. Protector Galley. Enlisted Jan. 28, 1777; discharged, after serving his time, by Capt. John Thomas, 28 Jan., 1780. LBP.

DYKES, RICHARD. H. D. 1834–5, Doc. 48, 7.

DYKES, ROBERT. Aud. Acct. XXXI, 348.

E

EAGLES, EDWARD. Gunner, Mosquito. LBP Charles de Kay.

EAST, SOUTHEY, of Accomac County. After service in the 9th Va. Regiment, in 1775–6, he was permitted to enter the Naval service and there continued till the end of the war. MC III, 213. Heirs in 1832 Southey W. East and Mary Bloxcom.

EDGCOMB (Edgecomb), THOMAS. Able seaman. H. D. 1834–5. Doc. 48, 8. War 5, 65.

EDGE, JOHN. Dragon, Sept. 1, 1777, to May 13, 1778. Deserted.

EDWARD (Edwards), ENOCH. Henry Galley, 1776. Brig Jefferson, 1779–1780.

EDWARD (Edwards), GEORGE, brother of Enoch. Enlisted on Henry Galley, Jan., 1777. Discharged in 1780. Brig Mosquito. B. W.

EDWARDS (Edward), ELLIS, of Wicomico Parish, Northumberland County. Reward offered for his apprehension in Virginia Gazette, Sept. 11, 1779. But see Certificate and discharge. LBP of Angel Baker. Also H. D. 1834–5. Doc. 48, 8 and MC II 13.

EDWARDS (Edward), RHODAM (Rodman), of Northumberland County. Tempest, Dec. 7, 1779. LBNB, Jan. 20, 1778. LBP, 1783.

EDWARDS, WM. Deserted from Dragon. See Va. Gazette, July 3, 1777.

EDWARDS, WM. JR. E 1.

ELAM, ROBERT. 2d Lieut. of Sloop Norfolk Revenge, appointed May 24, 1776 (2d Mate of Capt. Calvert). Heirs living in Norfolk, claim to land bounty rejected in 1833 because Elam resigned his commission.

ELBEY, PETER. Ex. Coms, 1776.

ELDER, CHARLES. Gunner, Safeguard Galley, March 1 to June 16, 1777. Discharged on account of "weakness of body". NBJ, Oct. 29, 1778.

ELLIOTT, ALEXANDER (after the war, of Rockbridge Co.). Midshipman. Served under Capt. George Elliott, Safeguard Galley. LBP John Flynt and of Hugh Bingham. MC II, 287.

ELLIOTT, CAPT. GEORGE (later of Fayette Co., Ky.). Safeguard Galley, Northampton, Dec. 18, 1778. NBJ. Commissioned July 22, 1776. In 1784 reported entitled to half pay. Will Oct. 17, 1814. USP. Among his children were John Elliott, of Dalbyville, Ky., Mrs. Montgomery (children: Joseph, Osiah, Elizabeth), who lived on Cumberland River; William, of Washington Co., Ky.; George, of Garrard Co. MC II, 306. Alexander Elliott and other heirs. BH, 179.

ELLIOTT, JOHN. Tempest. LBP Hugh Bingham.

ELLIOTT, JUDITHAN (or Jodithan), of Lancaster Co. Carpenter, Henry Galley, Jan. 17, 1777, to Jan. 11, 1780. LBP, 1784; 1851-2.

ELLIOTT, RICHARD. Safeguard Galley, March 1–June 16, 1777. Officer?

ELLIOTT, ROBT., Lieut. Captain of the Renown, B. W. R. C. In St. Eustatius, when Capt. Cox escaped from Tortola, and brought him back to the Virginia.

ELLIS, EDWARD. Seaman. H. D. 1834-5, Doc. 33.

ELLISTON, JOHN. Master. War 5, 65.

EMANUEL. A Negro. Tempest, Oct. 7, 1779.

EPPERSON, RICHARD, of New Kent Co. Entered as a midshipman with Capt. J. Thomas and served to the end of War. Ship Gloucester. Was at siege of York. Known after the war as "Navy Dick", or "Little Dick". He md. Margaret, dau. of Richmond Allen, and had an only child, Samuel (died about 1825), who had issue: Armistead Epperson, Richard W. Epperson, and Margaret B., md. Bennet Tompkins. LBP, 1850.

ESKRIDGE, EDWIN S., of Northumberland Co. Midshipman, Sept. 1778 to July, 1780. Protector Galley. Dragon. MC

II, 204. In 1786, Thomas Hobson, heir at law to Edwin Eskridge, decd.

ESKRIDGE, SAMUEL. Midshipman, Protector Galley, on which he continued till his death, Nov. 13, 1780. Left his brother George his heir, LBP, 1786–90. MC II, 354.

ESKRIDGE, WM. Midshipman. RC.

EVAN (Evans), PHILIP. Gunner. Dragon, Feb. 9, 1778 to Jan. 20, 1779. LBP John Flynt and of James Jennings.

EVANS, PHILIP. Carpenter. Dragon, Oct. 7, 1779. LBP. MC II, 269.

EVANS, JOHN. War 5, 65.

EVANS, VINCENT. Aud. Acct. 1779–80, 61.

EVANS, WM. Boatswain. H. D. 1834–5, Doc. 48, 8.

EVANS, —. Armourer, Henry Galley.

EWING (Ewin), JOHN. Pilot Boat Liberty. LBP Philip Bartlett.

F

FARISH, LARKIN, of Caroline Co. Marine on Mosquito, LBP De Kay. USP George Catlett.

FAUDRY, JOHN. H. D. 1834–5, Doc. 48, 8.

FENDLA, JOHN, of Lancaster Co. H. D. 1834–5, Doc. 48, 8.

FERGUSON, ROBERT, of King and Queen Co. Surgeon's Mate, Page Galley, LBNB, Feb. 13, 1778. Lewis Galley, Bounty land assigned as to a midshipman. BH, 1131.

FERGUSON, ROBERT. Steward. War 5, 71.

FIELD (Feild), THEOPHILUS. Lt. Dragon, March 10, 1779. Served to the end of the War. USP. He died intestate in Brunswick Co. between June 28 and Sept 28, 1789. Wife Martha. Tombstone on grave. Family Bible burned. Only heir in 1838, Mrs. Mary B. May. Letter of administration to John F. May of Petersburg, brother of Judge May. MC III, 441.

FIELDS (Field), JOHN. Steward and Clerk, Accomac Galley. LBP Wm. White, MC III, 175. Heirs in 1831: John D. Fields and Wm. B. Fields.

FIGG, JOHN. Brig Liberty. June, 1778.

Figg, Thomas. Brig Jefferson, Dec. 20, 1779; Jan. 20, 1780.
Fisher, Isaac. Diligence Galley. Heirs, N's Accomack, 65.
Fisher, James. H. D. 1833–4, Doc. 33.
Fisher, Wm. Dragon, March 15, 1778–May 20, 1778.
Fitzhugh, John. Brig Northampton. Henry Galley, NBJ, Sept. 10, 1778.
Fiveash, Peter. R. C. USP, Sailing Master of the Scorpion: imprisoned in Bermuda: returned with forty two other American prisoners in the Brig Dolphin, Capt. Thos. Seymour, which arrived at Yorktown, Jan. 17, 1783. He died in Hampton, July. 15, 1799, leaving four children: Alice Gardner, of Norfolk, John W., Fanny (md. Nathaniel Wilbourne), and Benjamin (died without issue).
Flatford, Thomas, of Prince William Co. H. D. Dec. 1826, 28.
Fleet, Henry. Midshipman, April 18, 1779, Certificate of Capt. Markham. LBP Wm. Mitchell.
Fleet, Thomas. H. D. 1833–4, Doc. 33.
Fleetwood, Isaac. Captain's Cook on Dragon in 1778. LBP Lewis Hinton. War 5, 70.
Fleming, John. Hero Galley, Nov. 4, 1777; Tempest, Oct. 7, 1779. H. D. Oct. 17, 1792. Stated he removed to Georgia before getting his discharge.
Flint, Thomas. War 5, 71.
Flynt (Flint), John, of Northumberland Co. Carpenter. Served three years. Discharge from Capt.Markham, LBP, Wm. Lowry, 1831. BH, 1129.
Fodron, John. H. D. 1833–4, Doc. 33, 12.
Ford, Joseph. Dragon from Feb 27, 1779 to July 4. Deserted.
Forrest (Forest), William, of Princess Anne County. Carpenter and Seaman. On Caswell, June, 1778. R. C.
Forrest, William. LBP, 1840.
Fortune, Gabriel. Able Seaman, Tempest, Dec. 7, 1779.
Fortune, James. H. D. 1834–5, Doc. 48, 8.
Foster, James. Lt. Marines, May 4, 1776 in Capt. Marsden's company. C. S. captain of a company lately commanded by Capt. Marsden, June 1, 1776. B, 1244.

FOSTER, PETER, of Kingston Parish, Gloucester Co. Carpenter's mate. Claimed to have enlisted as midshipman on Henry Galley, Capt. Robt. Tompkins, but received bounty as a carpenter, R. C.

FOSTER, PETER, of Hanover Co. Entered marine service early in 1776, continued twelve months on Brig Liberty, during which time she captured the Jane; then entered orderly sergeant, Capt. Thos. Meriwether's company, Gibson's regiment. In 1783 his trunk containing his certificate was burned, with his father's house. Died March 11, 1833, without issue; administration, March 23.

FOSTER, VOSS. Henry Galley. Deserted.

FOURJITT, JOHN. Lewis Galley, LBNB, Feb. 13, 1778.

FOUSHEE, WILLIAM. Surgeon. See VSR, July 1930, p. 29.

FOYLE, ROBT. Dragon, to March, 1778. Deserted.

FRANK. Mulatto. Seaman N. A. B.

FRANKS, JOHN. Manley Galley, NBJ, Nov. 5, 1776.

FRARY, JOHN. N 8, 18.

FRAZIER, THOS. Clerk and Steward. H. D. 1834–5, Doc. 488.

FREEMAN, CHARLES. Englishman. Deserted from Hero Galley. Va. Gazette, July 26, 1776. His costume described.

FREEMAN, EDWARD. H. D. 1834–5, Doc. 33 12.

FREEMAN, JOHN. Henry Galley, April 8, 1778.

FRESHWATER, WM. H. D. 1834–5, Doc. 48 8.

FROST (Frust), CARTER. Dragon, from Feb. 27, 1777 to July 4. NBJ, Sept. 3, 1778.

FRY, THOS. Dragon, April 7, 1777 to Jan. 29, 1779.

G

GAINES, THOMAS. Aud. Acct. XXV, 137.

GAINS (Gaines), JOHN. Cert. Capt. John Thomas.

GALLOWAY (Golway), JONATHAN. Safeguard Galley, June 16, 1777 to Feb. 13, 1778. (Jed) NBJ, March 7, 1778.

GAMMEL (Gamerel), JOHN. Protector Galley, LBNB, Jan. 30, 1777.

GARDNER, SAMUEL. Lt. marines, Caswell Galley, in N. C.

GARNER (Garney), PRESLEY, of Lancaster Co. Henry Galley, April 8, 1778.
GARTHWRIGHT, BEN. Marine, Capt. Hanway's Co. NBJ, Oct. 23, 1776.
GARTON (Gaston), BENJAMIN, of Lancaster Co. Able Seaman. MC II, 245.
GASKINS, THOS., of Northumberland Co. NBJ, Sept. 10, 1778.
GAUDGE, RICHARD. NBJ, Sept. 4, 1778.
GEORGE. Negro. Tempest, Dec. 7, 1779.
GEORGE, BENJ., of Lancaster Co. Brig Jefferson, Dec. 1779–Jan. 1780. B, 112.
GEORGE, BRISTER. War 5, 78.
GEORGE, DUKE. MC II, 345.
GEORGE, GLENDENNY. Sailing Master. LBP John Flynt.
GEORGE, JESSE, of Lancaster Co. 2d lt. Lewis Galley, Jan. 7, 1777; Protector; Dragon from Oct. 13, 1777 to May 3, 1778. USP, Testimony of Wm. James: after several years, spring before siege of York, George's Galley captured with all on board, including John Cummins, Zameth George, and John Tapscott. Martha Mason, however, stated that George was captured after the siege of York, together with all his men, while in the Rappahannock, and carried to England. Did not return till war had ended. USP. He died about Oct. 15, 1803. No will found. Heirs in 1834: Sally Francis (50), Monica George, Judy D., George, Mary C. I. George, Sally Trott, Fanny H. Ford (aged 46), Eliz. M. George, all of Lancaster Co., and Alice Drummond, of Elizabeth City Co. In 1835, Sally Francis and Fanny H. Trott, only surviving children. LBP, 1835. N's Lancaster, 27.
GEORGE, RICHARD. Hero Galley. Tempest, Oct. 7, 1779, LBNB, Feb. 13, 1778.
GEORGE, SAMUEL. Ship Gloucester.
GEORGE, WILLIAM. R. C. Heirs in Lancaster Co.: Thomas D. George and Lucy Simmons.
GEORGE, ZAMETH. On galley captured in Rappahannock. Married a sister of Martha Mason. See USP, Jesse George.
GERRINGS, LAWRENCE. N 8, 14.
GESTER (JESTER), JOHN. Enlisted Oct. 1777. LBP, 1785.

GIBBINS, THOMAS. Brig Northampton.
GIBBONS, THOMAS. Lt. C. S. 1776, 31.
GIBBS, JAMES, of Lancaster Co. USP. Bound apprentice to a sea captain, and when about 17 his master gave him up to be enlisted on Page Galley, Capt. Markham, in Carter's Creek. After a few days repairing rigging etc, they went out and cruised in the Bay about a year. Later Markham and greater part of the crew went on the Dragon lying near mouth of York. After his discharge he entered the merchant service; shipwrecked in the Bay of Biscay, losing his chest containing his discharge. Later he lived in Culpeper Co., Va. and then moved to Mason Co., Ky. In 1834 living in Greenup Co., Ky.
GIBSON, JAMES, of Elizabeth City Co. (brother of John below). Seaman, promoted gunner. Schooner Liberty; afterwards on Frigate Virginia, commanded by Com. James Barron, at time vessel was burned. Never married. "Zealous and active officer", testimony of James Barron, Jr. LBP, Dr. David Brown, and USP. MC III, 181. Jenny Trail of Norfolk Borough, heiress in 1831.
GIBSON, JOHN. "A Gibraltarian by birth", according to James Barron. Seaman and gunner. Attached to the Frigate Virginia at the time she was on the Stocks at Norfolk Navy Yard. Was on the new Patriot at time of his death, and served on others as occasion required. According to Mrs. Dameron of Norfolk, he died on board the boat Liberty, and she well remembered the parade of ceremony on the occasion of his burial at Hampton. He left one daughter, later Mrs. Jane Trale (Trail), of Norfolk. LBP John Flynt and Capt. Gray. USP. BH, 115.
GIDDEAN, LAWRENCE. Dragon. LBP, James Jennings.
GILBERT, EPHRAIM. C. J. 1776–7, 137.
GILL, CUDBERT (Cuthbert). Dragon, April 2, 1779.
GILL, THOMAS. N 8, 21.
GLASS, THOMAS. War 5, 77.
GLENDINING (Glendeny-Glenendy), GEORGE. Dragon from Sept. 1777 to Jan. 20, 1779. MC II, 292.
GLENN, THOMAS. Henry Galley, April 8, 1778.

GODWIN, JAMES. Lieut, June 18, 1776; Midshipman Brig Liberty, 18 May–30 July, 1776. Served three years. LBP George Rodgers.

GODWIN, JOSEPH, of Nansemond Co. Midshipman in 1779. Lt. "employed during whole war whenever his services were required". Godwin and John Archer transported troops from Norfolk and Portsmouth during the siege of York. "A Gentleman of property", will in USP. In 1838, heirs at law Stephen F. Hoockey and Eliza C. his wife, and Lucy Ann Jordan (will, Portsmouth, 1844, mentioning granddaughters Josephine Wilson and Emma Catherine Wilson), Godwin's dau. Lucy md. Col. Richard H. S. Lawson, and had issue: Joseph Godwin Lawson and Mary Frances Lawson md. Isam Hoockey, and had issue: Thomas Warwick Hoockey. MC III, 435. BH, 115.

GOFFIGAN, LABAN. Tues. June 18, 1776 appointed 1st Mate of Capt. Westcott's Cruiser" Patowmack". Lt. Scorpion, Jan. 1777. (commanding officer). Taken prisoner, carried to Bermuda, and held until end of war. Another account says that when he was released he got to France and Dr. Lee advanced 2274.15 francs to "bear his expenses home". Returned sometime after reduction of Navy on March 15, 1781. Died intestate in Norfolk Co. in Jan. 1795, leaving four children, one of whom, Henry, left an only child, Thomas H. Goffigan, living in James City Co. in 1781. USP.

GOFFIGAN, PETER, of Northampton Co. Pilot. MC III, 214. Heirs in 1832 Milly Spady and Emmeline Jones. N's Northampton, 11.

GOOSELEY, Capt. GEORGE, of York Co. One fourth owner of Brig Liberty, Feb. 16, 1776. Captain of Thetis. In 1788 master of the Brigantine Helen. MC III, 182. Sarah Campbell one of the heirs. MC III, 176, Sarah C. Gooseley and Ann M. Brown, in 1831.

GORDON, CHURCHILL. Midshipman, Tempest, Oct. 18, 1779. LBP. Returned home some days after the siege of York, according to declaration in March, 1835, of his brother, John Gordon, Sr., of Louisa Co. See also LBP John Stubbs.

Issue of Churchill Gordon: James A., John H., William L., Elizabeth A., Sarah L. (md. Ludwell Digges), and Ann S.

GORRELL, JAMES. Aud. Acct. XVIII, 689.

GOUDGE (Gooch), RICHARD. Lewis Galley. LBNB, Feb. 13, 1778.

GRANBERRY (Gransberry, or Cranberry), JOHN, of Nansemond Co. Sailing Master Jan. 24, 1778 to May 13. Sailing Master of the Dragon. USP, David Henderson.

GRANT, DANIEL. Gunner's Mate, 3 years. BH, 499.

GRANT, DANIEL. Deserted from Tartar, Va. Gazette, Sept. 11, 1779.

GRANT, THOMAS. Midshipman, Tartar. Brig Jefferson, Dec. 1779–Jan. 30, 1780. LBNB. According to one reference, Thomas Grant was a master's mate.

GRANT, THOMAS. Seaman. War 5, 78.

GRAVES, RICHARD C. Lt. Marines. Entered early in 1776.

GRAVES, RICHARD. Norfolk Revenge. NBJ, Aug. 30, 1776.

GRAVES, WM., of Elizabeth City Co. Lt. Row Galley. One account says he died in service in 1781, but USP puts his death in 1802. Heirs in 1846, Richard H. Graves and Sarah, wife of Robt. I. Barlow, of Williamsburg.

GRAY, CAPT. JAMES (died in Dec., 1783, in Warwick Co.). In service as lt. from March 16, 1776. Captain of Prison ship Gloucester; lt. in command of the Safeguard; LBNB, Feb. 13, 1778; ordered to take command of the Hero Galley at Gloucester during absence of Lt. Stratton. (Maxwell, Feb. 2, 1780). June 12, 1778 directed by Thomas Smith to proceed to Nantes with Brigantine Liberty. His brother Wm. Gray was his heir. USP. Heirs Eliz. Dammoret, wife of Wm. T. Topping, Wm. Topping, and Mary Ann Topping.

GRAY, ROBT. 2d lt. Raleigh. NBJ, Nov. 1, 1776.

GREAR, CHARLES. Surgeon. MC III, 166. Only heir in 1831, Wm. Grear.

GREAR, CHARLES. H. D. 1833–4, Doc. 33, 5.

GREEN, JAMES (George James), of Westmoreland Co. Manley Galley, Sept., 1777; later midshipman on Tartar. Served till summer of 1781. Removed to Fauquier Co.; md. in Feb., 1792, by "Parson Craig" to Frances Brown, whose mother was a Fletcher. Oldest son, Hedgman Green (b. 1793); Aaron Green was born in June, 1803. James Green died Aug. 25, 1847, in his 92d year. His widow lived in Rappahannock Co. USP.

GREEN, JAMES, of Culpeper Co. Midshipman. On Tartar up to Feb., 1780. Supernumerary in 1781. Always spoken of as "Lieut." In 1834, farmer. USP. See also LBP John Cheshire. MC III, 346.

GREEN, JAMES. Manley Galley, Sept. 11, 1779.

GREEN, WM. (son of Col. John Green, of Culpeper Co.). In early period of the war marched with the troops to Williamsburg; on his return entered the naval service under Capt. Callender. Appt. by C. S. July 20, 1776, 1st lt. Sloop Defiance. Succeeded Callender in command Dec. 6, 1776. The ship was captured, and Capt. Green remained a prisoner three years, after which time he made his escape. Then continued in service till the Navy was reduced. "A gallant chivalrous officer." LBP, BH, 1384. Capt. Green md. Lucy Williams, and had issue one son, Judge John W. Green, who, in 1823, had an old print of the ship Defiance with his father in uniform.

Judge John W. Green md. first, Mary Browne, and had issue: Wm. md. Columbia Slaughter (issue: John and Betty, md. James Hayes, of Richmond, issue); Raleigh H., Dr. Daniel S., U. S. A., issue. Judge Green md. second, Million Cooke, granddau. of George Mason, of "Gunston Hall", and had issue: John Cooke; Judge Thos. Claiborne, of W. Va.; George, issue: James Williams, issue: Lucy Williams.

GREEN, WM. Gunner. MC II, 290.

GREMBLEY, THOS. Safeguard Galley, June 16, 1777.

GRENIL, JAMES. Safeguard Galley, LBNB, Feb. 13, 1778.

GREY, WM. Recom. 1st. lt. Sloop Liberty; formerly 2d lt. Scorpion.

GRIFFIN, DR. CORBIN. Revenge Galley. Surgeon, Manley Galley, Aug. 3, 1776 till it was dismantled in 1779. In charge of the hospital at York till end of the war. USP. He died in York, leaving one child, Maj. Thomas Griffin, who had: Eliz. md. Robt. P. Waller, of Williamsburg, and

Mary md. John Waller, of Williamsburg. Mary Griffin Waller had issue: Wm. Waller and Catherine md. John M. Speed, of Lynchburg. Eliza (Elizabeth) had issue: Corbin Waller, and Mary md. John C. Mercer.

GRIGG (Griggs), JOHN. Safeguard Galley, June 16, 1777. Deserted. Brig Northampton, Sept. 10, 1778. NBJ.

GRIGGS, LEE. Brig Jefferson, 20 Dec., 1779, to Jan. 20, 1780.

GRODEN (Groton), CHARLES. Brig Northampton, Brig Liberty, June, 1778.

GRUMBLY, THOS. H. D. 1833-4, Doc. 33, 13.

GRYMES, JAMES. Ordinary Seaman. H. D. 1834-5, Doc. 49, 9.

GUNTER, JOHN, of Princess Anne Co. War 5, 78.

GUIRAUD, JOHN. Seaman on Brig Liberty, June, 1778.

GURNEY, PRESLEY (Gresley). See "Garney". N 8, 9.

GURRINGS, LAWRENCE. Dragon, Nov. 5, 1778, to Jan. 20, 1779.

GURTON, JOHN. Hero Galley. NBJ, Nov. 4, 1777.

GUTHRIE, CAPT. ALEXANDER. Schooner Peace and Plenty, employed in trade.

H

HAIL, EDWARD. H. D. 1834-5, Doc. 48, 10.

HAIR, PETER. War 5, 90.

HAIRLOW, JOSEPH. Deserted from Mosquito, Va. Gazette, May 26, 1776.

HAIRSTON, THOMAS. R. C.

HALEY (Haily), PETER. Seaman. E 1.

HALEY (Healey), SAMUEL, of Hampton, Elizabeth City Co. June 17, 1776, to Dec., 1778, Lieut. first Row Galley, the Lewis (Lt. Jos Saunders had command at time of destruction of Navy). Promoted by Capt. C. Saunders, April 23, 1777; captain of the schooner Hornet (trading department). Capt. of the Mayflower. Died Sept. 1, 1799. USP. MC III, 337. In 1834 Elizabeth Face, Sarah T., Mary, Robert S. Tompkins, Abby Haley, heirs at law of George Haley, who was heir of Samuel Haley. In USP, Wm. Face is named as administrator.

HALL, EPHRAIM. Marine. Discharged as infirm, Nov. 20, 1777. NBJ.
HALL, EPHRAIM. Accomac or Dilgence, and continued till galley laid up. See N's Accomack, p. 46. MC II, 233.
HALL, GEORGE. N's Accomack 26.
HALL, JOHN. Dragon, March 29, 1777, to Jan. 20, 1779. Cook.
HALL, JONATHAN. Dragon to Jan. 20, 1779. Cook. USP Lewis Hinton. Transferred from Gloucester to Dragon. NBJ, Aug. 29, 1778.
HALL, ROBERT, of Mathews Co. Master's mate, Henry Galley. In 1776 Sailing Master. Died before 1781, leaving Thomas Hall, Betsy Hall md. Fr. Brown; Mary Hall md. Peter Foster; Joicy Hall md. Mathew Gayle, and the children of Spencer Hall. In USP there is much about other descendants. 1847. LBP John Flynt. See also BH, 165 and 561. MC II, 265. Wm. Reynolds assignee of Thomas Hall decd, heir of Robt. Hall, 1786.
HALL, ROBERT, of Westmoreland Co. Master Commandant of Dragon. Jos. Sanders testified that Robert Hall commanded the Liberty in 1779, and from this to Brig Jefferson in Feb., 1780. USP. Robert Hall died May 31, 1802. Had three daughters that survived him; eldest Ann md. Andrew Montgomery; Elizabeth md. James Montgomery; Sarah md. Geo. C. Sedgwick (minister, who removed from the county). Ann had issue: Robt L. Montgomery; Eliza Ann md. John Powers, and Sarah md. John F. Morriss. Sarah Hall Sedgwick had issue: Robt. H.; Ann md. John H. Gibbs; A. J. Sedgwick, and Frances P. md. Thos. S. Wilson.
HALL, SPENCER (Spence). Henry Galley, 1776. LBNB, Nov. 1, 1777. Will made in Charleston, S. C.; proved Essex Co., Mass., Sept. 1, 1794. BH, 562.
HAM, VALENTINE. War 5, 12.
HAM, WM., of Elizabeth City Co. Lt. Entered service when a lad, remained till end of war, and afterwards entered the Revenue service. Commanded Sloop Experiment, Oct. 10, 1778, NBJ. Commanded Schooner Nicholson engaged in transporting provisions for the use of the army at the siege of Yorktown. Was a favorite of Commodore Barron.

HAMBLETON, ROBT. Gunner's mate, Mosquito. LBP De Kay.

HAMILTON, JOHN. Lt. Ship Pocahontas. Made prisoner along with Capt. Callender, and put on board a prison ship in New York, where he died between the 15th and 20th of November, 1780. MC III, 218. Only heir in 1832 Patsy Row. MC II, 204. Only heir in 1785 Patsy Hamilton, daughter.

HAMILTON, ROBERT. Safeguard Galley, from March 1 to June 16, 1777.

HAMILTON, THOMAS. Appointed Lt. marines, Nov. 14, 1776; 1st lt. Jan., 1777; capt. March 17, 1777, vice Arell (resigned or promoted). B, 1244.

HAMLETT, WM. Aud. Acct. XXV, 131.

HAMMENSON, WM. War 5, 85.

HAMMONS (Harmons), TYRE (Tyson?). Diligence Galley. LBP Solomon Powell, 1851. For heir in 1832 see N's Accomack, 35. War 5, 88 (Tyrer Hammons).

HAMMONS, STEVEN. War 5, 88. N's Accomack, p. 35.

HAMMONDTREE (Hamontree), JOHN. Protector Galley. LBNB. Jan., 1778. B, 244. MC II, 10.

HAMPHLETT, WILLIAM. Aud. Acct. XVIII, 435. See "Humphlett."

HANNAY, SPENCER. March 4, 1777-Nov. 1777 (Hanney).

HANSFORD, CHARLES, of King George Co. A remarkable personal statement concerning his adventures is found in his Pension papers in Washington.

HANSFORD, CARY H., of the Borough of Norfolk. Surgeon's mate. Served three years, Dragon. After the siege of York he served under Major Dick. Affidavit of Elizabeth Martin, Aug. 22, 1832: "Cary Hansford and Jonathan Calvert were both students of medicine with Doctors Taylor and Ramsay ** entered service of Virginia as surgeon's mates as early as 1778". Dr. Hansford "Alderman and eminent physician", of Norfolk, died in that city, Oct. 29, 1801. He left an only son, whose children were Maria T. Hansford and Wm. P. Hansford. USP. BH, 504, 1778.

HANSON, VALENTINE. Hero Galley. BH.

HANWAY, SAMUEL. Captain of Marines, appointed May 5, 1776. Born in Chester Co., Pa., Sept. 26, 1743; removed to Charles City County, Va., in 1768; then to the neighborhood of Petersburg; engaged in trade with the West Indies; then moved to Amelia County, where at the beginning of the Revolution, he raised a company of minute men; later became captain of marines, but resigned in December, 1776, and was succeeded by Lt. Benjamin Pollard. In 1781 he removed to Monongalia County, and on January 3, 1783, was appointed county surveyor. He was living in Morgantown in 1833, aged 90. An interesting affidavit by him is found in the USP.

HARCOM, ELISHA (Henry). Able seaman. Midshipman. Testimony of John S. Kesterson, of Northumberland Co., in 1838. Henry and Lott Harcom, sons of Wm. Harcom, enlisted together under Capt. Thomas, who had married their cousin. Elisha Harcom died of small pox, in Norfolk, shortly after the Revolution.

HARCOM, LOT (Lott), of Northumberland County. Midshipman. (Cadet) Protector Galley. Entered service Jan. 1, 1778, and served three years. See LBP John Flynt, 1822. BH, 571. MC 88, 283.

HARCUM, RHODAM. NBJ, Sept. 4, 1778.

HARCUM, SCOTT, of Northumberland County. Midshipman. Died soon after the war. BH, 570.

HARCUM, WILLIAM W. Aud. Acct. XXX, 5.

HARDAWAY, JOSEPH. Marine Jan. 20, 1783.

HARDEN, JESSE. Deserted from Mosquito. Va. Gazette, Nov. 26, 1776.

HARDYMAN, CAPT. JOHN (died Jan. 1, 1808, in Elizabeth City Co.). In 1781 or 1782 appointed captain of Marines. Recruited with Lts. John Clark and Lewis Webb for the Cormorant lying off Hampton. USP. Presumably the same officer who had been with the 2d State Regiment.

HAREY, JOHN. Corporal of Marines. Sloop Congress. LBP Wm. Skinner.

HARFORD, JOHN. Manley Galley, Aug. 3, 1776.

HARMAN, JERE. LBP Stephen Bloxsam.

HARMON, CURTIS. Henry Galley. LBNB.

HARPER, JULIUS. Manley Galley.
HARPER, WM. R. C.
HARRIS, CAPT. JAMES. For heirs, see N's Accomack, 22.
HARRIS, JOHN. Accomac Galley. Midshipman, Jan. 26, 1778.
HARRIS, JOHN. Lt. Died in June, 1780. LBP Wm. Tunnel, and USP John Harris.
HARRIS, JOHN. 1st Lt. Feb. 6, 1776-Nov. 1, 1776. Manley Galley.
HARRIS, CAPT. JOHN, of Accomac Co. (will, proved May 13, 1785). N's Accomack, 22.
HARRIS, CAPT. JOHN (said to have been born in Wales). Lt. Manley Galley in spring of 1776; recommended captain of the Brig Raleigh Oct. 31, 1776. Ordered, Oct. 24, 1776, to the command of the Mosquito; captured and confined in Fortune Jail, England; returned to Virginia late in 1779, and was put in command of the "Oliver Cromwell". He died in the spring of 1782. Copy of will in USP. On April 15, 1778 the Naval Board ordered necessaries delivered to Amelia, daughter of Capt. John Harris ** now a prisoner ** on his paying for the same".

Capt. Harris's wife, who was a Brough, died while he was in prison. His daughter Sallie md. her cousin, Dr. James Drew McCaw, and had issue: Dr. Wm. Reid McCaw, of Richmond; Dr. David McCaw, of Powhatan Co.; John McCaw, midshipman, U. S. N.; Georgina, married but left no issue.

An article on Capt. John Harris (with cut of a minature likeness), by General Walter Drew McCaw, U. S. A., son of the late Dr. James B. McCaw, appeared in the Virginia Historical Magazine, Vol. XXII, p. 160 et seq.
HARRIS, PETER. Nicholson. (Maxwell), Sept. 4, 1778.
HARRIS, SIMON, of Norfolk Co. Surgeon, Norfolk Revenge in 1776. Subsequently on Dolphin. Will probated in 1799. BH, 586 and 1405.
HARRISON, CUSTIS. Henry Galley. LBNB, Nov. 1, 1777.
HARRISON, JOHN. Master of the Ship Apollo (announced for sale in the Va. Gazette in 1780).

HARRISON, DR. JOSEPH. Doctor's mate. Captured on Brigantine Liberty. Died in prison in Halifax. In LBP appears the memorial of Catherine Harrison, John W. Davis and Anne his wife (formerly Temperance Anne Harrison) and Martha Gwaltney, widow (formerly Martha Harrison), all of the county of Isle of Wight, descendants and heirs at law of Joseph Harrison.
HART, DARBY. April 29, 1777, to Jan. 20, 1779. LBP James Jennings.
HART, ISAAC. Hero Galley. NBJ, Feb. 13, 1778.
HART, JOHN. N 8, 23.
HART, MICHAEL. Hero Galley. NBJ, Nov. 4, 1778 and Feb. 13, 1778.
HART, WILLIAM. Page Galley. LBNB, Feb. 13, 1778.
HARVEY, JOHN, of Northumberland County. Captain.
HASKINS, EDWARD. Safeguard Galley, March 1 to June 16, 1778. N 8, 11.
HASKINS, JAMES. Accomac Galley.
HASTENS, THOMAS. See LBP Wm. Tunnell, 1833.
HATCHER, WILLIAM. C. J. 1786-7, 165.
HATCHETT, ARCHIBALD. Captain, according to the testimony of his brother Edward. Service in Georgia. Claim rejected.
HAUTH, JOHN. Tempest, Dec. 7, 1779.
HAUTH, WILLIAM. Tempest, Dec. 7, 1779. N 8, 15.
HAW, PETER, of Lancaster County. H. D. 1834-5, Doc. 48, 10.
HAW, WILLIAM. Ship Gloucester. Voucher, 1783.
HAY, CHARLES. Hero Galley.
HAY, RICHARD. May 6, 1776, Marine service, recruiting. C. S.
HAYES, WILLIAM. Accomac Galley.
HAYNES, PETER. Ship Gloucester. N 8, 21.
HAYS, ALEXANDER. Dragon, Sept. 7, 1777, to Jan. 20, 1779.
HAYS, ELLEIK. Boatswain's mate. Dragon. LBP James Jennings.
HAYWOOD, RICHARD. War 5, 90.
HAYWOOD, THOMAS, of Gloucester County. H. D. 1834-5, Doc. 48, 10.
HEISTER, EZEKIAL. Ship Dragon, March 4, 1777, to June 23. Died.

HEMPHILL, EDWARD. N 8, 11.

HENDERSON, DAVID. Entered Dragon April 1st, 1777, and was immediately appointed Steward and Clerk, in which capacity he continued to act until he was appointed midshipman and resigned his Stewardship. USP. Petition, Oct. 23, 1821: he was then aged 67. He had the record book of the Dragon in his possession in Fredericksburg, in 1832. His pension was paid till Sept. 4, 1837, presumably the date of his death. In 1853 Alexander Henderson was his executor.

HERBERT, ARGYLE (Argil). Commander of the Norfolk Revenge, July 12, 1776; Caswell Galley, 1st. lt. Dec. 5, 1776; resigned April 29, 1779. MC II, 332. Heirs at law in 1834: Sally Tucker, a sister, and Frances Gill, a niece, of Mary Hunter, widow and devisee. BH, 1428.

HERBERT, BASCOM. Commissioned lt. Boat Liberty, Aug. 19, 1776. MC II, 343. Midshipman.

HERBERT, CHARLES. Hero Galley.

HERBERT, CHARLES. Lt. N 8, 3.

HERBERT, EDWARD. Marine, Jan. 16, 1776.

HERBERT, JOHN, of Elizabeth City Co. Carpenter and Midshipman on the Safeguard. Brother of Capt. Thomas Herbert. Entered war early and did not return. B, 895.

HERBERT (Pascal) PASCOW, of Elizabeth City Co. Brother of Capt. Thomas Herbert. USP. Lt. Kautzman testified Pascow Herbert was Lt. Boat Liberty from 1777 to latter part of 1780, when he was in company with him in making seven or eight prizes in the Bay. Capt. Thomas Herbert testified that Pascow continued lt. till 1781. Pasco Herbert died April 3, 1801. Issue: Barbara md. Roe Lattimer (and had among issue Pascow Lattimer); Amelia md. Robert Lively; John Curle (died s. p.), and Thomas I. (died s. p.). Pascow H. Lively in 1833, in Hampton, was attorney for heirs. His will pro. June 25, 1801 mentions wife Mary, daughters Barbara Curle and Amelia, and sons John, James and Curle. See also LBP Capt. James Gray and Dr. David Brown.

HERBERT, REUBEN. Master builder at the ship yard. C. S. 1776.

HERBERT, Capt. THOS. "Silverfist", so called from a silver device that took the place of his left hand he had lost. Of Elizabeth City Co., but lived in Portsmouth after the War. Uncle of James Barron, Jr.'s first wife. Lt. of the Brig Liberty; commissioned June 1, 1777. Made the voyage to Nantes and captured several Brigs. Later in command of a flotilla of small craft, at the time of the siege of York, for provisioning Washington's army and watching the movements of Ccrnwallis. He died Sept. 1, 1799. VSP. Heirs John Herbert, Amelia Lively, Barbara Lattimer, Garet H. Prendergrast, Geo. S. Blake, Frances C. Herbert, Thomas Herbert, Ed. Lattimer, Mary Ann Lattimer, and Margaretta Eliz. Tuttle, Eliz. C. Herbert wrote from 658 Fourth St., New York, in 1854 asking that her claim be paid. See also BH, 895–899.

HERBERT, WM. Hero Galley, Lt. Aug., 19, 1776.

HERN (Hearn), FRANCIS. Henry Galley, LBNB, Nov. 1, 1777. See "Horn".

HEWES, JAMES. NBJ, Oct. 16, 1778.

HEWLETT, WM. Brig Northampton. N 8, 19.

HEYWOOD, RICHARD. Henry Galley, April, 1778.

HIGDON, CHARLES, of King George Co. USP. Entered Manley in 1779, Capt. Wm. Saunders, Lt. Danl. Richardson; then on Jefferson, same officers; then on Tempest, same captain, but Lt. Parker. Also on Tartar. Living in 1840, aged 82, in Westmoreland Co. MC II, 240.

HIGDON, JOHN. Born in Westmoreland Co., near Miller's bridge, about 1758. Seaman, Manley; Jefferson; Tartar. John Higdon, one of the applicants for land bounty was born in Leedstown and in 1833 was living in Alexandria.

HIGDON, RICHARD (brother of John). Died a captive in Bermuda. LBP John Higdon.

HIGDON, RIDGLEY (Reginald). Dragon. At least two years a gunner's mate, and one year a powder monkey. Died in Alexandria Co. about the year 1816. LBP John Higdon.

HILL, JAMES. Served till May 5, 1780. B. W. 1784.

HILL, JOHN. Hero Galley. NBJ, Nov. 4, 1777.

HILL, MARTIN. Died on Ship Dragon. Served from Feb. 12 to Aug. 13, 1777. N's Lancaster, 23, 24.

HILLIS, WM. N. A. B.

HINTON, HENRY. NBJ, April 9, 1777. To be recommended lt. in case he recruited twenty men.

HINTON, LEWIS, of Lancaster Co. (b. Aug. 20, 1760), "an orderly colored man and respectable". Was enlisted on Dragon for three years, to take the place of his master, Thomas Hinton, who retired from the service on account of ill health. In USP, 1836, he gives an interesting account of his experiences in the Navy.

HINTON (Hinston-Hinson), SPENCER. Clerk. Steward. Lewis Galley. Ship Gloucester, July, 1779. N's Lancaster, 46. Only heir in 1834, Nicholas P. Buchan.

HINTON, THOMAS. Dragon, June 5 to Sept. 1, 1777. Discharged on account of ill health.

HINTON, WM. Aud. Acct. XV, 441. B. W.

HIPKINS, JESSE. On Mosquito. LBP James Dishman, of Caroline Co.

HOARE, BENJAMIN. Discharged as infirm, April 11, 1778.

HOBDAY, FRANCIS, of Gloucester Co. Pilot. Entered service early in 1776, and continued to end of war (Henry, Tartar, and Dragon). Piloted the French Fleet into York River, and when they went away he piloted some of the French vessels that remained. LBP. Testimony of Henry Hobday, Watlington Buchanan and Wm. Figg.

HODGES, JOSEPH. War 5, 89. (Norfolk).

HOG, CHARLES. H. D. 1833-4, Doc. 33, 13.

HOGDEN, MATTHEW. War 5, 88.

HOGG (Hog), RICHARD. Marine service recruiting, May 6, 1776; Lt. Marines, Norfolk Revenge Galley, March 18, 1777. NBJ, Nov. 16, 1776.

HOGGAN, HENRY. Dragon, July 23, 1777–Jan. 20, 1779.

HOLBARD, JESSE. Dragon, Sept. 2, 1779.

HOLT, HENRY. Midshipman. Said to have been lost at sea in the West Indies: statement of Capt. Wilson Boush, of Norfolk. LBP. Proved by testimony of Clarimond Colquhoun, in Petersburg, in 1831, that James Holt, decd, was

the elder brother of Henry Holt, midshipman, and that William C. Holt was the only child of James Holt.
For Holt Family, see Tyler's Quarterly, Vol. VII.

HOLT, STUART. Pilot, Eastern Shore.

HONEYCUTT, EDWARD. Lieut. See "Wonycutt".

HOPKINS, PATRICK, of Northumberland Co. Deserted from Tartar, Va. Gazette, Sept. 11, 1779.

HOPKINS, THOMAS. Marine. Jan. 16, 1783.

HORN (Hern), FRANCIS, of Gloucester (later Matthews) Co. Enlisted in 1776 or 1777 under Capt. Tompkins, as Sailing Master or sailmaker. See LBP.

HORN, RALPH R., of King William Co. After service in the 2d Va. Regiment, enlisted in Capt. A. Dick's marines. In prison in Barbadoes and in England. See LBP.
Horn's heirs in 1832 were: Robt. R. Horn, Mary R. Horn, John A. Stewart, Lucy M. Stewart, Wm. B. Horn, Anso Corso, Philip Horn, Martha H. Horn, Agnes M. Horn, and Susan Horn, of Caroline Co.

HORNBY, JOHN. Diligence Galley. See LBP, Solomon Powell. Heirs, N's Accomack, 24.

HORNSBY, JOHN, of Accomac Co. BH, 830.

HOUCHINGS, SAMUEL. Tempest, Dec. 7, 1779.

HOUGH, TIMOTHY. Hero Galley. NBJ, Nov. 4, 1777.

HOUSE, WM., of Elizabeth City Co. Gunner. BH, 826.

HOWARD (Heyward), THOS. First midshipman, Accomac Galley. MC III, 348. Heirs in 1834: Ezekial, Mary, Nancy, and Margaret Howard, and Polly, wife of Whittington Trader.

HOWE, BANNISTER, of Gloucester Town. Sailing Master, Henry Galley, Lt. Singleton, April 8, 1778. Died c. 1781. USP. BH, 1473.

HOWELL, —. Carpenter on Mosquito, USP Wm. Dishman.

HOY, CHAS. Hero Galley, NBJ, Nov. 4, 1777.

HUBBARD, AMOS. War 5, 86.

HUBBARD, CHAS., of the Parish of Christchurch, Lancaster Co. Dragon, March 15, 1777 to Jan. 20, 1779. LBP, 1783. USP. Married Sept. 3, 1782, Lucy —. Issue: Nancy, born Nov.

13, 1783; John, born in 1784. Charles Hubbard died April 20, 1794. Will in USP.

HUBBARD, JAMES. Ship Gloucester. B, 8, 21.

HUBBARD, JESSE. War 5, 86.

HUBBARD, JOHN. Warrant Officer. On Henry Galley until Nov. 21, 1776, when he was turned over to the Mosquito. On Henry again, Dec. 19, 1777, NBJ. LBP John Flynt. MC II, 283.

HUBBARD, WM. B. W. MC II, 301.

HUDGINS, REDGNAL. Sloop Defiance.

HUDSON, JOHN. Aud. Acct. XXV, 314.

HUGHES (Hughs), WM. Protector Galley, 3 years. NBJ, March 19, 1778.

HUGHLETT, GARRETT. Steward.

HUGHLETT, JOHN. Midshipman. MC II, 291. In 1788, Garrett Hughlett, heir.

HUGHS, WILLIAM. Gunner, Dragon, Oct. 7, 1779.

HUMPHILE, EDWARD. Safeguard Galley, March 1 to June 16, 1777.

HUMPHLETT, JOHN, of Elizabeth City County. Midshipman.

HUMPHLETT, THOMAS, of the Salters Creek section of Elizabeth City County. Lt., joined Navy in 1777. A prisoner in Charleston till after the evacuation. Entered Navy again and on Patriot till 1783. USP. Died Feb. 15, 1794, leaving his whole estate to his wife Elizabeth; will probated Feb. 20, 1794. The will of Rebecca Humphlett, heiress of Elizabeth Humphlett, was probated in Elizabeth City County, 28 May, 1840, leaving estate to Wm. Ivy Humphlett.

HUMPHLETT, WILLIAM. Voucher, 1783. Certificate of Com. James Barron.

HUMPHREYS, JAMES. Dragon. Ship Congress. LBP, James Jennings, in which it is stated that a number of men on the Dragon re-enlisted on the Jefferson.

HUMPHREYS, SAMUEL. LBP James Jennings.

HUNT, DANIEL. E 1. Board of War, Feb. 3, 1780 "Discharged after serving out term of enlistment."

HUNT, HENRY. Marine, Jan. 16, 1883.

HUNT, JOHN. War 5, 88.

HUNT, THOMAS. Armourer, Safeguard Galley, June 16, 1777.
HUNTER, DR. GEORGE, of Alexandria, Va. Sole physician and surgeon of the Sloop of War Congress, until his death, when the little fleet returned "in deep mourning", with his body. He was the son of Dr. John Hunter, and brother of Gen. John Chapman Hunter, of Fairfax Co. His mother Mrs. Elizabeth Hunter lived next door to Mrs. Hannah Hunter, who made an affidavit in LBP in 1831. Dr. George Hunter kept a Journal, which is quoted in LBP. MC III, 190. In 1831, J. C. Hunter, heir at law. BH, 1319-20.
HUNTER, THOMAS. H. D. 1834-5, Doc. 48, 9.
HUNTON, THOMAS, of Lancaster Co. (died in Middlesex Co., Aug. 17, 1792). Midshipman on Page in 1777. On Dragon. Lt. (?) Rhodam Kenner stated in LBP that he saw Hunton in the uniform and with the sword of officer at a Barbacue "where a good many officers and soldiers had met to congratulate each other that peace was again restored." LBP Thos. N. Hunton of Northumberland Co., Administrator. Hunton's children were: Polly B. md. John Gibson (issue, Albert); Frances md. James Brent (issue: William and Eliz. md. Wm. Porter); M. Hunton, died s. p.; Elizabeth md. Sydnor McCarty, of Richmond Co. (issue: John McCarty of Richmond Co.); Thos. Y. Hunton (issue: Susanna, unmarried); Jane F. Hunton md. Wm. W. Brown. N's Lancaster, 41, 42. MC III, 357.
HUPP, PHILIP. Marine soldier. See LBP Thos. and Wm. Givins.
HUPP, WM. Gunner.
HUSE, WILLIAM. War 5, 85.
HUSTON, ROBERT. Safeguard. LBNB, Feb. 13, 1778.
HUTCHESON (Hutchinson), WILLIAM. B, 155.
HYNT, JOHN. Aud. Acct. XXX, 5.

I

INNIS, JAMES. Commissioner of the Va. Navy. LBP, Wm. Mitchell.
INNIS, LEVY (Levi). War 5, 97.

IRONMONGER, GEORGE. Brig Northampton. NBJ, Sept. 10, 1778.

IVESON, DR. A letter written by Richard Harrison in Martinique, Dec. 27, 1777, to Thomas Smith, State Agent, stated that Dr. Iveson, of the Brig Mosquito, had been liberated from imprisonment, and had arrived in St. Pierre.

IVY (Ivey), CAPT. WILLIAM (born at "Sycamore View", Tanner's Creek, Norfolk Co., Va.). Lt. of the Scorpion, Capt. Westcott, Sept. 20, 1776; on Jan. 2, 1777 appt. 1st lt. Sloop Liberty, and on the 7th capt. vice Walter Brooke. An interesting sketch of Capt. Ivy in the "Virginia Historical Register", Vol. I, p. 185 (1848) states that sixty of his slaves were carried off in the course of depredations on his two estates. He died before July 16, 1778, the date of the administration of his estate. Heirs in 1834: Ann P. Ivy, Thos. J. Ivy, and Sarah H. Goodwin (nee Ivy). Thos J. Ivy was one grandson and Wm. N. Ivy another. MC III, 323.

J

JACK (negro). N 8, 10.
JACKSON, JOHN. Hero Galley. NBJ, Nov. 4, 1777.
JACKSON, WM. Safeguard Galley, March 1 to June 16, 1779.
JACKSON, WILSON. H. D. 1833–4, Doc. 33, 14.
JACOB the Dutchman. Sloop Liberty, Aug., 1777.
JAMES. Negro. Tempest, Dec. 7, 1779.
JAMES, CHRISTOPHER. Brig Jefferson, Dec. 20, 1779 to Jan. 20, 1780.
JAMES, EDWARD. Sloop Scorpion.
JAMES, HENRY. Steward, Safeguard, Scorpion. NBJ, May 15, 1777. Died in service in 1778. MC III, 438. Heir in 1838 his brother, the Rev. Daniel James, of Madison Co.
JAMES, MATHEW. Tempest, Dec. 7, 1779.
JAMES, MICHAEL, of Northampton Co. Lt. Brig Northampton, March 16, 1777. Tempest, Oct. 7, 1779. Commander of the Liberty, Aug. 3, 1784. USP. N's Northampton, 14, 16, 22.

JAMES, MICHAEL. Lt. N's Lancaster, 40.
JAMES, P. Brig Northampton.
JAMES, WALTER. H. D. 1834–5, Doc. 33.
JANEY, P. H. D. 1834–5, Doc. 33, 14.
JARVIS, THOS. Safeguard Galley. LBNB, Feb. 13, 1778.
JARVIS, WM., of Gloucester Co. Henry Galley. NBJ, March 27, 1777.
JEFFRIES, AARON. 1st lt. Schooner Revenge, Aug. 27, 1776; unable to recruit any seamen, resigned May 21, 1777. NBJ.
JENKINS, RICHARD. Aud. Acct. XXV, 131.
JENNINGS, JAMES, of Northumberland or Lancaster Co. Deserted from Dragon, Va. Gazette, July 3, 1779.
JENNINGS, JAMES, of Richmond Co. Enlisted at Fredericksburg,. Sept. 10, 1776, served to Jan. 20, 1779. Died in Richmond Co., leaving sons James and Smith Jennings, and grandchildren, George and Eliz. LBP. BH, 1331, 1473.
JENNINGS, JESSE. H. D. 1833–34, Doc. 33.
JENNINGS, JOHN, of Hampton. Sailing Master, Tartar. Transferred from Patriot to the Fly; ordered on separate command Aug. 11, 1779, and there continued two years until the Fly was run ashore on Cape Henry and taken by a British sloop of war. Then Jennings returned to the Patriot. Prisoner of war in 1781. Will recorded July 28, 1803. Issue: Thomas; Ann A. md. Wm. Morris; Jane md. Thos H. Williams; Lucy (s. p.); Charles (s. p.). LBP James Gray. USP.
JENNINGS, MICHAEL. Hero Galley. NBJ, Nov. 4, 1777, and Feb. 13, 1778.
JENNINGS, CAPT. THOMAS, of Elizabeth City County. Entered navy at age of 16, in 1778. LBP Capt. John Bright. After the war Capt. Jennings was Inspector of the Customs of Norfolk and Portsmouth.
JENNINGS, WM., of Elizabeth City County. USP. In his 81st year, Aug. 23, 1832 "Enlisted in 1777 as a seaman on board the Patriot under Capt. Richard Barron & remained continuously in service until the arrival of the French fleet under de Grasse. After the surrender he piloted the French 74 called the Northumberland to Martinique. On his return on the schooner Sally of Metompkin, belonging to

Col. Crocker, of the Eastern Shore, he was taken prisoner by the British 50 gun ship Chatham, commanded by Commodore Douglas, and was removed to the Jersey prison ship at New York; after four months he was exchanged through the interposition of Mr. Lenox a British Commissary, whom he had met on the Northumberland. After his return to Virginia he was received on the Patriot as a seaman, and so continued till after the proclamation of peace". B, 1162. Son, Robt. C. Jennings's affidavit in USP, in 1837.

JESTER, JOHN (Gester?), of Accomac County. Remained on Diligence Galley till she was laid up. LBP James Walker. N's Accomack, 49. MC III, 322. In 1834, heirs: James and Elizabeth Jester, Rachel Turlington, Kendall, Leah, Amey Jester, Henry and Griffin Winbro.

JETER, CLEMENT. War 5, 97.

JETT, JOHN, of Stafford Co. Manley Galley, Sept. 11, 1779. LDNB, Nov. 6, 1779. Tempest. B, 1163.

JOA (Jobbs), MOSES. War 5, 97. NBJ, Oct. 20, 1778.

JOIN, JOHN. 1st lt., July 20, 1776, first row galley.

JOHNSON, ISAIAH. R. C., 1831.

JOHNSON, JOHN. N's Accomack, 62.

JOHNSON, KENDRICK. Accomac Galley. Jobby Taylor acted as Boatswain, vice Johnson promoted. LBP Stephen Bloxsam. Boatswain, Lewis Galley, NBJ, Nov. 13, 1778. In 1835, Tabitha Maddux, only heir at law.

JOHNSON, JOSHUA, of Accomac Co. Died about six months after enlisting as Boatswain's mate to Wm. Stott. B, 15, 1146. N's Accomack, 67.

JOHNSON, ROBERT. Steward, Protector Galley. NBJ, Aug. 24, 1778. Manley Galley, Sept. 11, 1779.

JOHNSON, WM. Boat Liberty. Aug. 16, 1777, NJB. Able seaman, under command of John Crew. Voucher, 1783.

JOHNSTON, JOHN. BH, 1047.

JOHNSTON, JOSIAH. H. D. 1833-34, Doc. 33, 13.

JOHNSTON, WM. E., of Elizabeth City Co. Surgeon's mate, Defiance. Captured on Nicholson, Lieut. Jennings, and remained prisoner till end of war. USP. According to Nath.

Mitchell, of Lisbon, Ohio, Sept. 6, 1853, Johnston had no issue, but left his estate to a niece, who married ——— Tompkins, who had seven children, one of whom md. a Mr. Tabb, of Gloucester, whose only child, John T. Tabb, was the father of Mitchell's wife.

JOHNSTON, WILLIAM. Boat Patriot. Boat Liberty, Nov., 1779.

JOHNSTON, WILLIAM. Marine, Mosquito. Af. Moses Stanley and DeKay.

JONES, CHARLES. LBNB, June 10, 1777, and Aug. 22, Sloop Scorpion, Protector, Sept. 20, 1st lt. Patriot till captured, late in 1781, by British Frigate.

JONES, CHARLES. Seaman. N 8, 14.

JONES, EDWARD. N. A. B.

JONES, HENRY. H. D. 1833–34. Doc. 33, 13.

JONES, GABRIEL. Lt. marines. B, 1244.

JONES, JAMES. N 8, 15.

JONES, LEWIS, SR. 2d lt., Sloop Defiance. Brig Northampton. Recommended 1st lt., Protector Galley, Aug. 22, 1777. LBNB, Dec. 18, 1777. USP. He md. Oct. 4, 1789 Milly living in 1838. His will was probated Aug. 29, 1799. BH, 1016. N's Accomack, 35.

JONES, LEWIS, JR. Master's mate, Page Galley, June 17, 1776, to Oct. 28, 1779. LBP John Flynt. Wife Nancy. N's Lancaster, 23.

JONES, JOHN PAUL. Continental Navy.

Although John Paul Jones was not at any time connected with the Virginia Navy his heirs applied for land bounty in Virginia. The LBP include the memorial of the devisees and the following rather cryptic letter from Judge Francis Brooke to Gen. Lambert in Richmond:

St. Julien, June 26, 1838

My dear Sir

I have received your letter from Richmond, all I remember of John P. Jones I had from my Brother who was Surgeon of the Bon Homme Richard the whole of his celebrated Cruise, I think I remember when very young to have seen him in the year 1773, I was at school in Fred'g (Fredericksburg) and his brother William Paul was a Scotch

Tailer who made my cloths. on his death John came to Fredg to administer on his property. I think I saw him in the shop where I went for my cloths, this on seeing his picture years after I remember that it is a mistake that his brother was a merchant I do not think he remained long in Fredg the next year I think he was employed in the navy
***

Francis Brooke

"The memorial of the devisees of Commodore John Paul Jones respectfully represents

That their testator was s citizen of Virginia and a resident of the town of Fredericksburg when he accepted a commission in the Continental navy dated the 22nd day of Dec. 1775 as first lieutenant of the Alfred on board of which ship before Philadelphia he hoisted with his own hands the flag of freedom the first time it was displayed.

"That, as Captain of the Ranger in Quiberon bay, on the 14th of February he claimed and obtained from Monsieur LaMotte Piquet the first salute of the flag of the infant republic received from a foreign power.

"That he had been residing in Fredericksburg about two years previous to accepting his commission." &c., &c.

JONES, ROBERT (Robin). Gloucester, Nov. 4, 1777, NBJ. Northampton, Sept. 10, 1778. Tempest, Dec. 2, 1779. Certificate of Lt. Joseph Saunders.

JONES, ROBERT. Pilot. Captured on lookout boat in 1781. LBP John Rodgers.

JONES, WM., of Fredericksburg. LBP. Aged 60, in 1818. Enlisted in 1777, Protector Galley, at Great Ware House on Great Yeocomico; turned over to Tartar, Capt. Richard Taylor. After nine months, transferred to Ship Tempest. Discharged in 1780 at Chickahominy Navy Yard. MC III, 258. In 1833, Stanton Jones, devisee.

JOYNES, EDWARD, Accomac Co. On Accomac Galley till it was laid up: testimony of Elkanah Andrews. MC III, 267. In 1833, William and Edward Collins only heirs at law. N's Accomack, 3.

JOYNES, JOHN. R. C.

K

KAUTZMAN, JAMES. Lt. LBP. R. C.

KAUTZMAN, JOHN VALENTINE. Midshipman and Clerk, 14 April, 1777; lt. Hero Galley. Tempest. LBNB. Captured by detachment of British troops under Gen. Philips, April 27, 1781. Not exchanged. Lived in Henrico Co. several years. "Tyler in the Masonic Institute". Removed to Elizabeth City Co. near County Bridge just over the York line. Died just after the Jubilee in Yorktown in honor of Lafayette. His daughter Anne md. Samuel Williams, of King & Queen Co., and had Judith Williams of Stratton Major, and John Williams of Henrico. USP. Heirs, 1831, James Williams, Judith Williams, and Joseph Segar. BH, 243.

There was the will of John V. Kautzman probated in Henrico, June 14, 1799 that bequeathed property to Mistress Mary Bond, spinster, of Richmond, and to Sara, daughter of Wm. and Eliz. Baker. For this see USP John V. Kautzman.

KAY, JOHN. Lt. in land forces at Portsmouth; later in Marines; in 1781, Galley Henry. According to his eldest surviving child, Jonathan Kay, of Norfolk Co. (aged 84 in 1848), Lt. John Kay was attached to the Nicholson, captured by the enemy. LBP Philip Bartlett.

KELLY, JAMES. E 1.

KEMPE (Kemp), DR. THOS. Hero Galley. NBJ, Nov. 10, 1777. BH, 1150.

KENNER, HARRISON. Page Galley. LBNB, Feb. 13, 1778.

KENNER, HOUSON (Hawson). Protector, Aug. 20, 1777, to July 1, 1778. Midshipman, Dragon, Sept. 2, 1779. LBP John Flynt. MC II, 134.

KENNER, RODHAM (Rhodan), of King George Co. Protector. Dragon, Sept. 2, 1779. Died, Logan Co., Ky. BH, 224-225.

KENT, EDWIN, of Henrico Co. Midshipman, May, 1778. Md. Mrs. Minna Chetton, issue: Jesse (died about 1815) md. Frances Brook; Ludowick (no issue); Joel (no issue). Edwin Kent died in Lancaster Co., about 1815. MC III, 447. Heirs in 1838: Beverley and Edward Kent.

KENT, JESSE (father of Thomas, below). Enlisted with Lt. Pollard, on Revenge, July, 1779; midshipman; died in service. MC II, 235. In 1785, Thos. Kent, heir. N's Lancaster, 23.

KENT, JOSHUA, of Northumberland Co. Dragon, Sept. 10, 1778; Boat Fly; Tempest, Oct. 7, 1779. See petition of Charles Kent, only son of John, brother of Joshua. BH, 748.

KENT, THOS. Enlisted July 17, 1779. MC II, 245.

KENT, WM. Dragon, Jan. 30, 1779. Boat Fly. MC II, 244.

KEY, WILLIAM. USP. Born 14 Oct., 1766, in Chesterfield Co.; sister Mildred, who assisted in making his knapsack and clothes when he went into service; brother Bingham Key; a sister, who md. — Duncan and went to Illinois. William Key entered the militia service from Dinwiddie Co. in April or May, 1779; in summer of 1780, he thinks, he enlisted at Petersburg in Capt. Cook's company of marines: went on board of ship to guard James River; left schooner at Jamestown, when 18 received their discharges, again entered service as substitute for Wm. Spain and was present at the siege of York. He married previous to Jan., 1794, Elizabeth — (aged 22), of Halifax Co., N. C. They later removed to Sumner Co., Tenn., where he was a Methodist minister for many years. His widow died 28 July, 1844, leaving children Thomas, Peterson, James, Alfred C. and William Key, Nancy Davis and Harriet Robertson.

KILBY, JOHN. Continental Navy. Enlisted Aug. 1, 1776, Brig Sturdy Beggar. Temporary lt. Quarter Gunner on Bonhomme Richard. See "Scribner's Magazine", July, 1905.

KING, EDWARD. Safeguard Galley, 16 June, 1777.

KING, THOMAS. Safeguard Galley, March 1 to June 16, 1777.

KINGSTON. A negro man belonging to Sailing Master Jenifer Marshall. Kingston was "one of the foremost hands on board the Accomac.

KIRCH, JOHN. Marine. H. D. 16 Oct., 1792, p. 46.

KNIGHT, JACK. Negro. H. D. Oct. 1789, 7.

KNIGHT, JOHN. B. W.

KNOWLES, JOHN. Captain's mate, Dragon from Feb. 20, 1777, to Jan. 2, 1778.

L

LACY (Lacey), EDMUND. Aud. Acct. XXIX, 10.
LACY, EDWARD. Master at Arms. H. D. 1833-4, Doc. 33.
LACY (Lacey), RICHARD. Aud. Acct. XXIX, 10.
LAFAVOURS, NATHANIEL. Tempest, Dec. 7, 1779.
LAHERTY (Lurty ?), JOHN. Lt. appt. captain, NBJ, April 9, 1778.
LAMPKIN, JOHN, of Culpeper Co. H. D. Dec. 1823, 70.
LANCEFORD, ELIAS. War 5, 111.
LANDALL, ARNAM. Dragon.
LANDRUM, THOS., of Westmoreland Co. (son of "Parson Landrum", of King George Co.). Surgeon's Mate, Tartar. Tempest, Oct. 7, 1779. Practiced medicine at Port Royal. Will probated July 22, 1811. Left estate to Margaret Starke Landrum, his wife. His children were: Margaret C. of Westmoreland Co.; Elizabeth W., md. Collins; Thos. W. (Capt. U. S. A.); Lucy; Harriet, of King George Court House; and John B., who went to Ky. USP.
LANE, JOHN. Seaman, Jan. 16, 1783.
LANE, JOHN. Midshipman during war, Tempest. LBP Geo. Wray. Heirs in 1833: Wm. Clarke and Louisa Lane. BH, 786. N's Accomack, 28.
LANE, THOS. War 5, 113.
LANG (Ling), ALEX., of Accomac Co. Boatswain. Diligence Galley, LBP Wm. White and John Flynt. Died April 22, 1820. MC III, 170. Sarah Lang, devisee in 1831.
LANGLEY, WM. Sr. Midshipman. Caswell and Washington Galleys. H. D. Oct. 1794, 43. Norfolk Co. Petition, 1794.
LARKIN (Larkins), DAVID. Midshipman. LBP Hugh Bingham. Recommended 2d lt., Jan. 6, 1778, Safeguard Galley, NBJ.
LARKINS, REMANO (?).
LATCHER, WM. N 8, 14.
LATTIMER (Lattimore), EDWARD, of Smithfield, but at the time of his death "a native of Hampton". Recommended Jan. 30, 1777, 1st lt. of the Molly, Capt. Pasteur. He was the captain of a vessel owned by Purdie of Smithfield when the war

began. Died on the island of St. Eustatius, where one Uzzell stated that in 1786 he saw his tomb with inscription. Lattimer's wife was a sister of Capt. John Sinclair, and there were two sons brought up by their uncle. His son James died at sea near St. Eustatius, unmarried, and John was living in Smithfield in 1830. Lt. Lattimore's widow md. Col. James Bridger, of Isle of Wight Co. MC III, 445. Heir in 1838, Wm. Lattimore. BH, 1181.

LATTIMORE, SEMMICO (Senlia–Senica). Protector Galley, Tempest, Oct. 7, 1779. N 8, 15.

LAVIS, MATTHEW. Carpenter's Mate. War 5, 110.

LAWELL, THOS. Steward, Clerk. Diligence and Accomac. He lived at Drummond, Va.

LAWES, JOHN. Sailmaker, Brig Liberty, May 10 to July 30, 1776.

LAWES (Laws), JOHN, of Northumberland Co. Boatswain's Mate, Dragon, Jan. 20, 1777 to Jan. 20, 1779.

LAWS, TIMOTHY (brother of John and William). Gunner or Gunner's Mate, Mosquito, Tempest, Oct. 7, 1779. Nephew, Daniel Laws. BH, 1181.

LAWS, WM. Enlisted at a very early period of the war, on the Defiance.

LEE, JAMES. H. D. 1834–5, Doc. 33, 14.

LEE, JOHN. Lt. Capt. marines, June 20, 1776. B, 1244.

LEGIT, ROBT. Pilot. Captured on lookout boat in 1781.

LELAND (Leeland), ELLIS, of Northumberland Co. Henry Galley, Sept. 8, 1778.

LENARD, WM. Certificate of James Barron.

LENNIS, FRANCIS. Lt. Perished on Dolphin, 1779. LBP Simon Harris. MC III, 342. In 1834, Robt. Legate, only heir of James Legate, only surviving heir of Francis Lennis.

LEONARD, WM. War, 5, 111.

LEVELL, THOS. Tartar.

LEVELL, WM. Tartar.

LEVEWELL (Lovewell), WM. Aud. Acct. XXIX, 103.

LEWIS, AMBROSE, of Spotsylvania Co. Appt. April 15, 1776, Page Galley, LBNB, Feb. 13, 1778. On Dragon in 1779. "Soldier and sailor". LBP James Jennings.

Lewis, Charles. Dragon. April 13, 1776 to Jan. 20, 1779. LBNB, Feb. 13, 1778. LBP James Jennings.
Lewis, Daniel. Accomac Galley.
Lewis, John. Hero Galley.
Lewis, Matthew, of Elizabeth City Co. Carpenter's mate, Boat Liberty, Nov. 1779. USP. Wounded in service; died of a "mortification of the leg", July 25, 1795. Md. 19 May, 1780, Ann——, who after Lewis's death, md. Robt. James (died Nov. 23, 1819). She died July 4, 1835. Issue of Matthew Lewis: John, Thomas, and Margaret Lewis, who all married. BH, 737-739.
Lewis, Rowland. Hero Galley. NBJ, Nov. 4, 1777.
Lewis, Wyatt. N, 8, 13.
Libwin, Richard, Lt. Aud. Acct. XV, 368.
Lightburne, Henry. Lt. Page Galley, resigned May 12, 1778. NBJ.
Lightburne (Lightburn), Richard. Appointed July 17, 1776, mate: July 9, 1776. Lt. Schooner Adventure; Lt. on Hero till July 3, 1779, when he resigned his Commission. He died in Washington, Mason Co., Ky., in Nov. 1794. Testimony of Alvan Lightburne of Georgetown, Ky., in 1835, grandson and one of the heirs. Richard Lightburn, decd. of Scott Co., Ky., Sarah Pence, of Clay Co., and Lucy Jones, decd., of Scott Co., sole representatives of Lt. Richard Lightburn, and Alvin, Richard P., Martha C., John L., Thos. C. and W. L. sole representatives of Lt. Richard S. Lightburn of Scott Co. Patsy Jones, sole representative of Lucy Jones, USP. In 1834 Temperance Lightburne was the widow of Richard, Jr., decd. In 1851, Sarah Pence wrote from Independence, Mo.
Lightburne (Lightburn), Stafford, of Lancaster Co. Commissioned Aug. 2, 1776. In Command of the Lewis Galley. Resigned his commission May 12, 1778. Joined again as Lt. which office he held at least till end of 1781. On Tartar or Tempest, he was considered "a valuable officer". LBP Stafford Lighburne.
In the LBP is a memorial of Stafford H. Parker **brothers John S. Parker and Thomas Parker of Ky., Anne, Lucy W.

and Mary E. Parker of Port Royal, Mildred Green of Westmoreland Co., Mary, Lucy, Ann, Francis, and Juliet Summerson of Port Royal, Caroline Co., grandchildren and only heirs at law of the late Stafford Lightburne.

LILLY, CAPT. THOMAS, of Gloucester Co. Boatswain Jan. 14, 1776; captain Brig Liberty in 1776 and 1777. Capt. Ship Gloucester in Oct. 1777. Continued in service till end of war. Was in the "habit of strictest friendship and intimacy with Commodore Barron, who held him in high esteem".
A Journal of the Brig Liberty, in the handwriting of Capt. Lilly, was in the possession of Col. Darby of Richmond Co., who married Capt. Lilly's oldest daughter.

LINCEFORD (Launceford), ELLIS. Page Galley. LBNB, Feb. 15, 1778.

LINDSAY, JOHN. H. D. 1833-4, Doc. 33, 14.

LITCHFIELD, DANIEL. Officer. N's Accomack, 48.

LITCHFIELD, THOMAS, of Accomac County. MC III, 165. In 1830, Seymour Litchfield, only heir at law.

LITTLE, ADAM, of Scotland. Deserted from Scorpion Sloop, Capt. Westcott. Va. Gazette, Oct. 4, 1776.

LIVINGSTON, JUSTICE. Surgeon, Sloop Scorpion; Boat Fly; Ship Tartar. NBJ, Northampton, Sept. 1778. Certificate signed by Lt. Kautzman, July 26, 1780. Died April 1, 1785; will proved, King William Co., April 21, 1785. USP. Mentions wife Sarah: left Christian Frazer a diamond ring; to Wm. Frazer, silver watch; to Ralph Vaughan; to John Valentine all my wearing cloaths"; to Onley Moore; to Capt. Holster Hutchings."

LOCK, WILLIAM. Marine, Jan. 18, 1783.

LONG, ALEXANDER. See "Lang".

LONG, ISAAC. N 8, 15.

LONGITT (Longwith-Longworth), BURGESS, of Richmond Co. Gunner. LBP John Flynt.

LONGWAH, JOSEPH. Dragon. Deserted.

LOORELL (Lovrell), CHARLES. N 8, 30.

LOVELL, MORRIS. N 8, 38.

LOVELL, THOMAS. N 8, 12. R. C.

LOVEWELL, WILLIAM. Steward. H. D. 1834-5, Doc. 48, 12.

Lowe, John. Sailmaker. LBP George Rogers.
Lowe, Thomas (died in Philadelphia about 1818). Steward. Diligence Galley. B, 1152.
Lowe, Thomas. H. D. 1833–4, Doc. 33, 14.
Lowell, Thomas. Steward. Died in Philadelphia. BH, 1154.
Lowry (Lowrie), William. Entered service Feb. 2, 1777. LBP, 1784. Served three years. USP Capt. John Thomas. MC II, 14.
Loyd (Lloyd), Morris. Gunner's Mate, Safeguard Galley, June 16, 1777. LBP John Flynt and of Alexander Elliott. MC II, 286.
Lucas, Charles. Hero Galley, 1776; from Jan. 1777 to Jan. 1780. B, 1250.
Lucas, James. Henry Galley, 1776. N 8, 8.
Lucas, John. Dragon. LBP James Jennings.
Lucas, William. Master at Arms, Henry Galley, Clerk.
Lumbar, Thomas, of Accomac County. Gunner's Mate. Died in Philadelphia. For heirs, see N's Accomack, 24, and BH, 587 and 870.
Lumbar (Lumber), William, brother of Thomas above. Gunner. Died in Philadelphia. MC III, 164. Heirs in 1830, Martha Melson, Audley Lee and Mary, his wife; James and Wm. Lumbar.
Lunsford, Elias. R. C. 1834 (Lunceford). Aud. Acct. XVII, 306.
Lurty, John, of King George Co. (born in England in 1750). 1st lt. of the Dragon, Capt. Callender; 1st lt. Page Galley, Aug. 2, 1776; Appt. April 17, 1777 to command galley building at Fredericksburg. Commanded Marines on the Northampton. After the war, was in command of a Revenue Cutter and died in this service 1795 at Hampton. In LBP are mentioned Wm. B. Lurty (Mary, wife and relict) and Nolley Proctor (son of Mary Lurty md. Absalom Proctor), of Mason Co., Ky.
USP. Capt. Lurty, who md. Rosa Bronaugh, had also a son Robt. Lurty, who died in Bracken Co., Ky. and had children William and Elizabeth. For other descendants of Capt. Lurty see Munsell's "American Ancestry", Vol. III,

p. 34. He had a son Moore Lurty, who was an officer in the War of 1812, and had among issue: Senator Beverley Hooe Lurty, of what is now W. Va., who was the father of Major Warren Seymour Lurty, C. S. A., of "The Oaks", Harrisonburg, Va. BH, 1165.

LUTRELL (Lutterell), RHODAM (Rodham). B. W. Aud. Acct. XXIX, 103.

LYBURN, HENRY. Pilot of vessel fitted out by Col. Fielding Lewis, 1776.

LYBURN, RICHARD. Aud. Acct. XVIII, 271.

LYELL, FENWICK. Surgeon. C. J. 1776, 61.

LYONS (Lyon), JOHN, of Nansemond Co. Surgeon's Mate under Dr. Pell on Capt. Westcott's vessel. Surgeon's Mate to garrison at Hampton Jan. 17 to March 17, 1779. Hero Galley, Sept. 13, 1778, NBJ. Died Feb. 10, 1795. USP. MC III, 329. Heirs at law in 1834, John Keeling and Mary Ann Keeling.

M

McADAM, JOSEPH, of Westmoreland Co. Surgeon's mate. BH, 835.

McALISTER, WM. N. A. B.

McALLEY, JAMES. Musician, Jan. 20, 1783.

McARVEY, STEPHEN. Dragon.

M'CLEAN, LEWIS. Caswell and Washington Galleys. Norfolk Co. Petition, 1794.

McCLENAHAN (McClanahan), ELIJAH. Armourer. NBJ, Aug. 5, 1778. B. W.

McCLURE, JAMES. N 8, 11.

McCLURG, JAMES. Surgeon. Director and physician to the General Hospital at Williamsburg. LBP James Gray and of Dr. Griffin Corbin.

McCLURG, WALTER (son of Dr. James McClurg). On Liberty and Patriot some time in June, 1776. After reduction of the Navy he was called on for the crew of the Liberty, etc. LBP. For McClurg family, see "William and Mary College Quarterly", Vol. I, p. 164.

McCoy, Caleb. War 5, 134.
McCrewley, John. H. D. 1833–4, Doc. 33, 14.
McCrowdy, John. Hero Galley. NBJ, Nov. 4, 1777.
McDaniel, James. American Congress. C. S., March 27, 1776. Dragon. LBP James Jennings.
McDonald, James. Gunner, Sloop Liberty, Aug., 1777.
McDonald, Thos. Aud. Acct. XVIII, 82.
McGraw, James. Safeguard, March 1 to June 16, 1777.
Macheax (Michaux), Jacob. Aud. Acct. XVIII, 535.
McIntyre, Charles. Hero Galley. NBJ, Nov. 4, 1777.
McIntyre, Christopher. Hero Galley, Nov. 4, 1777, to Feb. 13, 1778. LBNB.
Mackaway, Stephen. Dragon. LBP James Jennings.
Mackner, Nicholas. N. A. B.
McLaughlin, Daniel. Safeguard Galley, June 18, 1777.
McLean (M'Clean), Ann. H. D. Oct. 1794, 43. For her husband, who served on the Caswell Galley. Norfolk Co.
Maclin (Mclin), Edward. Accomac Galley.
McNichols (McNickle-McNichol). Born Sept. 29, 1737, in the Parish of Inverary, Scotland. Surgeon on Mosquito. Captive in Fortune Jail, Gosport, Eng. Returned to Virginia, and was on Tempest, Oct. 7, 1779. Died in New York City. B, 923. See also VSR, July, 1930, p. 29. For heirs, see Henrico Petition, 1843.
McPherson (McPicaren), Mark. Steward. Tempest. B, 23. LBP John Stubbs.
McPickren, Spencer. Aud. Acct. XVIII, 537.
McWilliams, Joshua. Midshipman. Tempest. NBJ, June 14, 1779. B. W.
McWilliams, Wm. Page Galley. LBNB, Feb. 13, 1778. LBP Presley Neal.
Madison, Gabriel, of Hanover Co. (brother of Capt. Rowland Madison and of George Madison, later Gov. of Kentucky). Lt. marines till 1779, when he became supernumerary owing to a severe wound in right leg. Later served as capt. under Gen. George Rogers Clarke. Slightly wounded at Battle of Blue Licks. Married in what was then Fayette Co., on Dec. 12, 1784, Myra ———, who died between years 1840 and

1845, in Jessamine Co., Ky. Capt. Madison, after the Revolution, was col. of militia. He died April 15, 1804. Heirs in 1845: Jane L., wife of Wm. Robertson, M. D., of Woodford Co., Ky.; Elizabeth Allen, widow, Lucy McMurtry, widow, Gabriella, wife of Strother S. Hawkins, and Martha, wife of Charles Alexander. USP.

MADRID, ELISHA. Accomac Galley. LBP Wm. Tunnell.

MAGLON, JOHN. Dragon.

MAHON (Mabon?), JOHN. Marine. LBP Wm. Lowry. MC III, 332. Heirs in 1834, Eliz. Sadler and Sarah Repast.

MAHORN (Mahon, or Maborn), GEORGE, of Northumberland Co. Dragon, Feb. 17, 1777, to Aug. 30, 1779. LBP Wm. Jennings.

MAHORN, JOHN. Dragon. LBP James Jennings.

MAILEY, JAMES. Able Seaman. H. D. 1834-5, Doc. 48, 13.

MAINS, THOMAS. Quartermaster. Certificate of Capt. Thomas.

MAIRS, THOMAS. Seaman. H. D. 1834-5, Doc. 48, 13.

MALCOMB, JAMES. "an officer of merit" appointed Dec. 1, 1778, to command of ship Tempest "small class Frigate of about six or seven hundred tons and carried from 30 to 36 guns", stated Capt. Saunders who was in command of Tempest about 1780. On invasion of Arnold and Philips the Navy which had previously during the war signalized itself by the most gallant service was captured or otherwise destroyed. Malcomb was taken prisoner and so remained till end of war. In 1849 Sarah Davis and Sarah Hodges, of Norfolk Co., were his heirs. USP.

MALLORY, JOHN. War 5, 115.

MALONE, JERRY. Tartar. NBJ, Sept. 3, 1778.

MALONE, TERRY. Brig Northampton.

MALTMORE (Maltimore), JAMES. H. D. 1834-5, Doc. 48, 13.

MANES (Moones?), THOS., of Northumberland Co. Deserted from Tartar. Reward $100, Va. Gazette, Sept. 11, 1779.

MANHOW, GEORGE. Aud. Acct. XVIII, 94.

MARBURY, SAMUEL. 2d lt. marines. Congress. LBP Wm. Skinner.

MARCH, RICHARD. 2d lt. Cruiser Revenge. Resigned July, 1776. C. J. 1776, p. 87.

March, Wm. Midshipman. MC II, 278. Richard March, Jr., representative.

Marcum, Wm. W. Aud. Acct. XXII, 209.

Mariner (Marriner), Laban (Levin). Accomac Galley. N's Accomack, 54, 68.

Markham, Capt. James. Appointed about April, 1776, by Council of Safety to command one of the vessels fitted out for defence of Rappahannock. Page Galley, Sept., 1776, and in 1777 appointed to command Tempest Dec. 1, 1780. Captain of the Dragon from April 1, 1777, to April 7, 1780. Taken prisoner at Osborne's; parole dated April 28, 1781. Died Sept. 1, 1816. USP. In 1854 his grandson Geo. B. Goode, of Janesville, O., was one of the heirs. See also LBP Presley Neale and BH, 1209.

Marks, Anthony. N 8, 14.

Marks, John. War 5, 132. Discharged Feb. 3, 1780.

Marley (Marleys), James. Brig Jefferson, Dec. 20, 1779-Jan. 20, 1780.

Marlow (Marley?), James. Tempest, Oct. 7, 1779.

Marriner, Jeoffrey (See Mariner above). H. D. 1834-5, Doc. 48, 13.

Marsden, John. Capt., Marines.

Marshall, Benjamin. Master-at-Arms. N's Accomack, 35-36. BH, 1144.

Marshall, James. Midshipman. MC II, 503. Heirs at law in 1841, Edwin, Ugenia, John, James, and Norvell King.

Marshall, James, of King George Co. (died in Elizabeth City County circa 1788). Captain. From 1778 made trips to the West Indies. Died on one of these trips. Mrs. Ann Payne testified she saw Capt. Marshall at the Liberty Ball at Hampton. LBP. His children all died under age except Ann Collier, and Jane md. Walter Haughthorn, of Warwick Co., who left two children: Frances md. Thomas Young, of Elizabeth City Co., and Thomas Haughthorn. BH, 1193.

Marshall, Jenifer (died April 1, 1792). Sailing Master. Accomac Galley. "A valuable officer" testified Wm. Thornton, in USP. Served till galley was dismantled. LBP. Left service in July, 1781. USP. In 1832 Power of attorney from

Elphemia Walston, daughter and only heir to Vespasian Ellis. Claim to half pay allowed. Letter from Philadelphia of Wm. T. Conquest, Sept. 10, 1860. Euphemia Marshall (d. Dec. 7, 1837) md. first, Maj. Wm. Conquest, and had among issue: William Thomas Conquest (b. 1816), who had among issue: Pleasonton Laws Conquest md. Emma Parker; issue: Pleasonton L. Conquest, Jr., md. Elise Gamble; Emma md. James C. Wheat, and Edwin Parker Conquest md. Eugenia Fairfax.

MARSHALL, JOHN. Deserted from Tartar, see Va. Gazette, Sept. 11, 1779.

MARSHALL, JOHN. Boatswain's mate. See N's Accomack, 35. BH, 684.

MARSHALL, JOSEPH, of Norfolk Co. Sailing Master, Accomac Galley, 3 years. B, 648 and 1090.

MARSHALL, JOSEPH, of Elizabeth City Co. Sailing Master. Schooner Scorpion, until last of year **1781**, when he was captured at sea and held a prisoner in Bermuda till after the signing of peace treaty. Died about July 1, 1812. Heirs in **1851**: Ann A. Collier and Fanny Young, daughter of Virginia Marshall. USP.

MARSHALL, KINGSTON. War 5, 131.

MARSHALL, THOMAS. Aud. Acct. XXII, 209.

MARTIN, EDWARD. Safeguard, Oct. 13, 1778. NBJ.

MARTIN, JAMES. Irishman. Deserted from Hero Galley. Reward offered by Capt. Muter, Va. Gazette, July 20, 1776.

MARTIN, JAMES. Doctor, Caswell Galley. NBJ, May 27, 1777.

MARTIN, JOSEPH. Discharged as infirm, April 10, 1778. NBJ.

MASE (Muse), JESSE. Aud. Acct. XXX, 147.

MASON, ABEL. H. D. 1834–5, Doc. 48, 13.

MASON, JOHN. Hero Galley, Nov. 4, 1777. NBJ.

MASON, JOHN. Seaman, Nicholson, Sept. 4, 1780. (Maxwell).

MASON, WM. War 5, 133.

MASSENBURG, ALEXANDER, of Hampton. Midshipman. Captured by British Cruiser and taken to Halifax, and did not return until some time in 1780. Ship commanded by Capt. John Rogers, who died in prison. The Liberty was a large man of war and mounted as many as 18 guns. Massenburg also served on the Henry Galley, Capt. Tompkins; later on the Nicholson: captured and imprisoned till 1783. USP. Mrs. Anne Payne recalled seeing Massenburg and Dr. Johnston in their respective uniforms at the Liberty Ball, in Hampton. George G. Massenburg was one of his heirs. Among the documents in the USP is a letter from John Darby, of Richmond Co. with excerpt from pay roll of Brig Liberty, Capt. Lilly, July 30, 1777.

MASSENBURG, WM. H. D. October, 1795, 16, 60. Mariner. Heir, Geo. Massenburg.

MASSEY, PETER. Dragon. R. C.

MASTER, ELLISTON. Aud. Acct. XXX, 168.

MASTERSON, THOMAS (commonly called "Marsden"). Midshipman, Tempest, Feb. 12, 1776. Lived on the Island in the lower part of Lancaster Co. In LBP, his only heirs at law were Thomas and John Marsden "who now reside in said Island".

MAUGHON (Moughon), GEORGE. Boatswain. In R. C. John N. Sale attested in 1835, that George Maughon md. a Miss Adams of Matthews Co. and left two children: Wm. and George. Elizabeth Sadler (nee Maughon) stated that she had been informed by her uncle George Moughon, her father John Maughon, her uncle John Nuttall, said to be a gunner in the Va. Navy, and by many others that George Maughon was boatswain upon a lookout boat of the Dragon, commanded by Lt. Joshua Singleton; that they were taken as prisoners of war to the West Indies and not released until end of War; her uncle George died about 1815, and left a will. In the petition of Mathias Moughon appears: "George H. Moughon is residing in the county of Gloucester and Wm. N. Moughon has been at sea for several years without returning home."

MAUGHON (Moughon-Mohon), JOHN. Marine. BH, 1191.

MAXWELL, JAMES. Superintendant General of the Shipyard; Commissioner of the Navy; not entitled to bounty land. Commanded a trading ship, the Cormorant, at the end of the war. She was once lying at Broadway above City Point.

Maxwell wore "a cockade in his hat". Will probated in Norfolk, Oct. 25, 1795, USP. Wm. Maxwell, administrator in 1845. See also BH, 1048.

MAYNES, WM. Manley Galley.

MAYS, JAMES, of Charlotte Co. Marine under Capt. Hanway. Served three years. In LBP, 1783, Nancy Chaffin, Sarah Mays, Elizabeth Chaffin, Prudence P. Mays, Jane Dunton, and Tabitha Green, children and only heirs at law of James Mays.

MAYS (Mayes), WM. Carpenter. Ship Tartar.

MEALS (Meale), SAMUEL. Aud. Acct. XVIII, 117.

MEARS (Meers), BARTHOLOMEW, of Accomac Co. Quartermaster and then Gunner. Enlisted Aug. 6, 1777. 2d Mate, Accomac Galley. BH, 653–4.

MEARS, EDWARD.

MEARS, SOUTHY. N's Accomack, 35.

MELONY, JEREMIAH. N. A. B.

MELSON, LEVIN. Carpenter's Mate. Accomac Galley. MC III, 166. Heirs in 1830, Levin Melson, Nancy White, Henry Cary, and Thos. Melson. N's Accomack 20; BH, 1160.

MELVAN, MATHEW. N 8, 39.

MENER, ISAAC. War 5, 133.

MENIR, JOHN. Certificate of Byrd Chamberlayne.

MERCER, ISAAC. USP. Sailing Master of the Safeguard; continued till the boat was dismantled; Lt. commanding the Boat Nicholson, NBJ. In 1786, in Lancaster Co. William, and George Garner, and Martha Morris, heirs of Isaac Mercer, decd. MC II, 230.

MERCER (or Menos), SAMUEL. Boatswain's mate, Boat Liberty.

MERIWETHER, JAMES. Appointed Nov. 5, 1776, 2d lt. marines in Capt. Thos. Meriwether's Company. On Brig Northampton. On Irish vessel captured by the Liberty. 2d lt. State Service. Feb. 19, 1777. Lt. in Capt. John Rogers' company of cavalry until June 1, 1781, after which he was in the continental service. Jefferson Petition, Nov. 9, USP. G. W. Meriwether stated that there were two James Meriwethers in service; one the son of David Meriwether, the other his (G. W.'s) uncle, of Dabney's Legion, who died in Oct. 1803. James Meriwether of Jefferson Co., Ga. was a Lt. in Illinois Troops, Light Dragoons. Susanna Meriwether, widow and Executrix, Louisville, Ky.

MERIWETHER, THOMAS. Captain of Marines. Afterwards in the land service. He removed to Georgia with his niece, Jane Pattison, who md., 1st, Eleazer Early and, 2d, Geo. T. Hawkins, Esq. of Florida. In the will of Thomas Meriwether, Jefferson Co., Ga., he left his brother James a copy of his mother's picture "as soon as a good artist could be obtained to execute it". Geo. W. Meriwether, of Louisville, Ky. was his attorney in 1851.

MERRY, JOHN. Brig Northampton. NBJ, Sept. 10, 1778.

MESSEARES (Messieres-Messuere, Messares), FRANCIS. Lt. Tartar. Resigned, Jan. 12, 1778, NBJ.

METCALF, GEORGE. Quartermaster. LBP.

METCALF (Midcalf), GORDON. Brig Northampton, NBJ, Sept. 10, 1778. MC II, 178.

METCALF (Midcalf), WALTER. Brig Northampton. Ordinary Seaman, from June 10, 1776 to June 19, 1779. MC II, 232.

MIARS, THOS. War 5, 134.

MICHAUX, JACOB. Patrick Co. Petitions, Dec. 20, 1826.

MICKING, EDWARD. Aud. Acct. XXV, 251.

MILES, NORTHAM. H. D. 1833–4, Doc. 33, 15.

MILES, WM. Accomac Galley. For heirs, see N's Accomack, 62.

MILLER, JAMES. Marine, enlisted Jan. 16, 1783.

MILLER, JAMES. N 8, 35.

MILLER, ROBT. Lt. Orange Co. Petitions, March 14, 1781.

MILLER, ROBT. N 8, 6.

MILLER, WM. NBJ, Jan. 20, 1778. Tempest, Oct. 7, 1779.

MILLS, JOHN. War 5, 134.

MILNER (Milliner), JAMES (died before Jan. 1787). 1st lt. Accomac Galley, Oct. 16, 1777; Aug. 1778. For heirs, see N's Accomack, 28.

MILNER (Miliner-Milliner), ROBT. Recommended 2d. lt. Accomac Galley, Oct. 16, 1777. LBNB. In R. C., Custis Bull, a neighbor of Milner, gives an account of the traitorous action of Lt. Ishmael Andrews, and states that Lt. Milner protested and remonstrated and declared he would not serve under such an officer. He left the galley for about three weeks, but after Lt. Andrews was dismissed, he returned and performed duty as long as the galley was in service. For heirs, see N's Accomack, 20. MC III, 164.

MINDER (?), JAMES. Dragon. LBP James Jennings.

MINNY. Negro Pilot. C. J. May, 1776, 19.

MINOR, NICHOLAS. Ex. Coms. 1776.

MINTER, JAMES. Henry Galley. LBNB, Nov. 1, 1777. B. W.

MITCHELL, JOSEPH. Oct. 7, 1779.

MITCHELL, RICHARD, of Gloucester Co. Tempest. Entered as Carpenter under Lilly.

MITCHELL, RICHARD, of Lancaster Co. Midshipman, Tempest. Heirs at law, Wm. B. Mitchell and Francis B. Lemorne.

MITCHELL, ROBERT. Master, Tempest, Oct. 7, 1779. Midshipman. BH, 23.

MITCHELL, Ross, of Elizabeth City Co. (died in 1796). Carpenter's mate on the Liberty, Pilot, LBP, Dr. David Brown. Piloted the privateer Marquis Lafayette on her remarkable exploit of passing through the whole British fleet in 1781. In 1832, Elizabeth Jones stated that Ross Mitchell left three children: John, Helen, and Ross (drowned while an apprentice). John Ross md. Sally Pasteur, and had issue: Susan Mitchell; Helen md. Isaac Smith, of Princess Anne Co. In LBP, 1840, there is a memorial of the "only heirs" at that time, John Ripley and Ann, his wife, daughter of Ross Mitchell.

MITCHELL, THOMAS. Living in Frederick Co. in 1835. See Report of Secretary of War, 1835.

MITCHELL, WM., of Caroline Co. Marine, LBP De Kay. Living in 1837. See USP George Catlett.

MITCHELL, WM., of Yorktown. Recruiting as early as Jan. 11, 1776; capt. of marines; resigned Nov. 5, 1776; quartermaster at York; captain in state line for three years. B, 1244.

MITCHELL, WM., of Caroline Co. Enlisted on Defiance, Capt. Callender, for one year, after which he joined Capt. Dick's Marines. Captured on Mosquito. Escaped from Fortune jail. After his return joined Capt. Wallace's company of infantry. See USP George Catlett.

MOHUN, JOEL, of Norfolk. Died in State Ship Virginia. Wife Elizabeth.

MOLICKS, WM. Safeguard. LBNB, Feb. 13, 1778.

MONGHON, GEORGE. R. C. (See Manghan, above).

MONGHON, JOHN, of Matthews Co. (See Manghan, above.)

MONTAGUE, RICHARD. Midshipman, July 7, 1777; Jan. 20, 1778, 1st lt. marines; resigned, Aug., 1779. In USP, an affiant, Spencer Clark, stated that Montague was taken prisoner, and did not return till the close of the war; he assisted him in taking his baggage home from the wharf at Tappahannock. For Richard Montague's descendants see "History and Genealogy of Peter Montague** and his Descendants", by George Williams Montague.

MOODY, JAMES. 2d lt. marines; captain of Sloop Congress before March 1776, at which time he entered the land service.

MOON, WM. War 5, 125.

MOOR, STEPHEN. Accomac Galley. See N's Accomack, 33.

MOORE, ALEX. Midshipman. LBP John Flynt.

MOORE, CHARLES. War 5, 126.

MOORE, DUNFORD. Ablebodied seaman, Henry Galley. Dragon, March 4, 1777 to Nov. 24, 1778. "Faithful to the end", according to Lt. Singleton.

MOORE, EDWARD. Henry Galley. R. C.

MOORE, JOHN. Ship Gloucester. NBJ, Oct. 9, 1778. Lived and died in Lancaster Co. Administration, Sept. 20, 1802. Sailing master on a galley, and then on Dragon. Had two children: (1) Ann md. James Bowen, and had Wm. and a dau.; (2) Judith md. Wm. Danson, of Lancaster Co., and had John, Wm., Lewis, Ann, and Alice Danson (md. Beverly Kent: issue Francis). USP, conflicting claim with John Moore, below.

MOORE, JOHN, of Accomac Co. Sailing master of Lewis, March 1, 1778. Died early in summer of 1798 in Accomac Co. His only child md. Shadrach W. Outten, who removed to Hampton. According to USP, John Moore shipped as a seaman with Capt. Richard Taylor, on the Hornet, March 25, 1776. Issue of Shadrach W. Outten: Eliz. md. John Baynes; Mary (unmar. in 1846); Powell G.; Margaret md. Charles Bryan; Augustus; John; Martha Jane Outten. N's Accomack, 12.

In 1905 Geo. W. Wood, of 19 W. Queen St., Hampton, stated that John Moore was his wife's mother's grandfather.

MOORE, LOTT. Dragon.

MOORE, LUNSFORD. Dragon, March 4, 1777–Sept. 23, 1778.

MOORE, STEPHEN. Diligence. MC III, 322. Only heirs in 1834 Levi, John, and Rachel Moore, Caty, widow of Asa Crockett, and Lucy, wife of Geo, Scott. N's Accomack, 35.

MOORE, WM. Seaman. H. D. 1832-3, Doc. 33.

MOORE, WM. Aged 78 in 1835. Entered April 22, 1776. Marine on Mosquito. Taken prisoner. After the War he removed to Rock Castle Co., Ky. See LBP and USP Charles De Kay.

MORGAN, JAMES. Page Galley. LBNB, Feb. 13, 1778.

MORGAN, WILLIAM. Boat Liberty.

MORRIS, ANTHONY. Ship Gloucester, Nov. 1777. Sarah Morris only heir at law.

MORRIS, CHARLES. Pilot. Hero Galley.

MORRIS, CHRISTOPHER. Henry Galley, Pilot. Died leaving four children: William, Nancy, Edward, and Polly.

John Cunningham in 1802 made affidavit "I have frequently heard my mother say that James Wood and Christopher Morris were both Pilots from or near to this place: that they were taken prisoners by the Enemy in the time of the Revolutionary war; they were carried to York (New ?) and remained as prisoners until the conclusion of peace." It was also stated in this affidavit: "The pay of a Pilot is equal to that of a Lieutenant in the Navy." R. C.

MORRIS, CHRISTOPHER. Hero Galley. N 8, 10.

MORRIS, LLOYD. B. W.

MORRISON, ANTHONY. LBP, 1834. N's Lancaster, 29.

MORTIMER, JAMES. Dragon. Of Northumberland County.

MORTON, EDMUND. Lt. from Dec. 1, 1776, to Nov. 3, 1783. B. W. Miscellaneous Petitions, 1791 (Nov. 21, 1778). MC III, 430. In 1838, Eliz. C. Donaldson, sole heir.
MORTON, EDWARD. N 8, 23.
MORTON, EDWARD. Lt. 1777, vice Jeffries. On Schooner Revenge. Died in prison in 1779. Had a wife, who, while he was a prisoner, received pay, clothing, etc.
MORTON, WM. Lived on Mill Creek near Hampton. Testimony of James Legget, who removed to Princess Anne Co.
MOSES, JOAB. H. D. 1834-5, Doc. 35, 7.
MOSS, FRANCIS. Armourer, Henry Galley, 1776. NBJ, Nov. 1, 1777.
MOSS, JOHN. Aud. Acct. XXII, 3.
MOSS, STARK (Starkey?), of Nansemond Co. Carpenter's mate, Henry Galley, 1776. BH, 1257.
MOSSIR, CHRISTOPHER. Hero Galley. NBJ, Nov. 4, 1777.
MOTCALF, GEORGE. B. W. See "Metcalf".
MOTT, JAMES. Tempest, Dec. 7, 1779 (Of Northumberland Co?).
MOTT, THOMAS. Gunner's mate. Voucher, 1784. B. W.
MUIR, JOHN. War 5, 127. B. W.
MULLOK, WILLIAM. Safeguard from March 1. ——.
MURDEN, EDWARD (Norfolk County?). War 5, 153.
MURPHY (Murphey), PATRICK. Safeguard Galley, June 16, 1777.
MURRAY, DAVID. Master's Mate, Accomac Galley. Welburn made affidavit in LBP that Murray lived in the neighborhood of Chincoteague. Sailing master all during war. MC III, 166. N's Accomack, 26.
MUSE, JESSE. Midshipman, Page Galley. Tempest, June, 1778. Commander, Manley Sept. 11, 1779. MC II, 243. In 1786 Jeremiah Muse, heir at law of Jesse Muse, decd.
MUSE, JOHN. Lt. Page Galley, Oct., 1777, and VSR, p. 6, July, 1930.
MUTER, CAPT. GEORGE. Appointed captain by the Council of Safety, March 16, 1776; by Governor, July 16, 1776, Hero Galley. Resigned and became Lt. Col. in the land service. Removed to Woodford Co., Ky. Died May, 1811. BH, 1055.

N

NEAKINS (Nicken), JAMES. Dragon. LBP Jas. Jennings.
NEAKINS, NATHANIEL. Dragon. LBP Jas. Jennings.
NEAKINS, WM. Dragon. LBP Jas. Jennings.
NEALE (Neil-Neal), PRESLEY . (Died Jan., 1805). Midshipman, Tempest, Oct. 7, 1777. Dragon, Aug. and Sept., 1779. Lived in Westmoreland Co., near Wakefield. The Rev. John Neal, of Fauquier Co., was his son. In 1835 his only heirs were: Thomas Rice, Lucy Rice, Elias Edmunds and Sophia (Rice) Edmunds, his wife.
NEEHAM, FRANCE. Ex. Com. 1776.
NEGROES on Hero Galley, Nov. 4, 1777. NBJ. Pluto, Jack, Bachus, Boston, William and George.
NEGRO JAMES. Tempest, Dec. 7, 1779.
NEGRO KINGSTON. Accomac Galley, 1779.
NEIL, JOHN. Dragon, May 3, 1777, to March 28. Deserted.
NELMS (Nellums), MENDETH (Meredith), of Nansemond Co. H. D. 1834-5, Doc. 48, 13. War 5, 141.
NELSON, LEVIN. N 8, 6.
NELSON, WM. Brig Jefferson, Dec., 1779, to Jan. 20, 1780.
NESSELL (Nessels), EPHRAIM. N 8, 11.
NEWBILL, ZACHARIAS. N 8, 39.
NEWBY, WM., of Lancaster Co. Carpenter, enlisted about year 1778, Aug. 22, 1780 (Maxwell).
He left a son Wm. P. Newby, of Culpeper Co. Other heirs Thos. G. Rains, who md. Anne Newby; Daniel P. Mitchell and his wife, Virginia; George Warren and George Channel.
NEWBY, WM. Marine. On Protector and then on Dragon. Statement of Wm. Lowry, in Northumberland Co., in 1838.
NEWHOUSE, ANTHONY. Safeguard, 1st March to June 16, 1777; removed to Brig Northampton. On Safeguard, Feb. 13, 1776. LBNB.
NEWLY (Newby), WILLIAM. War 5, 142.
NICHOLAS, JOHN. Hero Galley.
NICHOLS, JAMES. Hero Galley. Nov. 4, 1777, NBJ.
NICHOLS, RICHARD. Hero Galley, Nov. 4, 1777. NBJ.

NICHOLS, NATHANIEL. Hero Galley. NBJ, Nov. 4, 1777, to Feb. 13, 1778.
NICHOLSON, JOHN. H. D. 1834–5, Doc. 48, 14.
NICHOLSON, JOHN. Captain. B. W.
NICHOLON, WILLIAM. Ex. Coms. 1776.
NICHOLSON, CAPT. WILLIAM, of Accomac County. Captain of a Continental Frigate. Removed to Elizabeth City County, where he died and where his heirs lived. Served four or five years up to the siege of Yorktown. One of his sons was County Surveyor of Elizabeth City County, and Edmund Rudd married one of his grandchildren.
Note: "He became entitled to land bounty as though he had served in the Virginia line."
NICHOLSON, WM. In USP is the claim of a Wm. Nicholson that he was an officer in the Va. Navy, with French documents stating that he served under Commodore Paul Jones.
NICKELBURN, JOHN. Aug. 19, 1778. N 8, 39. Deserted.
NICKEN, AMOS, of Northumberland Co. On Congress. USP Wm. Skinner.
NICKEN, EDWARD. Able Seaman. H. D. 1834–5, Doc. 48, 15.
NICKENS (Nicking, Nicken, Neakins), HEZEKIAH (brother of James). On Gloucester. Died a prisoner.
NICKING (Nicken), JAMES. See also Neakins. Enlisted about 19 July, 1777, and continued to end of war. On Gloucester. On Dragon, Sept. 2, 1779. Another statement sets forth that he enlisted Aug. 1, 1777. Honorably discharged by Markham, June 2, 1780. Living in Stafford Co. in 1840, aged 85. Memorialists residing in Frederick County: son James Nickens: daughters Elizabeth Nickens and Indy Pollard. NBJ. James Nicken a boy delivered from Hero to Capt. Thomas Pollard.
NICKENS, JOHN. Aud. Acct. XXIX, 78.
NICKENS (Nicken), NATHANIEL. "Ornary" Seaman, Tempest, Aug., 1778. See also "Neakens".
NICKENS (Nicken), RICHARD, of Lancaster Co. USP. S 5830. Aged 82 in Dec., 1832. Entered service as a private in the Navy, under Thomas Pollard, with whom he went to Hampton. Then served eighteen months on the Hero, Capt.

Chamberlin, stationed in Hampton Roads and on contiguous coasts. Was removed to the Tempest, 18 guns, Capt. Sanders, and was on her eighteen months, after which he was discharged by Capt. Steele, who had charge of Chickahominy shipyard. Never was in any regular battle, but in frequent skirmishes.

NICKENS, WILLIAM. Drummer. Served three years. R. C.

NIGHTINGALE, MATTHEW, of Northumberland Co. Wicomico Parish. Boatswain, Protector. Given discharge at the end of his term, by Capt. Thomas, Sept. 11, 1779. MC III, 435. James Nightingale, heir.

NITT, JOHN. H. D. Oct. 1795, 39, 74.

NORMAN, WM. Dragon, Sept. 2, 1779.

NORTH, BOLLING. Manley Galley, Sept. 11, 1779.

NORTH, WM. Aud. Acct. XV, 227.

NORTHAM, MILES. Norfolk Petitions, Dec. 10, 1829. BH, 363.

NORTHRUP, JOSEPH. War 5, 143.

NORTHRUP, STEPHEN. War 5, 143.

NORTON, MILES. E 1.

NUTALL, JOHN. Seaman. H. D. 1834–5, Doc. 48, 14.

NUTT (Nut), THOMAS. Dragon, Sept. 2, 1779. MC II, 10.

NUTTALL, IVERSON, of Gloucester Co. Gunner, Dragon, Feb. 27, 1779, to June 20, 1779. Midshipman, Sept. 2, 1779. LBP Presley Neal.

NUTTALL, JOHN. Gunner's mate, Dragon, Feb. 27, 1779, to June 20, 1779. David Henderson attested that John Nuttall was in service as a midshipman on the Dragon in the spring of 1777.

O

OATS, WM. War 5, 149.

OBRIAN, DANIEL. Deserted from Capt. Taylor, Va. Gazette, Sept. 11, 1779.

O'DANIEL, JOHN. Tempest, Oct. 7, 1779.

O'HARROW, JAMES. On cruise in Brig Liberty in 1777. See petition of John Paul. H. D. Oct. 16, 1792.

OLDHAM, SAMUEL, of Northumberland Co. H. D. 1834–5, Doc. 48, 14.

OLDNER, JOSHUA. R. C.
OPIE, GEORGE HEALE, of Fairfax Co. Clerk. C. J. 1777–8, 50.
ORDERS, JOHN. Safeguard Galley from March 1 to June 15, 1777.
ORRILL, JOHN. N 8, 11.
OSBORNE, WM. Boatswain, July 8, 1778. NBJ. In charge of Sloop Experiment.
OVERSTREET, HENRY. Lewis Galley. LBNB, Feb. 13, 1778.
OVERSTREET, JOHN. Died in service. N's Lancaster, 22, 23.
OVERSTREET, SAMUEL. Dragon, Dec. 2, 1777 to Dec. 3. Discharged.
OWEN, EPHRAIM. Dragon, Sept. 16 to Dec. 3, 1777. Discharged.
OWEN, JOHN. Dragon. War 5, 149.
OWENS, EVAN. Dragon, Sept. 12 to Nov. 29, 1777. Discharged.

P

PAGE, WM. Dragon. NBJ, June 11, 1777.
PALMER, THOS. War 5, 154.
PARADISE, MERRILL (Merrill). Accomac Galley. War 5, 15.
PARKER, GEORGE. War 5, 157.
PARKER, RICHARD. 1st. lt. Diligence Galley. Commander after the capt. resigned. Was at sea with Michael Parker several years before the war. Supernumerary May, 1780. USP. MC III, 180. Died Nov. 11, 1811. Heirs in 1832: Mary Ann, wife of Edmund Chandler; Henry and James Stakes, children of Nancy Stakes. Mary Ann Chandler and Nancy Stakes, daughters of Lt. Richard Parker. N's Accomack, 70.
PARKER, ROBT. Seaman. Accomac Co. H. D. 1833, Doc. 33, 15.
PARKER, THOMAS (son of Clement). Midshipman. Diligence Galley, 1777. LBP Solomon Powell. For heir see N's Accomack, 59.
PARKER, WM. Boat Fly.
PARKER, WM. Dilligence Galley. Lt. Jan. 29, 1777. N 8, 12.

PARKER, WM. HARWAR. Lt. Tartar. When vessel was captured he made his escape by swimming ashore, being frequently shot at before reaching it. Later served in the army. Statement of Frances Blackwell (nee Parker), of Fauquier Co., in 1830. USP. In 1845 Wm. E. Parker, of Southampton Co., was attorney for Hannah Parker, administratrix. Lt. (later Capt.). Wm. Harwar Parker, son of Richard Parker, of "Lawfield" had issue: I. Col. Richard Elliott Parker (born in Westmoreland Co., Dec. 27, 1783: died at "Retreat", Snickersville, Va., Sept. 9, 1849). U. S. Senator: member Court of Appeals md. Elizabeth, dau. of Dr. Wm. Foushee, and had: (1) Richard, Member of Congress: Judge of the General Court that tried John Brown: md. Evelina Moss; (2) Mary md. John S. Milloon: (3) Juliet, s. p. (4) Margaret, s. p. (5) Charlotte md. Dr. Wm. McCormick: (6) Eliz. md. A. F. Crenshaw. II. Foxhall A. (born 1788), Commodore, U. S. N.; Commandant U. S. Naval Academy; md. Sarah, dau. of Gen. Robt. S. Bogardus, and had issue: Robert Bogardus, Foxhall, Wm. Harwar, C. S. N.; Richard Leroy, Daingerfield, U. S. N., Mary Jay, Octavia, Virginia Adela. III, Col. Wm. C. Parker, IV, John, of Southampton Co., who had Col. John A. Parker, died in 1890, aged 89; V. Juliet md. Leroy P. Daingerfield.

PARRISH, JOHN, of Elizabeth City Co. LBP, affidavit of Mrs. Ann Payne. The brothers John, William and Mark Parrish were pilots, probably for three years. John Parrish left nine children: Martha md. Nathaniel Harris (issue: John and Ed.) Frances md. Abraham Cooper (issue: Eliz. md. Capt. Middleton; another dau. md. Charles Ropery; Mary md. Henry Roubet; Martha md. Samuel Skinner, and had James Skinner of Norfolk, and Samuel and Thos. Skinner of Richmond; Elizabeth md. John K. Lattimer; Susan; Barbara; Catherine. BH, 304.

PARRISH, MARK (son of John Parrish, will, Nov. 11, 1777). Pilot. BH, 304.

PARRISH, WM., of Norfolk. Dau. Mrs. Eliz. Jones. BH, 308.

PARTRIDGE, SAML. Gloucester.

PASLET, THOS. Hero Galley.

PASTEUR, BLOVET (Bluet), of Elizabeth City Co. War 5, 154.
PASTEUR (Pasture), CAPT. JOHN, of Smithfield. Commanded a vessel in trade, before the Revolution. Independence Galley. Lookout Boat Molly. Capt. Pasture died Aug. 22, 1794. His will names: wife Honour; daus. Polly and Elizabeth; Charles (died s. p.) and Solomon Wilson Pasteur. In 1836 Elizabeth was the widow of David Boykin, and Mary the wife of Jos. B. Hodsden. USP. MC III, 325.
PASTEUR, ROBT. Aud. Acct. XVIII, 376.
PATE, MATTHEW. Boat Fly. N 8, 30.
PATE, ROBT. MC II, 283.
PATTERSON, JOHN, of Elizabeth City Co. Midshipman and Clerk, Jan. 16, 1783. BH, 389.
PAULLIN, CHARLES. Mosquito. Died in Fortune Jail, Eng. USP Thos. Herbert.
PAYNE, BERRIMAN (Merriman). Lt. Aud. Acct. XXII, 469.
PAYNE, JOHN, of Northumberland Co. Pilot. Master. Lost on the Hiram. He had a bro., John Sr. B, 389.
PAYNE, JOHN. Sailing Master. Died in July, 1787 or 1788. N's Lancaster, 41.
PAYNE, MERRYMAN, of Lancaster Co. (will pro. April 20, 1780); md. Betsey Hughlett; no issue. 2d. lt. Safeguard; recom. 1st lt. Aug. 12, 1777. BH, 391.
PAYNE, WILLIAM. Appt. 1st lt. Sloop American Congress, April 16, 1776. B, 1244.
PEA, GEORGE. Tempest, Dec. 7, 1779.
PEAD, JOHN. NBJ, Nov. 4, 1777. Hero Galley, Capt. Chamberlaine; lost one of his eyes in the service.
PEATON (Peatons-Peatow), SOLOMON. Caswell Galley. Tempest, Oct. 7, 1779.
PEEPHALL, GEORGE. Safeguard Galley. LBNB, Feb. 13, 1778.
PEERS, VALENTINE, of Fairfax Co. Lt. marines, Capt. marines. Congress. Major in Land service. Died June 6, 1830 at Mayville, Mason Co., Ky. LBP Wm. Skinner. B, 1244.
PEIRCE, JOHN. War 5, 154.
PEIRCE, THOMAS. B. W.

Pell, Joseph S., of Norfolk City. Surgeon from July, 1776. Pell was probably on the Norfolk Revenge, Capt. Westcott, commanding, sunk May 29, 1777. BH, 396, 1335, 1436.

Pell, Simon. Surgeon. N 8, 22.

Penn, John. War 5, 154.

Perkins, James. N's Lancaster, 23.

Perkins, Joshua. N's Accomack, 59.

Perkins, Nimrod, "a freeman of Colour", Diligence Galley. In LBP Wm. White, Elkanah Andrews stated, in 1831, that, so far as he knew, he and Perkins were the only survivors of the crew of the Diligence and Accomac Galleys. BH, 396–7.

Perkins, Thos. Enlisting men for the Tartar, June 3, 1777, NBJ. N's Lancaster, 23.

Peter. A Negro. Able Seaman, War 5, 157.

Peter, Richard. E 1.

Peters, James. Henry Galley. LBNB, Nov. 1, 1777. MC II, 277.

Peters, Samuel. Tempest, Oct. 7, 1779.

Pettigrew, Abel. H. D. 1834–5, Doc. 35, 10.

Pettigrew, Richard (died Oct. 5, 1835). N's Accomack, 65. USP, Leah Collins, his daughter, 40 years of age in 1838.

Pettygrew, Edward. War 5, 156.

Pettygrew (Pettigrew), John, of Accomac Co. Lt., Sept. 22, 1778. "Lived near where the galleys were launched", LBP Wm. Skinner: John Pettigrew died in Milford, Kent Co., Delaware (will pro. July 20, 1812). For heirs, see N's Accomack, 25, 26. MC III, 174.

Pettygrew, Levin (Gavin), brother of John. Did not return home. LBP Wm. White, MC III, 174.

Peyton, Solomon. Aud. Acct. XXV, 314.

Philips (Phillips), Jacob. Accomac Galley. Boatswain, Diligence, 1779. LBP Solomon Powell, 1857. N's Accomack, 24, 59.

Philips, John. Sergt. marines, Sloop Congress.

Philips, William, of Accomac County. MC III, 177. Heir, March 26, 1831, Jacob Philips.

Philipson, John. Dragon, Feb. 25, 1777–Oct. 29, 1778. N 8, 39.

PICKERIN, MATHEW, of Wicomico Parish, Northumberland Co. Deserted, see Va. Gazette, Sept. 11, 1779.
PICKETT, FRANCIS, of Caroline Co. Marine on Mosquito. See USP George Catlett.
PICKETT, JOHN. Boat Liberty, 1784. LBP Dr. P. Bartlett.
PICKRELL, SPENCER. Sailor. MC II, 10.
PICKRENT, SAMUEL, of Northumberland Co. B, 244.
PIERCE, EDWARD. H. D. 1833–34, Doc. 33, 15.
PIERCE, JOHN. Midshipman, Tempest, B. W.
PILLS (Pell ?), JOSEPH. Surgeon. H. D. Oct. 1791, p. 50.
PINN, JOHN. B. W.
PINSHAW, PURSLEY. LBP James Jennings.
PIPENHOLT, GEORGE. Hero Galley.
PIPPEN (Pipin), BANNISTER. Henry Galley, 1778. Died in service about midsummer, 1781. USP Dr. John Reynolds. MC II, 350.
PIPPEN (Pipin), WM. Henry Galley. NBJ, May 27, 1778.
PITT (Pitts), JOHN. Accomac Galley. Apt. Surgeon, Oct. 6, 1776. MC III, 178. In 1831 Ann H. P. Hall, sole heiress of Ann Beard, sole heiress of Robt. Pitt, sole heir at law of John Pitts. N's Accomack, 23, 29.
PLAYL, JOHN. Dragon, Feb. 18, 1777. Deserted Aug. 18, 1778.
PLUTO (negro). H. D. Oct. 1793, 43.
POLLARD, BENJAMIN. Recommended lt. marines March 29, 1776. Captain. One of the original members of the Society of the Cincinnati in the Commonwealth of Va. Died intestate in 1807; his only children were Benj. Pollard and Margaret, wife of George Loyall. BH, 320.
POLLARD, GEORGE. 1st lt. Hero Galley, 1776.
POLLARD, ROBT. (?) Lt. Norfolk Revenge, NBJ, May 8, 1777.
POLLARD, THOMAS, of Lancaster Co. Lt. recruiting in Oct. 1776; LBNB, Jan. 31, 1777. Lt. Norfolk Revenge, Dec. 1, 1777. Later, capt. in land service. N's Lancaster, 27.
POMEROY, ESAU. E 1.
POMEROY (Pumeroy), ISAAC, of Fairfax Co. LBNB, Nov. 4, 1777.
POOL (Poole), JOHN, of Elizabeth City Co. Enlisted in 1778 under Barron. LBP Thos. Bulley.

Pope, Joseph. LBNB, June 20, 1778.
Pope, Momas. N 8, 39.
Pope, Thomas, of Lancaster or Northampton Co. Deserted, Va. Gazette, July 3, 1779. But see H. D. 1834–5, Doc. 48, 14.
Pope, Wm. Midshipman. BH, 323.
Pope, Wm. Ship Gloucester, NBJ, Oct. 9, 1778. Transferred to Tartar, NBJ, Feb. 7, 1779.
Pope, Wm. Lewis, or First Row Galley.
Poplar, Hack. Patriot in 1778. R. C. of John Christian.
Portlock, Archibald. Caswell and Washington Galleys, Feb. 13, 1778 to April 3, 1779, Norfolk Co. Petition, 1794. John Portlock, claimant.
Powell, Benj. Brig Liberty.
Powell, Francis, of Nansemond Co. 2d Midshipman. BH, 327.
Powell, Francis. Hero Galley.
Powell, John. Brig Liberty, June, 1778.
Powell, S. Brig Liberty. N 8, 20.
Powell, Samuel, of Accomac Co. Quartermaster. BH, 330.
Powell, Samuel. War 5, 158.
Powell, Solomon. Second mate, Diligence Galley, Quartermaster. LBP. N's Accomack, 30. BH, 329.
Power, John. Ex. Coms. 1776.
Powers, Jacob. Dragon, Jan. 22, 1777 to Jan. 20, 1779.
Prayl (Playl), John. War 5, 158.
Price, Ebenezer. Quartermaster. LBP John Flynt. MC II, 262.
Price, Edward. Safeguard, June 16, 1777. LBNB, Feb. 13, 1778.
Price, John. On cruise in the Brig Liberty. See H. D. Oct. 16, 1792.
Prim, John, of Stafford Co. Cook, Manley Galley, Sept. 11, 1779.
Pritchett (Prichard), George. Aud. Acct. XXX, 163.
Probat, Monson. B. W.
Procure, Thos. Dragon, Sept. 2, 1779.
Prosser, John. Henry Galley. War 4, 156.
Purcell (Purcill), Charles. War 5, 154.

Purcley, Thos. Hero Galley. NBJ, Nov. 4, 1777.
Pursar, Wm. Died in service late in 1777. MC III, 281. In 1833, Wm. and Molly Parrish, heirs. BH, 1177.
Pushaw, Presley. Dragon. LBP James Jennings.

Q

Quarles, Francis. N. A. B., 1838.
Quarles, James. Lt. Marines. Appointed March 3, 1776, Capt. Cocke. B, 1244.
Miscellaneous Pets. 1791 (1777).
Petitioners, John Allison, James Quarles, Ben Pollard, Thos., Meredith, Thos. Hamilton, Windsor Brown, and John R. Davies stated that they had been turned over to the land service after serving in the marine.

R

Ragsdale, Godfrey. In USP, in 1828, is found an interesting account of his career. Student at William and Mary College: entered Col. Bland's cavalry, in which he became lt. and quartermaster. Sergt. marines, June 16, 1783. Godfrey Ragsdale was md. in Fayette Co., Ky., Jan. 13, 1789, by Rev. Lewis Craig, to Elizabeth Mitchell, whose bro. Andrew was of Trimble Co. Godfrey Ragsdale died Feb. 16, 1835. His widow, born March 14, 1777, was living in Oldham Co. in 1855. In the USP is found a record of the birth dates of their twelve children.
Railey, James. H. D. 1834-5, Doc. 48, 16.
Raines, Henry. Taken prisoner on Mosquito. After the war he went to Hardin Co., Ky. USP James Dishman.
Ralls, Capt. George, of Elizabeth City Co. Captured at sea twice. LBP Dr. Brown.
Rambourg, John. Dragon, March 17, 1777 to Jan. 20, 1779.
Ramsay, John. Seaman.
Randall, Benjamin. Drowned shortly before Aug. 19, 1776, NBJ. Norfolk Revenge.

RANGER, JOSEPH. Dragon. LBP James Jennings. MC II, 242.

RANKIN, WM. Carpenter's mate, Safeguard Galley, March 1 to June 16, 1777.

RANSOME, AUGUSTINE, of Gloucester Co. B, 347.

RANSOME, THOS. Ward of Henry Buchanan. Boatswain on Brig Liberty. On Dragon. Died 1823. BH, 346–348.

RANSOME, THOMAS. Sloop Liberty, Aug. 1777.

RAWLEY, JAMES. War 5, 171.

READ, DANIEL. N 8, 11.

READ (Reid, Reed), FRANCIS, of Kingston Parish, Gloucester Co. 1st Midshipman, Henry Galley. LBP.

READ, JOHN. Hero Galley. N 8, 10.

REAVES (Reavis, Reives, or Reeves), JAMES. Dragon, Feb. 8, 1777–Jan. 20, 1779. Able Seaman. Served till close of War. Heirs Elizabeth and Lucinda Phillips. N's Lancaster, 29.

REDD, JOHN. H. D. Oct. 1894, 43. Caswell and Washington Galleys. Norfolk Co. Petition, 1794.

REDMOND, ISAAC. Pilot. Captured on lookout boat in 1781. LBP, John Rodgers.

REED, DANIEL. Safeguard Galley. Deserted.

REED, JOHN. Boat Liberty, November, 1779.

REEVES, CAPT. HENRY. "Flag" going to Charleston, Nov. 8, 1780. See VSR, July, 1931, p. 23.

REILLY, BARNEY. Cook, Safeguard Galley, March 1–June 15, 1777.

REVELL, JOHN. Gunner's Mate. LBP "when the ship to which he was attached was in harbour he would join the troops on land." See N's Accomack, 23 and 34.

REVERE (Rivere), WYATT, of Lancaster Co. See also "Rivier" below. MC III, 192. In 1831 Lee Ann Ruddle and Cordelia Charlton, heirs at law. MC II, 367–368 "late Soldier of Moreen Page Galley", June 11, 1796, of Wilkes Co., Ga.

REYBOURN, GEORGE. Prisoner. Pressed into British service.

REYNOLDS, JAMES. Sergt. Marines, July 30, 1783.

REYNOLDS, JOHN. Lt. Marines. Appt. Dec. 2, 1776 vice Waller promoted. B, 1244.

REYNOLDS, DR. JOHN. Surgeon, LBNB, Oct. 11, 1776, Protector, Tartar, LBP, Wm. Skinner. After surrender resumed his practice in Yorktown. In USP he is said to have removed to Eastern Shore. Died about 1815. Wm. Lanis, only nephew and heir in 1836. N's Northampton, 28.
RICHARDS, JOHN. Clerk.
RICHARDS (Richard), JOHN. Page Galley. Gunner, Sloop Congress. LBP Wm. Skinner.
RICHARD, JOHN. Sloop Scorpion.
RICHARD, JOHN. Purser on Dragon. USP John Gibbs.
RICHARDS, JOHN, of Spotsylvania Co. H. D. Dec. 1818, 63.
RICHARDS (Richard), LEWIS. Dragon, Sept. 2, 1779.
RICHARDS, WILLIAM. Lt. April 14, 1778. Resigned, Jan. 12, 1779.
RICHARDSON, DANIEL, of Westmoreland Co. Midshipman, Manley Galley, 1776; lt. Manley Galley, Nov. 17, 1778. Resigned July 1, 1779, LBP, Wm. Mitchell. Died intestate in Fredericksburg, Jan. 17, 1800. His son Thos. R. H. Richardson died in Washington. In USP Elizabeth Richardson, in 1837, claimed to be the sole heir, as granddaughter, of Lt. Richardson. In 1850 a Mrs. Sarah Ann Owens claimed to be an heir. Among the papers presented in the pension claim is a leaf from the family Bible of Thos. R. H. Richardson, containing date of death of Dan. Richardson and Ann, his wife. Also Henry Thorp Sr., died in Nov., 1773. MC III, 195.
RICHARDSON, JOHN. Page Galley. LBNB, Feb. 8, 1778.
RICHARDSON, JOHN, Northampton. LBNB, Feb. 12, 1778.
RICHARDSON, SOLOMON. H. D. 1834–5, Doc. 48, 16.
RICHARDSON, WM. Accomac. Diligence Galley. Three years.
RICHARDSON, WM. Marine. H. D. 1832–3, Doc. 33.
RICHARDSON, WM. Lt. Resigned.
RIDDLE (Riddell), DR. GEORGE. Surgeon's mate, Brig Liberty. NBJ, Nov. 29, 1776.
RIGGS, GEORGE B. LBP Wm. Tunnell. BH, 362. N's Accomack, 61, 67.
RIGGS, WM. Accomac Galley. BH, 868. N's Accomack, 61, 67.

RILEY, EDWARD. Marine. Deserted. Va. Gazette, Supplement, Sept. 6, 1776.

RIVIER (Rivers-Reverr-Rivears), WIATT (Wyatt), of Lancaster Co. Armourer Marine. Page Galley, Capt. Markham. Dragon (seaman), to Jan. 20, 1779, Aug. 22, 1780, MC II, 367 and 386, June 11, 1796, in Wilkes Co., Ga. In LBP it is stated: "An armourer ranks as any of the above mentioned kind of officers—carpenters, gunners' mates, boatswain's mates, and other petty officers."

ROBERTS, ABRAHAM. Brig Jefferson, Dec. 1779 to Jan. 20, 1780. LBNB.

ROBERTS, GEORGE. War 5, 169.

ROBERTS, GODFREY. Safeguard Galley, June 16, 1777.

ROBERTS, JAMES. Diligence Galley. LBP Solomon Powell.

ROBERTS, PHILIP. Aug 4, 1777 to Feb. 18, 1778. Deserted.

ROBERTS, THOS. Tempest, NBJ, June 19, 1778.

ROBERTS, WM. Hero Galley, Tempest, Feb. 1778; died in service, Feb. 1780. MC II, 236. Heir at law, in 1786, Margaret Roberts, wife of Wm. Roberts, decd.

ROBERTSON, JOHN. Safeguard Galley, March 1 to June 16, 1777. LBNB.

ROBEY, ROBT. Tempest, Dec. 7, 1779.

ROBINS, JOHN. First Midshipman, Lt. Tempest, Oct. 9, 1779. LBP George Wray and John Stubbs. MC III, 318. Heirs in 1834: James Crewison and Ellen C. Lewis.

ROBINSON, JAMES, of Louisa Co. Hero Galley. See advertisement by Benjamin Pollard in Supplement to Va. Gazette, Sept. 6, 1776.

ROE, WM., of Westmoreland and later of Fauquier Co. Surgeon's mate, Feb. 12, 1777 till Feb., 1780. Affidavit of Capt. Wm. Saunders, who lived in Leedstown. Wm. Roe rented a house and had his sister Sally keep house for him. Will probated, April 23, 1798; bro. Henry Roe, of Westmoreland Co.; bro. John Roe; sister Sarah Baker, wife of Richard Baker; their children John, Betsy, and Richard Henry Baker, (died young). Betsy Baker md. James English, had issue: Major James A. Baker. USP. MC II, 231.

ROGERS, GEORGE. Mate, Feb. 22, 1776, Brigantine Greyhound (employed in trade).
ROGERS, GEORGE. Captain. Coms. lt. Aug. 3, 1776, Mosquito. Captured with Brig Liberty and died a prisoner in N. Y. USP. MC III, 255. Heirs in 1833: John and Elizabeth Rogers.
ROGERS, HENRY. Seaman. Accomac Galley. N's Accomack, 49. MC III, 242. Hargis family, heirs.
ROGERS (Rodgers), JOHN, of Elizabeth City Co. Lt. and capt. (died Jan. 1, 1816). Brother of Capt. George Rogers. 2d lt. Brig Liberty. Captured in 1778. Capt. in 1780. USP. In LBP, in 1834, claim of John Rogers and Elizabeth D. Rogers, grandchildren of Capt. John Rogers.
ROGERS, MELVIN. Brig Northampton. NBJ, Sept. 10, 1778. Tempest, Dec. 7, 1779.
ROGERS, WM., of King George Co. Boat Liberty. LBP Wm. Bartlett. BH, 1206-7.
ROLLEY (Rolly), JAMES. Gunner's mate, Oct., 1777, Diligence Galley. LBP.
ROMAS (Roman-Rowmas), ADAM. Carpenter's mate, Diligence Galley. N's Accomack, 36.
ROOTES (Rotes), DANIEL. 1st lt. Schooner Speedwell. Trading Dept., Aug. 3, 1776. Council Journal, 1776-1777, p. 89.
ROSE, CLEMENT. Brig Northampton.
ROSE, DUNCAN. Lewis Galley, Feb. 13, 1778. LBNB.
ROSE, ELIJAH. Accomac Galley. LBP Wm. Tunnell.
ROSE, WM. Northampton. NBJ, Sept. 10, 1777.
ROSS, JOHN. 3d lt. Norfolk Revenge, Nov. 1, 1777.
ROWLEY, JAMES. Aud. Acct. XXIX, 8.
ROYSTER, JOHN. Steward, Brig Liberty, May 18-July 30, 1776. LBP George Rogers.
RUDD, BENJ. Ship Tartar. LBP Dr. P. Bartlett.
RUDD, JAMES. NBJ, Oct. 23, 1778.
RUDD, JOHN. Boat Liberty, Nov., 1779.
RUN, MATTHEW. Mosquito, 1776.
RUDMAN, JOHN. Master's mate. LBP John Flynt.
RUSSELL, DR. Surgeon, Manley Galley, Aug. 3, 1776.
RUSSELL, JOHN. Dragon, July 15 to Sept. 17, 1777.

Russell, Thos. Brig Jefferson, Dec. 26, 1779 to Jan. 20, 1780.

Russell, Vincent. MC II, 173.

Rust, Benjamin. Lt. Oct. 23, 1778. Boat Patriot, Dec. 16, 1778. NBJ. Midshipman, Dragon, June 9, 1777, to Jan. 20, 1779. Certificate of Capt. Callender. LBP James Jennings and of Wm. Mitchell. Died at Tappahannock; will, 1787. BH, 1332. MC III, 221. In 1832, Lettice S. Smith, sole heir.

S

Salke (Salkie), John. Hero Galley. NBJ, Nov. 4, 1777, and Feb. 13, 1778.

Salisbury (Saulesberry), Moses. Armourer. N's Accomack, 25, 29. BH, 1835.

Sanders (Saunders), Lt. Joseph. Born in Lancaster Co. in June, 1757. Enlisted March 7, 1777, under Thos. Downing, recruiting officer. Placed on the Dragon, then on the stocks in Fredericksburg. Helped to rig the ship; later had charge of the Magazine, took part in the engagement off the Capes; promoted to Master's mate; was in charge of a galley that served as a lookout; lived for a while in Lancaster Co. after the war; in 1789 removed to Brunswick Co., where he devoted his time to "domestic economy and Religion". In 1822 he removed to Tennessee, and a year later to Lawrence Co., Ala. His declaration in the USP is very valuable. For his family, see "Early Settlers of Alabama", by Col. J. E. Saunders, with notes, etc., by Elizabeth S. B. Stubbs.

Sandford, Lawrence. Appointed by the Council captain of the Brig Adventure.

Saunders (Sanders), Capt. Celey (born about 1740 near Dumfries). In command of the Lewis Galley in Sept., 1776 and in 1777. Commander of Tempest, Dec. 17, 1779. MC III, 344. Captain from April 1, 1776 to end of war. Heirs in 1834: Ann B. Taylor, John B. Saunders, Mary M. Green, and Jane V. Hunter, heirs of John Saunders, sole heir of Celey Saunders. Capt. Saunders is said to have died in the Halifax, Nova Scotia prison about the end of the war.

Captain Celey Saunders' grandson, John Loyall Saunders md. Martha Bland Selden, at Westover, in 1834. John Loyall Saunders was a captain in the U. S. Navy. His eldest daughter, Elizabeth Selden Saunders, was the wife of Col. Walter H. Taylor, of General Lee's staff, and his youngest daughter md. George McIntosh. See "The Researcher", Vol. I, p. 195.

SAUNDERS, RICHARD. Henry Galley, March 4, 1777 to Jan. 20, 1779. LBNB.

SAUNDERS, RICHARD. Midshipman. H. D. Doc. 48, p. 7. 1833–4.

SAUNDERS (Sanders), CAPT. WM. Lt. and capt. of the Brig Adventure, August, 1776. Ordered to command of Manley April 18, 1777, late commander being dead. Commander of Tartar. USP. MC III, 322, captain from April, 1776 to the end of the war. Heir in 1834, Elizabeth Murray, who appointed Reuben Saunders of King and Queen Co. her Atty. Reuben Saunders md. Capt. Wm. Saunders' daughter Lavinia, and they were the parents of Major Wm. A. Saunders, who md. Emeline Motley, and had among issue: John Richard Saunders, Attorney General of Virginia.

SAVAGE, JOSEPH and HENRY. Surgeon's mates. Heirs in Ky.

SAVAGE, RABLE. War 5, 186.

SCARBOROUGH, NICHOLAS. Henry Galley, 1776. LBNB, Nov. 1, 1777.

SCHOFIELD, ROBT. Dragon. War 5, 182.

SCHOFIELD (Scholfield), WM. H. D. 1834–5, Doc. 48, 17.

SCOTT, JOHN. Manley Galley. LBNB. LBP, testimony Thomas Jett, of Westmoreland Co.

SCOTT, JOHN. Northampton Brig. Discharged, Feb. 12, 1778. NBJ.

SCOTT, RICHARD. Tempest, Dec. 7, 1779.

SCOTT, THOS. Manley Galley, Sept. 11, 1779.

SCOTT, WM. War 5, 186.

SELBY, JACK. N's Accomack, 62.

SELDEN, LT. Lt. Selden was recruiting for the ship "Cormorant" in 1782. It is not clear whether this was Lt. Samuel Selden or Lt. Joseph Selden (BH, 1325).

SELDEN, WILSON CARY, of Loudoun Co.; aged 71 in 1818. After service as a surgeon's mate to a regiment of artillery, he commenced his public service in the Marine Hospital at Hampton. Afterwards served at York and at Williamsburg, and then served in South Carolina as a Regular Surgeon of the Army. On a trip to the West Indies, for the benefit of his health, he was captured by the enemy, &c. &c. See LBP.

For descendants, see "Seldens of Virginia and Allied Families", by Mary Selden Kennedy.

SERVANT, RICHARD. 1st lt. armed Boat Liberty, under his uncle Capt. James Barron. Lost his life near Cape Henry in defense of his vessel, in action with several British privateers. Heirs in 1830: Richard B., Samuel B., Robert, Elizabeth, and Ann Servant, only heirs of Richard B. Servant, only heir of Lt. Richard Servant. LBP.

SERVANT (Scervant), SAMUEL. Entered service June 24, 1777.

SHARPLESS, DR. JOHN. Surgeon, Manley Galley, Aug. 3, 1776. MC II, 301. Warrant to Courtney Sharpless, widow of John Sharpless (Jan. 2, 1790).

SHEARMAN (Sheerman), MARTIN. Midshipman, of Northumberland or of Lancaster Co. LBP John Flynt.

SHEFFIELD, ROBERT. Aud. Acct. XXX, 92.

SHEILD, JOHN. N 8, 31. Lt. marines Nov. 23, 1776.

SHEPHERD, JOHN. H. D. 1834-5, Doc. 48, 17.

SHIELDS, JOHN. Captain marines. (Died before 1784)

SHORT, JOHN. Brig Northampton. Tartar. NBJ, Sept. 3, 1778.

SIBERY, GEORGE. Tempest, Dec. 7, 1779. N 8, 15.

SIMMONDS, JERRY. Brig Jefferson, Dec., 1779, to Jan. 20, 1780. (Maxwell).

SIMMONS, JEREMIAH (Same as foregoing?). Page Galley. LBNB, Feb. 13, 1778.

SIMMONS, RICHARD. LBNB, Dec. 10, 1777.

SIMPSON, ELISHA. Diligence Galley. MC III, 266. In 1833, Leah A. Cannon and Mary Munday, heirs.

SIMPSON (Sampson, Sympson), HANCOCK (Hammock). Accomac Galley. N's Accomack, 21. Coxswain. MC III, 165.

SIMPSON (Sympson), SELATHIAL. Master at Arms. LBP Solomon Powell. MC III, 538. Only heir in 1851: Leah Cameron.

SIMPSON, WM. (brother of Elisha, above). Diligence or Accomac Galley. N's Accomack, 55.

SIMPSON, WM. Cook. LBP Wm. Tunnell.

SIMPSON, WM. Gloucester, in 1777.

SINCLAIR, CAPT. JOHN. In command of the Nicholson in 1777. See Auditor's Papers, Virginia State Archives.

SINCLAIR, THOS. Sailor. NBJ, March 20, 1778.

SINGLETON. Negro. Accomac Galley.

SINGLETON, JOSHUA, of Gloucester Co. Recom. 1st lt., Nov. 26, 1777. Took charge of the Henry Galley, April 8, 1778, a short time before Capt. Westcott commanded her. Lt. Dragon, Sept. 12, 1779. Living in 1835. Pensioner. See also Gloucester Petitions, Dec. 23, 1830. A 6988.

SKINNER, ELISHA. War 5, 185.

SKINNER, CAPT. WM., of Hampton. 1st lt. and then capt. of the Congress, Sept., 1776; served till the ship was dismantled June 1, 1780. Died intestate and without issue. Sisters Peggy, Betsy, Molly, Nancy, and Fanny, and brothers John and Thomas. Peggy md. Thos. Sands; Nancy md. Wm. Moody; Fanny md. Wm. Dobbins; John Skinner md. Frances Lively; Thomas Skinner left five children, all of Elizabeth City Co. Capt. Skinner was lost at sea in January, 1805. See LBP.

SMART, RICHARD. Master's mate. Tempest, Oct. 7, 1779. Ship Gloucester. NBJ, Oct. 9, 1778.

SMART, ROBT. Master's mate. LBP John Flynt.

SMITH, JAMES. Dragon. LBP James Jennings.

SMITH, JOHN. LBP.

SMITH, CAPT. THOMAS WILDRIDGE. NBJ, Oct. 16, 1778.

SMITH, WM. Boatswain, Mosquito. Prisoner in England. MC III, 225.

SMITH, WM. Manley Galley, Sept. 11, 1779. LBNB, Nov. 6, 1777. Discharged Feb. 3, 1780.

SMITH, WM. JR. E 1.

SMITH, WOOLEN. Sailing Master. LBP James Jennings.

SNALE, THOS., of the Borough of Norfolk. Lt., died of cold and exposure in the winter of 1780, after assisting in saving his ship and cargo. Wife Elizabeth (nee Ivy) was living in 1838. USP their only child, Nancy Snale, became the second wife of Wm. Herbert, and left one child, Mary Ann Herbert. William Herbert, by his first wife, nee Godfrey, had a son Thomas, who died in 1825, leaving an only child, Wm. W. Herbert. MC III, 431. Heirs in 1837: Wm. M. Ivey, Thos. I. Ivey, Ann R. Bonny, and Sarah B. Godwin. BH, 1380.

SNEAD (Sneed), ROBT., of Accomac Co. Surgeon, Diligence Galley. Brother Bowden Snead. Thomas Bonnewell md. their sister. USP. MC III, 170. In 1830, John W. Snead, of Beaver Co., Pa., heir. N's Accomack, 22, 23.

SOLOMON, SAMUEL. Voucher, 1787.

SORRELL, CHARLES. On Henry Galley till turned over to the Mosquito.

SORRELL, JAMES. Gunner's mate, Protector. Tartar. LBP, affidavit of Edward Sorrell, of Northumberland Co. USP James Dougherty.

SPAIN (Spann), THOS. Discharged from Henry Galley; unfit for duty. NBJ, April 26, 1777.

SPAT, JOHN. Ex. Coms, 1776.

SPEAKE, JOSEPH, of Charles Co., Md. 1st lt. Safeguard Galley until after July 6, 1779. Appt. to command Boat Nicholson, June 24, 1777. LBNB. Returned home a short time before his marriage in Aug., 1782. Died March 28, 1798. Widow Mrs. Cornelia Speake. USP. In 1834, Eliz. Chunn, surviving daughter, and John A. Mathews, Henrietta Speake, and Joseph Cooksey, only grandchildren. John A. Mathews was the son of Amelia Speake Mathews, and Joseph Henry Cooksey, the son of Charlotte G. Speake Cooksey. Henrietta was another daughter of Lt. Speake. In USP Thos. Speake declared that Joseph Speake commanded the sloop of war Washington.

SPEAKES, LEONIDAS. Safeguard Galley, May 1-June 16, 1777.

SPENCER, ABRAHAM. Carpenter, Jan. 16, 1783.

SPILLMAN, GEORGE. Enlisted at Fredericksburg in Capt. Dick's marines. On Mosquito. LBP Charles DeKay.
SPRATT (Spratts), JOHN. Able Seaman. H. D. 1834–5, Doc. 48, 17.
SPRIGG, ABRAHAM. LBP James Jennings.
SPRIGG (Spriggs), NATHAN. Hero Galley, NBJ, Nov. 4, 1777; Tempest, Oct. 7, 1779. N's Lancaster, 40.
SPRIGGS (Sprigs), ABEL. Mulatto. Deserted from Dragon, Va. Gazette, July 3, 1779.
SPRIGGS, WM. Hero Galley. LBNB, Feb. 13, 1778.
STAFF, WM. Aud. Acct. XVIII, 509.
STANBACK, LITTLEBERRY. Able Seaman. Certificate of James Barron. BH, 1213.
STANDLEY, WM. Safeguard Galley, from March 18 to June, 1777.
STANFORD, REUBEN. Boatswain, Sloop Liberty, Aug., 1777.
STANLEY, MOSES, of Caroline Co. On Mosquito. After imprisonment of 32 months, he escaped along with fifteen other seamen. USP Geo. Catlett. Aged 82 in 1840.
START, DERBY. Aud. Acct. 1779–80, 193.
STEELE, THOMAS. Dragon, Dec. 1, 1778 to Dec. 21.
STEELE, WILLIAM. Lieut. from Aug. 20, 1776 to April 26, 1781. Boat Nicholson, Sept. 15, 1779; Tempest, Oct. 7, 1779. Taken prisoner by Arnold; paroled by Gen. Phillips. Lived in Staunton for a while after the war. Married a widow. Died, Dec. 17, 1792 in the Parish of Orangeburg, S. C. Will names son Wm. Govan Steele; his wife; and an unborn child. In 1838, Wm. G. and I. A. Steele of Charleston, S. C., were the only devisees. LBP and USP.
STEPHENS, JOSEPH. H. D. 1834–5, Doc. 48, 16. (Joseph Stevens, Seaman, War 5, 183).
STEPHENS (Stevens), SIMON. Cook. Diligence Galley, LBP Solomon Powell, 1831. MC III, 264. In 1833, Mary Stephens only heir at law.
STEPHENS, STEPHEN (brother of Simon). Both served on Accomac, one as cook and the other as seaman till galley was laid up. "The galleys were carried across the Bay to be armed, and on their return the men were immediately

enlisted. Among the first were the brothers Stephens."
MC III, 264. In 1833, Mary Stephens only heir at law.

STEVANS, JOHN, of Caroline. Petition of Francis V. Sutton. R. C.

STEVENS, CAPT. JOHN. B. W. R. C. According to affidavit of Wm. White of Caroline Co., he and Stevens were from the same neighborhood; Stevens after serving in the land forces at Gwynn's Island, etc., obtained commission of capt. in Navy; on his return from a voyage to France for ammunition, was taken prisoner as he attempted to get into Charleston, and was held in St. Augustine until Dec., 1779. BH, 1444.

STEVENS, WM. War 5, 183.

STEWART, FRANCIS. Aud. Acct. XXV, 35.

STEWART, GEORGE. Appt. Jan. 10, 1778, Muster Master and Purchasing Agent to Accomac and Diligence Galleys. LBNB. Heirs in 1851–2 James S., Mary Jane, and Sarah Ann Corbin. N's Accomack, 30. BH, 1446.

STEWART, JAMES. Boat Nicholson. NBJ, Feb. 13, 1778.

STEWART, ROBT. LBP Salathiel Simpson. BH, 1446.

STEWART, THOMAS. Sept. 4, 1780. (Maxwell).

STIRES, THOMAS. War 5, 182.

STONE, JOHN. Sergeant Marines. Sloop Congress. LBP Wm. Skinner.

STOTT (Stotts), WM. Boatswain, Safeguard. Died in service. LBP Joshua Johnson.

STOTT, WM., of Northampton Co. N's Northampton, 29, 35. B 451, 1344.

STOTT, WM. Ship Gloucester.

STRATTON, HENRY. Lt. marines, Henry Galley, Oct. 20, 1776; 2d lt. Hero, 1776, commanding, Sept. 14, 1777, LBNB, Dec. 5, 1777. In 1779, in command of the Schooner Alliance, captured in 1780 off the Virginia Capes. H. D. Oct. 17, 1792. B, 685, 1244.

STRATTON, THOMAS. Lt. Safeguard Galley, May 4, 1776, C. S. Resigned Aug. 25, 1778, NBJ.

STROTHER, BENJAMIN, son of Anthony and Behethland (Storke) Strother. Born on June 25, 1750 in Fredericksburg; md. Catherine Price; died in Jefferson Co., Oct. 22, 1807. 1st midshipman of the Tempest. Recruiting at Frazer's Ferry. According to Nath. Craghill, of Jefferson Co., Midshipman Strother was "an active officer performing a great deal of duty and business on board the ship to which he belonged." LBP. He was later in the land service. USP. In 1832 heirs: Catherine Crane, Margaret Moore, Mary S. Duffield, John Strother, and "the present representatives of Elizabeth Pendleton, decd". [Catherine Thornton Nicklin, Benj. Strother Pendleton, and James W. Pendleton.]

See the Genealogy of the Strother Family, by Major John Bailey Calvert Nicklin in Tyler's Quarterly, Vol. XI, p. 113. Col. Benjamin Patten Nicklin, U. S. A. is the representative of Midshipman Benjamin Strother, in the Society of the Cincinnati in the State of Virginia.

STUART, FRANCIS. (See "Francis Stewart" above). H. D. 1834-5, Doc. 48, 17.

STUBBLEFIELD, PETER. Lt. in Capt. Gabriel Jones' marines, NBJ, Sept. 10, 1776.

STUBBS, JOHN, of Gloucester County. Midshipman. Tempest. Appointed lt., Feb. 21, 1778. Entered service late in 1776. In the R. C. of the heirs of John Stubbs is found an affidavit of Henry Buchanan, setting forth that he was well acquainted with John Stubbs of Gloucester, and that the said John Stubbs was a lt. in the Virginia State Navy on board the Henry Galley commanded by Capt. Robert Tompkins, and that the said Stubbs served till the vessel was laid up or dismantled in the year 1781 and that he never resigned his station. In R. C., 1847-48 "The representatives of John Stubbs respectfully represent that he was a midshipman in the Navy of Virginia during the war of the Revolution and attached to the ship Tempest. He entered the service in the latter part of the year 1776; he quitted sometime in September, 1781".

On Jan. 24, 1849, Arthur Emerson, Clerk of the Court of Norfolk County, wrote: "The Court doth certify upon satisfactory evidence** that John Stubbs who was a midshipman in the Virginia State Navy **died in 1788, leaving six children: viz., Thomas, William, James C., Samuel, John, and Elizabeth Stubbs.

Thomas, William, and James C. died, each of them leaving no children and leaving their brothers Samuel and John and sister Elizabeth their heirs at law. John Stubbs (son of John Senr) died leaving three children, Elizabeth, Francis, and Cykey his heirs at law.

That Samuel Stubbs died leaving seven children, viz: John S. Stubbs, Thomas W. Stubbs, S. S. Stubbs, Sarah DeNeufville, Mary Booker, Frances Clarke, and Samuel N. Stubbs. That Elizabeth Stubbs (daughter of John Stubbs senr) married Edmund Borum and died leaving five children, viz: Samuel S. Borum, John S. Borum, Frances Mathews, Elizabeth Brown and Mary Roberts her heirs at law. The Court therefore certifies that Elizabeth, Franklin and Cykey Stubbs (children of John Stubbs Junr decd), John S. Stubbs, Thomas W. Stubbs, Sarah Deneufville, Mary Booker, Frances Clarke, and Samuel N. Stubbs (children of Samuel Stubbs deceased), Samuel S. Borum, John S. Borum, Frances Mathews, Elizabeth Brown and Mary Roberts, children of Elizabeth Brown aforesaid are the heirs at law of John Stubbs senr deceased as aforesaid."

But see also claims of another John Stubbs' heirs, BH, 1212. John S. Stubbs, son of Samuel Stubbs, md. Stella L. H. Armistead, dau. of Dr. Robert Alexander Armistead, of Mecklenburg Co. and later of Portsmouth, Va., and had: Anne Wright Stubbs md. Col. Wm. H. Stewart, issue; Mary S. Stubbs (second dau. of John S. Stubbs) md. the Rev. Wm. Gould Woodbridge, M. A., D. D., and had issue: William Witherspoon Woodbridge md. Pearl Logan, issue: Mary Charlotte Woodbridge, Martha Winifred W. Baunsgard, Jean Woodbridge Grant, and Wm. W. Woodbridge Jr., of Seattle, Washington.

STUBBS, John. Seaman. N 8, 15.

STURDIVANT, CAPT. JOEL, of Dinwiddie Co. C. J. 1776–1777, 9. Died in service. BH, 449.

STURDIVANT, JOHN. Recom. lt. Manley Galley, Sept. 8, 1777, NBJ. Resigned April 24, 1779. See LBP John Griffin.

STURDIVANT, LEWIS. Manley Galley, Sept. 1779, LBNB, Jan. 3, 1777.
STURRS (Sturr), THOS. Voucher, 1783.
SULLIVANT, JOHN. Dragon, June 15, 1778 to Jan. 20, 1779.
SUMMERS, GAWIN. N 8, 12.
SUMMERSON, GAVIN. Gloucester Galley. NBJ, Oct. 9, 1778.
SUMMERSON, GEORGE. Lt. (?) Appointed by C. S., 1776. Lewis (first row galley). NBJ, Aug. 25, 1778.
SWAN, EDWARD, of Maryland. Deserted from the Dragon.
SWIFT, PHILIP. Dragon, May 3, 1777 to Jan. 20, 1779.
SWOPE, JOHN. Lieut. Dragon, Oct. 7, 1777.
SWOPE, JOHN. Surgeon, Sept. 2, 1779. See VSR, July 30, 1930, p. 29. USP. Liberty & Galley Henry. Died in Nansemond Co., Jan. 1, 1793. Served to Nov. 30, 1781. Walter Swope (of Philadelphia in 1846), late of Gloucester Co., N. J., one of the heirs at law.

T

TANKERSLEY, BENJ. War 5, 195.
TANKERSLEY, JOHN. War 5, 195.
TAPER (Tapore), JOHN. Hero Galley, NBJ, Oct. 24, 1778. N's Lancaster, 30.
TAPSCOTT, EZEKIAL, of Lancaster Co. Dragon, March 19, 1777 to Jan. 20, 1780. LBP James Jennings.
TAPSCOTT, JOHN, of Lancaster Co. Dragon. LBP Wm. Jennings.
TARLICK, JOHN. Dragon, Sept. 2, 1779.
TARPLEY (Tapley), THOS. Hero Galley, NBJ, Nov. 4, 1777; Boat Nicholson, Oct. 27, 1778.
TARPLEY, WM. Hero Galley, NBJ, Nov. 4, 1777; Boat Nicholson, Oct. 27, 1778, NBJ.
TATE, JESSE. Dragon, Sept. 19, 1777 to Jan. 20, 1779.
TATE, ROBT. Certificate, John Markham.
TATUM, THOS. Carpenter's Mate. H. D. 1834-5, Doc. 48, 18.
TAYLOR, ANIS. War 5, 195.
TAYLOR, AYRES, of Accomac Co. Accomac Galley. Will probated June 21, 1821. See N's Accomack, 66.

Taylor, Benjamin, of Orange Co. (born Nov. 11, 1759, eleventh son of George Taylor). Midshipman on vessels commanded by his brother Richard. Tartar, Oct. 10, 1777. LBP, John Flynt. Never married.

Taylor, Daniel. Accomac Galley. BH, 689. N's Accomack, 55.

Taylor, Giles. Heirs, N's Accomack, 67, 71.

Taylor, Jabez (Jaybee, Jabua). Boatswain on Accomac. N's Accomack, 60.

Taylor, Jesse. NBJ, Sept. 10, 1778.

Taylor, John, of Orange Co. (born Jan. 27, 1751, seventh son of George Taylor of Orange Co.). Midshipman, Aug. 13, 1777; promoted 1t. Aug. 13, 1777; captured by the British, and died in the old Jersey prison ship at New York, Jan. 6, 1781. Served under his brother, Capt. Richard Taylor.

Taylor, John. Clerk of the Navy. Aud. Acct. XIII, 15.

Taylor, John, of Northumberland Co. Deserted from Tartar, Va. Gazette, Sept. 11, 1779.

Taylor, Major. Marine, Jan. 20, 1783.

Taylor, Michael. N 8, 15, 35.

Taylor, Capt. Richard, of James City Co. This claim by heirs was rejected on the ground that there was but one Capt. Taylor in the Navy.

Taylor, Capt. Richard. Sixth son of George Taylor of Orange; born Jan. 6, 1749. Captain of the Schooner Hornet in Sept., 1776; captain of the Tartar; commanded a squadron; captured several British vessels; was twice wounded, the last time so severely that he had to withdraw from the service, June 19, 1779. Operated on late in 1779, by Dr. Wellford. Died Aug. 30, 1825. Will recorded in Oldham Co., Ky. USP. In 1833 grandchildren: Richard Taylor Robertson; Eliza Robertson md. Thos. K. Byrne; Mary Ann Robertson md. James B. Anderson; great-grandson, Richard Taylor Jacob (John J. Jacob, guardian, Jefferson Co., Ky.) H. D. Oct. 30, 1792.

Taylor, Severn. Accomac Galley. N's Accomack, 35.

Taylor, Capt. Thomas, of Accomac Co. Accomac Galley. Protector Galley.

TAYLOR, THOMAS. Seaman. Of Accomac Co. LBP Wm. Tunnell. BH, 716.

TAYLOR, TIMOTHY. Midshipman, Brig Liberty, May 11 to July, 1776; July 30, 1777. LBP George Rogers.

TEACKLE, JOHN. Paymaster. Diligence and Accomac Galleys. LBP Solomon Powell.

TEMBLIN, WM. Tempest, Oct. 7, 1777.

TEMPLE, ALEXANDER. Dragon, from July 31, 1778 to Jan. 29, 1779. MC II, 145.

TEMPLE, HUMPHREY. Mate Thetis. BH, 1049.

TEMPLE, SAMUEL. Boat Liberty, Nov. 1779.

TENNANT (Tenant), JAMES. Master, Norfolk Revenge. Commissioned July 12, 1776. Recommended 1st Lt. Jan. 1777. LBNB.

TERRANT, CESAR. Pilot. LBP. Dr. David Brown, affidavit James Burke: "During the action between Commodore Taylor (of the Patriot) and a British privateer at the South of the Capes of Virginia he steered the Patriot during the whole action and behaved gallantly. Taylor was wounded by getting his thigh broken." Terrant entered service in 1776 or 1777, and served till capture of Yorktown. BH, 1219.

TERRELL, WM. Safeguard. March 1 to June 18, 1777.

THARP, ———. Dragon. NBJ, Sept. 3, 1778.

THATCHER, WM. Dragon, March 30, 1778 to Jan. 20, 1779. Died in service. N's Lancaster, 23, 24.

THETWOOD, ISAAC. Dragon. B, 1332.

THOMAS, CHARLES CAPTAIN, of Nansemond County. B. W. 25 Feb., 1834 Wright Carney stated that his father Wright Carney (commander of Letters of Marque in the Revolution), of Norfolk County, speaking of events of the war and persons engaged therein, mentioned Capt. Charles Thomas as "having command of a vessel in the Navy", and also of the hostility of the British and Tories towards Capt. Thomas and other prominent individuals in his neighborhood. The enemy made many unsuccessful efforts to take Capt. Thomas. They burned his home and destroyed his property. Thomas served from 1778 to 1781, sometimes as captain of the

Ropewalk at Warwick and sometimes as captain of a vessel. According to the testimony of Wm. Duval of Buckingham in 1834, Capt. Thomas was "well acquainted with such Cordage & Cable Rope as sailed our Navy."

His will, dated May 24, 1785, was probated June 11, 1787 (copy in LBP). Names wife Ann: seven children: John, James, Charles, Ezekial (who left two children, Martha J. Bernard and Henry Thomas), Tolvin, Lydia, and Elizabeth md. Ezekial Powell, and left Nancy Beaman and Susan Kelly.

THOMAS, CORNELIUS. H. D. Oct. 1795, 16, 60. Carpenter. Cornelius Thomas, heir.

THOMAS, DANIEL. Dragon, Jan. 23, 1777 to June 16, 1777.

THOMAS, HUMPHREY. War 5, 196.

THOMAS, FRANK. Tempest, Dec. 7, 1779.

THOMAS, JAMES. Testimony of James Barron, Jr. Thomas a "man of colour late of the Borough of Norfolk, who served through the War in the Capacity of Boatswain, with exemplary conduct, as I had frequent opportunities of witnessing it. In the year 1779 he served as a Boatswain of the Brig Northampton (originally commanded by Capt. Francis Bright). He was a fellow of daring and though a man of color was respected by all the officers who served with him." Petition of Nancy Bell, of Norfolk Co., a "free woman of colour", daughter of James Thomas, "a free man of Colour".

THOMAS, JAMES. Boatswain. BH, 1216.

THOMAS, JAMES. Seaman. H. D. 1834-5, Doc. 48, 18.

THOMAS, CAPT. JOHN, of Nansemond Co. He was buried on Mason Creek, adjoining Wm. Langley's plantation. He is said to have died about July 1, 1796, and left a widow Elizabeth (nee Gordon), and three children William, Mary, and Ann. In R. C. there is much information concerning his descendants.

THOMAS, CAPT. JOHN, of Northumberland C. H., by birth an Englishman according to the supposition of Chas. Broadwater (died July 1, 1796). 2d lt. Ship Congress, 1st lt. Protector Galley, which was destroyed by the British in Great Wicomico. After this Thomas and his men were transferred to the Dragon. One affiant stated that Capt. Thomas went to France on a ship commanded by Capt. Blackwell, and was bringing one of the prizes to the U. S., when the ship was wrecked on the shoals of Cape Hatteras. He retired about Jan. 24, 1780. "A devoted Patriot". In 1832 Wm. Thomas of the county of Alexandria, and Thomas Thomas were his heirs. USP.

THOMPSON, AMBROSE. Tempest, Oct. 7, 1779.

THOMPSON, CHARLES. Resigned 2d lt. Capt. Davis's marines and succeeded by James Bankhead, Sept. 30, 1776.

THOMPSON, JAMES. H. D. 1834–5, Doc. 48, p. 17.

THOMPSON, ROBT. Aud. Acct. 1780, 80.

THORN, JAMES. N 8, 11.

THORNTON, CHARLES. Resigned lt. marines, Capt. Dick's company, Oct. 30, 1776. NBJ.

THORP, JAMES. Safeguard Galley, June 16, 1776. R. C., of Thos. J. Thorp, George W. Thorp, and Hawkins C. Thorp, of Louisville, Ky.

THORP, WM., of Caroline Co. Seaman, Mosquito. He and George Catlett made their escape from Fortune Jail by bribing the jailer, then took a little boat, and got to France: returned to America in the spring of 1781.

THRALL (Throll), JOHN, of Lancaster Co. Enlisted as midshipman, Jan. 22, 1776, and served as such to May 4, 1778; and as lt. till July 8, 1779. Resigned. Certificate, Jesse George. MC II, 235.

THWING, JOHN. Hero Galley, Nov. 4, 1777. LBNB, Feb. 13, 1778.

TIMBERLAKE, RICHARD, of Lancaster Co. Deserted from Tartar, Va. Gazette, Sept. 11, 1779. But see Doc. 48, p. 18, 1834–5.

TIVY, THOMAS. N. A. B.

TOBEY, THOMAS. Accomac Galley.

TODROW, JOHN. N 8, 15.

TOM. Negro. War 5, 196.

TOM. A Negro. Ordinary Seaman. Doc. 48, p. 18, 1834–5.

TOMLINSON, JOHN. War 5, 196.

TOMLINSON, WM. War 5, 196.

TOMPKINS, CHRISTOPHER. 2d lt. Henry Galley, 1776: also Nov. 1, 1777. Resigned Jan. 14, 1779. Captain. LBP Wm. Mitchell, etc. MC II, 315; III, 189. In 1831, Ann D. Shirley, granddaughter and sole heiress at law. USP. He md. March 13, 1783 Martha ——, who later md. Oney Dameron, of Norfolk in July, 1796. Mrs. Dameron's will, dated Oct. 29, 1842, mentions her son-in-law David Duncan, of Randolph-Macon College and her son-in-law Oney S. Dameron.

TOMPKINS, CAPT. ROBERT, of Gloucester Co. Superintended the building of the Henry Galley and became her captain in June, 1776. According to the testimony of Henry Buchanan, Capt. Tompkins continued in the service until the British fleet came up in York river in August, 1781, which prevented the gallies from rendering any effectual service. Another affidavit states that he died in service. Heir, his son Christopher. MC III, 323. In 1834, sole heir, Ann D. Tompkins md. Ambrose Shirley. See Kentucky Year Book, 1895, p. 86. Elsewhere James V. Tompkins is referred to as an heir.

TOMPSON, AMBROSE. Brig Jefferson, Dec., 1779-Jan., 1780. LBNB. Tempest, Dec. 7, 1779.

TOOL, RICHARD. Gunner, Henry Galley. The petition of Elizabeth Caston, granddaughter, stated that her grandfather entered service in 1778. Sarah, widow of Richard, petitioned in 1794. BH, 1994. He died on the Galley Henry in Feb., 1778.

TOOLEIK (Toolick), JOHN. Dragon. LBP James Jennings.

TOPMAN, JOHN. N 8, 12.

TOOLES, SAML. Lt. C. J. 1776, 137. Captain of the Schooner Revenge (galley) vice Dean appointed Superintendent of Shipbuilding.

TOWNSEND, JACOB. Cook, Safeguard Galley, March 1-June 14, 1777. LBNB.

TOWNSEND, THOMAS. Accomac Galley.

TOWNSEND, THOS. Accomac Galley.

TRAKAS (Traks), NICHOLAS. H. D. 1833-4, Doc. 33, 17.

TRAVIS, CHAMPION. Member Navy Board.

TRAVIS, EDWARD. Captain, April, 1776, Manley Galley. Capt. Brig Raleigh, captured by the enemy. Commanded at times the ship Thetis and the Tartar. USP. Capt. Edward Travis lived later on Jamestown Island. He died in 1784 while on the way to the Virginia Springs. He left a son Joseph Hutchings Travis, and a postumous son, Edward, was born shortly after his death. Joseph H. Travis lived in Brunswick Co., but spent much time on his estate in King William Co. Edward Travis lived at one time in Mecklenburg Co., but later removed to Tenn. In USP is found a copy of the will of Capt. Travis, March 28, 1784; probated, James City Co., June 13, 1784. His executors were his two brothers, Champion and John Travis, John Coles and John Tucker. His widow md. Mordecai Booth, Esq. BH, 1448.

TRIPLETT, DANIEL (son of John Triplett and his wife nee Popham). Lt. Sloop Congress. Safeguard Galley, June 6, 1777. LBP Wm. Skinner. "A brave and meritorious officer", declared Peter Triplett, "thought highly of by Gen. Washington."

TRIPLETT, GEORGE. Lt. marines early in 1776; then went into the infantry.

TRIPLETT, PETER, of Culpeper. "In 1776 Peter Triplett was on the Congress; in 1778, in Gibson's 1st Va. Regiment; later on Congress again." Living in 1840, aged 88.

TRIPLETT, REUBEN, of Prince William Co., near the Loudoun line. Sailed early in 1776 from Alexandria as a marine on the Liberty, commanded by Walter Brooke. Peter Triplett attested he saw Reuben Triplett in Philadelphia during the war.

TROOP, WM. Sloop Liberty, Aug., 1777.

TUCKER, SILAS. Master. LBP John Flynt. MC II, 363.

TULIE (Tarlick), JOHN. Dragon, Feb. 7, 1777-Jan. 20, 1779.

TULLY, MATHEW. Dragon, June 25, 1777, to Jan. 24, 1778. Discharged by Navy Board. BH, 1048.

TUMBLIN, WILLIAM. Brig Jefferson, Dec., 1779-Jan. 20, 1780.

TUNNELL (Tunnells), JAMES, of Accomac County. Accomac Galley. N's Accomack, 61, 70.

Tunnell, Joseph (died 1788), of Accomac County. Accomac Galley. BH, 742.

Tunnell, William. 3d Mate, Accomac Galley. Seaman. BH, 1219.

Tunnell, William. Quartermaster, Accomac Galley. In LBP, 1833, Elkanah Andrews made affidavit that he was well acquainted with William Tunnell, Joseph Tunnell, William Riggs, Geo. B. Riggs, Laban Marriner, Wm. Miles, Elisha Madrid, Miles Northern, Elijah Rose, Thomas Taylor, Thomas Townsend, George Becket, James Collens, Stephen Collens, Daniel Taylor, Severn Taylor, Ayres Taylor, Spencer Wartens, John White, Thomas Hastens, Daniel Lewis, Jacob Phillips, James Warrington, James Tunnell, and Joseph Webb. B, 1263.

Tupman, John. Sailing Master. Manley Galley, Oct. 6, 1778. NBJ, Sept. 11, 1779. Tartar from Nov., 1779 to Jan., 1780. USP. Resident of Westmoreland Co. In April, 1798, went on a ship to the West Indies and all hands lost (one affidavit affirms that he died in 1801). Heirs in 1832: John Tupman, of Adair County, Ky., and Nancy Settles (nee Tupman). The latter had issue: Louisa md. John Clarke; Matilda md. Thos. Smith; Emily md. Thos. Stubbs; Sally md. Sansy Stubbs.

Turlington, Laban. H. D. 1834–5, Doc. 48, 18.

Turner, John. On cruise in the Brig Liberty in 1777. See petition of John Paul. H. D. Oct. 16, 1792.

Turpin, John, of Northampton Co. Midshipman, Manley Galley, March 9, 1777; Sept., 1778. MC III, 538. Heirs in 1851: John S. Turpin, Eliz. S. Walker, and Ann W. Turpin. Master. N. 8, 33. BW. N's Northampton 33.

Turpin, Scott. N 8, 17.

Tutt, James. Midshipman, Dragon, June 25, 1777 to Jan. 24, 1778. LBP James Jennings. In Culpeper petition, Feb. 1, 1822, James Tutt stated that he entered the Revolutionary service as a private in the marine corps, and when this branch was disbanded he joined the 2d regiment of Va. troops as a cadet under Capt. Thos. Minor. He was marched to Williamsburg, where, meeting Capt. Callender of the Dragon, he was prevailed upon to transfer to the naval service, in which he was appointed a midshipman. BH, 1048. James Tutt's dau. Ellen md. a Mr. Spillman, and his dau. Polly md. Silas Hickman, of Morgan Co., Ohio.

TYGER, MAN. LBP James Jennings. Dragon.

TYLER, HENRY, of Prince William Co. (will proved Sept. 5, 1820). Midshipman, Tempest, 1779. Did not return home until after the siege of York. In 1834, Alice P. Tyler and Mary Ann Baird (wife of Thomas E. Baird), children of Thos. G. Tyler, of Stafford Co., brother of Henry Tyler, of Prince William, sole heirs of Henry Tyler, midshipman.

U

UMPHRIES, JAMES. Dragon, May 12, 1776, to Nov. 4, 1778. Died in service.

UMPHRIES, SAMUEL. Dragon, Aug. 12, 1777, to Jan. 20, 1779.

UMPRESS, ROBT. Sailor, Sloop Liberty, Aug., 1777.

UNDERHILL (Undrill), CAPT. WILLIAM. Recommended to command Accomac Galley, Oct. 16, 1777. LBP Dr. Robt. Snead. MC III, 164. Heirs in 1830 Thomas Underhill and Elizabeth Trader, wife of Farrar Trader, of Philadelphia. N's Accomack, 24, 27.

V

VALENTINE, CAPT. JACOB, of Princess Anne Co. His marines ordered to the Manley Galley in 1776, from the Mosquito. Lost an eye at Valley Forge from catching a violent cold. See H. D., Oct. 1793, p. 33. Died in the summer of 1811. See statement of Elizabeth Ogg in Norfolk Order Book, Nov. 24, 1834, p. 417. Capt. Valentine had two sons, Edward and Jacob.

VASEY, JAMES. LBP.

VASEY, PETER. Dragon. WBP James Jennings.

W

WADDY, SHAPLEIGH (Sharpley), of Northumberland Co. Midshipman. Cadet, Protector Galley, March 21, 1778, NBJ. BH, 1221.

WALKER, JAMES. Accomac Galley. MC III, 264. In 1833, Mary Melson, only heir at law. N's Accomack, 50. B, 244.

WALKER, JOHN, of Accomac Co. Hero Galley, NBJ, Nov. 4, 1777.

WALKER, JOHN, of Northumberland Co. Dragon, Va. Gazette, July 3, 1779. R. C.

WALKER, JOSEPH. N's Accomack, 54.

WALL (or Well), JOSEPH. Tempest, Dec. 7, 1779.

WALLACE, ROGER. Ordinary seaman. H. D. 1834-5, Doc. 48, 19.

WALLACE, WILSON. Brig Jefferson, Dec. 20, 1779 to Jan. 20, 1780.

WALLACE, WILLIAM, of Norfolk Co. Caswell Galley. According to the testimony of William Creekmur, he was a sailor under Capt. Willis Wilson, and continued through the war. MC III, 179. Heirs in 1831 William, Cary, and Joseph Wallace, Lucretia (?) Willey. and Rebecca Garrett.

William Wallace has many descendants, including the Wallaces of Wallaceton, Norfolk Co., Va., the Garretts of Norfolk Co., Norfolk, and Berkley, and the late Col. Wm. H. Stewart and R. E. B. Stewart, of Portsmouth, and Charles A. Stewart, of East Falls Church, Va.

WALLAGE (Wallace), EDWARD. Boatswain's Mate. H. D. 1832, Doc. 33.

WALLAT, DANIEL. Ex. Coms. 1776.

WALLEN, JAMES. N 8, 17.

WALLER, EDMUND, Lieut. Marines (Capt. Dick) vice Bankhead resigned. Later Major in land service. B, 1241.

WALLER, JAMES. Boat Liberty.

WALTER, JOHN. Hero Galley. LBNB, Nov. 4, 1777.

WALTERS (Waters ?), ISAAC. LBP.

WALTERS, SPENCER. See N's Accomack, 61.

WARD, JOHN WYATT. Able Seaman. H. D. 1834-5, Doc. 48, 19.
WARWICK, JOSEPH. Pilot's mate of the Mosquito.
WARRINGTON, JAMES. Accomac Galley. Doc. 48, 14, 1834-5.
WARRINGTON, STEPHEN. Quartermaster, Accomac Galley. See N's Northampton, 14 and BH, 1431.
WARTON (Wharton), JOHN, Boatswain. LBP Wm. White.
WASHINGTON,—. H. D. 1833, Doc. 33.
WATER (Waters, or Watters), ISAAC, Boatswain's mate. LBP John Flynt. MC III, 172. In 1831 Thomas and Sally Waters, heirs. N's Accomack, 32.
WATERMAN, JAMES. War 5, 215.
WATERS, ISAAC. N 8, 6.
WATERS, JAMES. War 5, 211.
WATERS, SAMUEL. Aud. Acct. XVIII, 144.
WATKINS, GEORGE, Pilot. "Acted with Honour" during the whole war. Capt. George Ralls stated that Watkins set out with him from Hampton, on the Schooner Jenny, and was appointed pilot on Feb. 17, 1777. B, 193.
WATKINS, JAMES. Able Seaman. H. D. 1834-35. Doc. 48, 18.
WATKINS, JAMES. Lt. Served three years. BH, 856.
WATKINS, WILLIAM. Marine, 20 July, 1783.
WATKINS, WILLIAM (died circa 1791), Pilot. Served three years. According to the affidavit of his daughter, Mary Servant: "while serving on board of the boat Patriot or Liberty commanded by one of the Barrons he received a severe wound in the ankle and when he recovered from the wound he received a lieutenant's commission and continued to the end of the war." "The uniform of her father worn in the Revolution remained in the family many years as also did the ball which was extracted from his ankle." He was treated by Dr. McClurg. He had two brothers in the naval service. Capt. James Watkins (Lieut. James, above ?), the vessel under his command having been captured and carried into the port of Charleston by a British cruiser, died there a prisoner. The other brother George, a pilot in the Virginia State Navy, died sometime after the war,:— Testimony of Jeremiah (X) Cain. July 18, 1834. B, 857.

William Watkins, Lieut. H. D. 1834 Doc. 35, 12.

WATSON, JOHANNES. Recommended Oct. 16, 1777, LBNB. Captain Diligence Galley. NBJ. Resigned July 24, 1779. In October, 1822, Bloxsam heirs. See N's Accomack 10 and BH, 1237.

WATSON, CASTILLO (Castileo). War 5, 214.

WATSON, THOMAS. N 8, 40.

WATTS, SAMUEL. Lewis Galley, LBNB, Feb. 13, 1778. Tempest, June 19, 1778; NBJ. Luke Ashburn made affidavit that he served three years on the Page Galley; he knew Watts well on the Lewis Galley in 1776; that the latter was still there when he (Ashburn) left.

WEAVER, AARON. Princess Anne Pets., Jan. 3, 1812.

WEAVER, ELISHA. Aud. Acct. XV, 610.

WEAVER, ELIJAH, of Lancaster County. On Dragon or Tempest. Served three years. Testimony of a single witness in 1834—a neighbor Richard Nickin, who spent half his time on the Dragon and half on the Tempest.

WEBB, FOSTER, JR. Appt. paymaster and muster master for eastern side of Chesapeake, Feb. 18, 1778. George Webb, Esq., security.

WEBB, FRANCIS, born 1759, son of James Webb and his wife Mary (Smith) Webb, of Essex Co., Va. Midshipman of the Dragon. LBP and USP.

"[Francis Webb] went on board a private armed vessel (a privateer ?). This was about the commencement of the Revolutionary War. He was only about 16. Every one on their little craft was either killed or wounded but their Captain John Evans and a negro boy. My father was shot in the ankle, which caused one of his legs to be shorter than the other. Although they were all so disabled, they managed to save their vessel. For his gallantry he received the appointment of midshipman in the Virginia Navy, and was stationed on board the Ship 'Dragon', where he served the principal part of the Revolutionary War." MS of Midshipman Webb's son John Webb.

Midshipman Francis Webb md. in 1786 Frances Walker, (B. 1764-D. 1809). He removed to Hancock Co., Georgia in 1810, and there died the following year. They had among issue: James Webb and John Webb. For Family History, see Tyler's Quarterly, VII, and "The Webb and Allied Families" by J. Adger Stewart, Esq., of Louisville, Ky., who is the representative of Midshipman Webb in the Society of the Cincinnati in the State of Virginia.

WEBB, JAMES. Hero Galley, NBJ, Nov. 4, 1777; Feb. 13, 1778; Tempest, Oct. 7, 1779.

WEBB, JAMES, of Elizabeth City Co., Pilot. Living in 1838. See R. C. of Wm. Ham.

WEBB, JOHN. Appointed Aug. 16, 1779 paymaster and muster master of the Navy in the room of Foster Webb, Jr. resigned. He was also clothier to the Navy. See H. D. Feb. 28, 1784, p. 225. And Hanover Petitions, Nov. 22, 1787.

WEBB, JOPLEY (Tarpley ?). N 8, 18.

WEBB, JOSEPH. Accomac Galley. N's Accomack, 64. MC II, 173.

WEBB, LEWIS. Lt. marines with Capt. Hardyman, on the Cormorant.

WEBB, ROBERT, Pilot. Accomac Galley. Lived near where galleys were launched. Died about the time the Accomac was laid up. LBP Wm. White. MC III, 171. Heirs in 1831: Betsey Young, Jonathan Young, Thorowgood and Sarah Ann Young, children of Wm. Young, brother of Betsey and Jonathan.

WEBB, TARPLEY, of Lancaster Co. Tempest, Dec. 7, 1779.

WELCH, PATRICK. War 5, 215.

WELTON, JAMES. Safeguard Galley, March 1—June 3, 1777.

WEST, JAMES. Page Galley. Dragon, Jan. 20, 1779, NBJ, Sept. 10, 1778.

WEST, JOHN. Page Galley. LBNB, Feb. 13, 1778.

WESTCOTT, WRIGHT, Captain of the "Potomack" (Scorpion), Dec. 1776. After the Revenge Galley was sunk Westcott commanded the Henry. One of the retained officers of the Virginia Navy. He was guardian and near relative of Stephen Wright, who started with him to Martinique; they were captured by the Cerberus and thrown into prison.

Among the other prisoners were Lt. John Crew and Joseph Marshall, the Sailing Master, USP. Capt Westcott died Feb. 1, 1784. His daughter Fanny Davidson was his only heir.

WHALE, JOHN. Dragon, March 30, 1778 to Jan. 20, 1779.

WHARTON (Whorton), JOHN, of the Parish of Kingston, Gloucester County. Boatswain, on Henry Galley in York River. Served three years. BH, 759.

WHARTON, PHILIP. Lewis Galley. LBNB, Feb. 1, 1778.

WHITE, GALEN (Galin). War 4, 403.

WHITE, JACOBUS, of Accomac County. Carpenter, Diligence Galley. Served three years. BH, 760–761. See also N's Accomack p. 22. MC III, 176.

WHITE, JAMES. Marine. Jan 26, 1780.

WHITE, JOHN. Henry Galley, 1776. Brig Northampton. NBJ, 10 Sept., 1778.

WHITE, JOHN. Accomac Galley.

WHITE, JOHN. Dragon. Sept. 2, 1779.

WHITE, JOHN. Surgeon's Mate. Accomac Galley. N's Accomack, 29, 60.

WHITE, JOSEPH, Master Pilot. According to the affidavit of Henry Nuttall. Joseph White was pilot of the Liberty in 1777; they captured a ship bound from Liverpool to Quebec laden with Naval Stores, and brought her into Little York. About 1780 White went in a Letter of Marque to St. Eustatia, which port Rodney had a short time previously taken possession of and kept the Dutch flag flying to decoy the Americans. White was thus captured and died there in prison.

J. Murdaugh testified that White had a son in Portsmouth, Virginia. LBP, heirs in 1833, Jane and Richard White.

WHITE, ROBERT. Midshipman (?). N's Accomack, 29, 69, and 88. MC III, 449.

WHITE, WM. Surgeon's mate. Died in Worcester Co., Md. (will, 1821). MC III, 171. Heirs in 1831: Littleton S. and Eliza H. White. N's Accomack, 21.

WHITE, WM. Marine, Jan. 16, 1783.

WHITE, WM. One Wm. White is said to have been sent to France, and on his return was made a prisoner, when trying to get into Charleston.
WHITE, WM. S. Surgeon's mate. N's Accomack, 29.
WHITEHEAD, JOHN. LBP.
WHITEHEAD, SAMUEL, of Princess Anne Co. Able Seaman. H. D. 1834–5, Doc. 48, 19.
WHITFIELD, HAINS. Certif. James Barron.
WHITFIELD, HAISIAS. Aud. Acct. XVIII, 435.
WHITFIELD, HARRIS. War 4, 211.
WHITEHURST, JOHN. H. D. 1833–4, Doc. 33.
WHITING, HENRY. In LBP John Archer, Mrs. Ann Payne attested that a Harry Whiting was lt. on the Brig Liberty at the time it was captured.
WHITT, RICHARD. Dragon, May 20, 1777 to June 4. Discharged for bad behaviour.
WHORTON, JOHN. War 5, 213.
WILDER (Willder), GEORGE, of Northumberland County. Able Seaman. Dragon, March 30, 1778–Jan. 20, 1779. Honorable discharge by Capt. Markham.
WILDER (Wilders), JAMES. War 5, 209.
WILES, REUBEN, of Princess Anne County. LBP, Wm. Forest. H. D. 1834–35, Doc. 49, p. 19. Caswell and Washington Galleys. Norfolk Co. Petition.
WILKERSON, WILLIAM. Manley Galley, Sept. 11, 1779; Tempest, Dec. 7, 1779. N 8, 15, 17.
WILKINS, JOHN. Henry Galley. April 8, 1778. Tempest, Oct. 7, 1779.
WILKINS, NATHANIEL. Dec. 7, 1779.
WILKINSON, Stephen. Henry Galley, 1776. Mosquito, 1776. LBNB, Nov. 1, 1777.
WILKINSON, WILLIAM. Manley Galley, Sept. 11, 1779.
WILL. Negro. N 8, 10.
WILLETT, DANIEL P. Steward. Dec. 1779; Jan. 20, 1780. LBNB.
WILLIAM THE DUTCHMAN, Sloop Liberty, Aug. 1777. (Auditor's Papers.)
WILLIAMS, JAMES. Henry Galley. Nov. 1, 1777.

WILLIAMS, JAMES. Boy. Sloop Liberty, Aug. 1777. (Auditor's Papers.)

WILLIAMS, JOHN. In the Virginia State Archives is a rejected claim of one William Williams of Scott County, Ky., who represented himself to be the son of a John Williams, officer in the Virginia Navy.

WILLIAMS, JOHN, of Elizabeth City County. Pilot. Served three years. BH, 777.

WILLIAMS, JOHN. Mosquito, 1776.

WILLIAMS, JOHN. Henry Galley.

WILLIAMS, JOHN. Manley Galley. NBJ, Nov. 5, 1776.

WILLIAMS, JOHN. Hero Galley, to take charge, Dec. 5, 1776. NBJ, Nov. 4, 1777.

WILLIAMS, JOSHUA. Caswell and Washington Galleys, Feb. 13, 1778 to April 3, 1779. Norfolk Co. Petition, 1794. James Williams, claimant.

WILLIAMS, MEREDITH. Hero Galley. NBJ, Nov. 4, 1777.

WILLIAMS, MOSES. Princess Anne Petitions, Jan. 3, 1812. MC II, 14. B, 1220.

WILLIAMS, WM. Henry Galley. NBJ, Nov. 1, 1777.

WILLIS, HENRY. Midshipman. Died in service.

WILLIS, HENRY. Dragon, Sept. 3, 1778. NBJ.

WILLIS, JAMES, of Matthews Co. Manley. Henry. R. C. B, 778.

WILLIS, WALTER. Diligence Galley.

WILLIS, WM. N's Accomack, 46.

WILLSON, JOHN. Tempest, Oct. 7, 1779.

WILSON, ALLEN (or Alvin), of Richmond Co. Midshipman, March 1, 1778 to Jan. 20, 1779. Lt. Dragon. In LBP, Eliz. Thompson testified: "he was the son of my aunt Betsey, who resided at that time in Richmond Co. He died in service. Two coats, one of fine blue cloth and one of red, were brought to the house after his death. I heard aunt Isabella Wilson say Alvin was the son of Uncle Martin Wilson." Martha C. Potts of King George Co. stated that she was a sister of Alvin Wilson.

WILSON, HARRY. Aud. Acct. XXVII A, 306.

WILSON, HENRY. Ordinary Seaman. H. D. 1833–4, Doc. 33.

WILSON, JOHN. Hero Galley.
WILSON, JOHN. Henry Galley, 1776 until Nov. 21, when he was turned over to the Mosquito.
WILSON, JOHN. Tempest. B, 25.
WILSON, JOHN. Midshipman, Liberty, July, 1777. Tempest, Dec. 7, 1779. LBP. Heirs: Cyrus Wilson and Elizabeth Yerby, of Lancaster Co. N's Lancaster, 30.
WILSON, JOSEPH. Master's mate, Brig Liberty, May 18 to July 30, 1776. LBP George Rogers.
WILSON, JOSEPH. Midshipman. N's Lancaster, 31.
WILSON, LEMUEL. NBJ, Jan. 27, 1779.
WILSON, SAMUEL. Tartar, 28 Sept. to 28 Nov., 1779. N 8, 13. Sailing Master, see USP Laban Bayly. From Nov. 1779 to 1780.
WILSON, WM. Discharged as infirm, Nov. 20, 1777. NBJ.
WILSON, CAPT. WILLIS, of Portsmouth, Va. Recommended captain of the Caswell Galley, Sept. 7, 1776 (another record gives Dec. 1). Appointed to command Jefferson, Dec. 4, 1780. One of the retained captains of the Navy. USP. Will, Dec. 2, 1796; proved Dec. 17, 1798. He died Sept. 11, 1798. Administrator, Saml. L. Wilson. Heirs in 1836, son William Wilson and others. In 1832 Jacomine F., wife of Richard Halstead, and Elizabeth, wife of James Courtney, are mentioned also as heirs.
WIMBRO, EBERN (Eben Winbrough), of Chincoteague; will proved April 2, 1817. BH, 807. N's Accomack, 64.
WINDER, JAMES. LBP James Jennings.
WITCHELL, MR. ROBERT. Boatswain at Chickahominy Shipyard, Sept. 15, 1780. Maxwell (Dec. 16, 1780).
WOLLAGE, EDWARD. Boatswain's mate, Henry Galley.
WONYCUTT, EDWARD, CAPT., of Norfolk County. Lt. appointed by Committee of Safety, on recommendation of Capt. Taylor. Captain (?) Brigantine Greyhound (employed in trade). USNP. Died June 1, 1811. Mary, wife of Robt. Morrissett, administratrix. MC III, 152. In 1833, Mary Shays, sole devisee.
WONYCUTT (Wonneycutt), RICHARD, of Norfolk Co. Lt. Dec. 4, 1776, (1st Mate), Hornet.

WOOD, ALLEN, Pilot, Dragon to June 28, 1779. Son of Allen Wood of Hampton. He md. a daughter of James Leggit, in Hampton, and went elsewhere to live, according to John S. Westwood. Jane Wood, of York Co., however, stated that Allen was taken prisoner, and, when he attempted to escape, was hung. MC III, 450. In 1838, James, William, Robert, Samuel, John, Cary, Martha, and Jane Wood, sole heirs of James Wood decd., who was sole heir of his brother Allen Wood, who died in service.

WOOD, JAMES. Lt. marines.

WOOD, JAMES, of Elizabeth City Co. Pilot. See LBP James Jennings. BH, 791.

WOOD, JAMES. Tempest, Dec. 7, 1779.

WOOD, JOHN. Dragon. LBP James Jennings.

WOOD, PHILIP. Dragon. LBP James Jennings.

WOOD, THOMAS. Dragon. LBP James Jennings.

WOOD, THOMAS. Mulatto. Deserted from Dragon, Va. Gazette, July 3, 1779.

WOOD, WM. Pilot, of Elizabeth City Co. Tempest. B, 23.

WOOD, WM., of Elizabeth City Co. Supposed to be on Capt. Calvert's Galley, after deserting from Edmund B. Dickinson's company, first regiment, Va. Gazette, Sept., 1776.

WOOD, WM. Sailor. NBJ, Sept. 9, 1778.

WOODS, THOS. N 8, 14.

WOODS, WM. Tempest, Oct. 7, 1779.

WORDEN, JESSE, of Hanover or Henrico Co. Deserted, Va. Gazette, Sept. 13, 1776.

WORSHAM, MILES. Accomac Galley.

WORTON, JOHN. Boatswain, Henry Galley, 1776.

WORTH, BOLLING. NBJ, Oct. 20, 1778.

WORTH, WM. E 1.

WRAY, GEORGE. Acting Midshipman, Tempest, 1777; Oct. 7, 1779. Seaman, Dec. 7, 1779. LBNB. In 1855, Mary D. Cooper, of New Orleans, granddaughter. USP.

WRIGHT, PATRICK. Midshipman and captain. Appointed to new galley, May or June, 1776; served to Aug. 2, 1777, when he entered the State Artillery.

WRIGHT, STEPHEN, of Norfolk. See LSP John Crew. Stephen Wright crossed to Yorktown as ensign in one of the vessels commanded by Capt. John Archer. Later acted as a sort of aide to Capt. Wright Wescott of the Scorpion. Was captured and imprisoned in Bermuda. Affidavit of Col. Stephen Wright in 1850.

WRIGHT, WESCOTT (Westcott, Wright?). H. D. 1833-4, Doc. 33, 6.

Y

YEATS (Yates), ROBT. Safeguard March 1 to June 16, 1777. Deserted.

YOUNG, JOHN. March 24, 1783.

YOUNGER, JAMES, of Norfolk Co. Born in 1757; living in 1833. Marine; enlisted under Lt. John Smith; finally sent on board the Independence, Capt. Matheson; then on Schooner Dolphin, Capt. Thos. Bryant; wounded in a battle off Tangier Island; afterwards, enlisted with Capt. Johnson in land service, and was at siege of York. LBP Thos. Christie.

YOUNGHUSBAND, CAPT. ISAAC, of Richmond, Feb. 21, 1776, in command of the Mosquito. Resigned. His brother, John Younghusband, a native of Great Britain, was granted naturalization Nov. 21, 1782. H. D.

*INDEX

A

Abercrombie, Col., 102.
Accomac (galley), 68, 83, 85.
Adams, John, 9.
Admiralty Court, 121.
Adventure (ship), 12, 16, 17, 86.
Alliance (schooner), 29, 83.
Allison, Capt. John, 9, 16.
American Congress (ship), 8.
American Fabius (ship), 135.
Anderson, John, 42.
Andrews, Lt. Ishmael, court martial, 68.
Antelope (ship), 38.
Antigua, 26, 35, 37.
Apollo (ship), 135.
Arbuthnot, Admiral, 98, 99.
Archer, Lieut. John, 49.
Ariadne (ship), 37.
Armistead, Robert, 97.
Armistead, William, 97.
Arnold, General Benedict, 93 et seq.; 103, 113.
Aurora (ship), 17.
Avery, Col., 99.
Aylett, Col. William, 23 et seq.; 43.

B

Bailey, Charles, 17.
Bailey, Thomas, 44.
Ball, John, 23, 30.
Baltimore, 18, 45, 120, 127.
Baltimore (brig), 84.
Banks, Mr., 11.
Barbadoes, 38, 39.
Barge, 128 (Note).
Barges, Battle of, 128.
Barrett, Capt. John, 12.
Barrett, Jonathan, 42.
Barron, James (captain and afterwards commodore), 11, 18, 59, 69, 70, 77, 87, 106, 120, 121, 123, 124, 126.
Barron, James Jr., 69, 108.
Barron, Capt. Richard, 11, 18, 49, 70, 84, 106, 136.
Barron, Samuel, 55.
Bayne (Baynes), Capt. John, 49.
Bermuda, 22, 58, 105, 106, 126.
Betsey (boat), 29.
Betsey and Peggy (boat), 87.
B. Hero (sloop), 27.

Biddle, Capt., 11.
Biffin, John, 9.
Bingham, John, 45.
Blacksnake (privateer), 75.
Bland, Col. Theodorick, 79.
Blaws, James, 10.
Blonde (ship), 118.
Bolling, Lieut. Robert, 84.
Bond, Capt. Hance, 53.
Bonhomme Richard (ship), 12.
Boston (ship), 81.
Boucher, Commodore John Thomas, 9, 16.
Boush, Capt. Goodrich, 20.
Bowker's Wharf, 10.
Bowman's Folly, 63, 64, 65.
Brave Fier Roderique (ship), 52.
Brehan, Dr., 40.
Bright, Capt. Francis, 12, 19, 58.
Brittain, John, 60.
Broadwater, Charles L., 9.
Broadwater, Col., 16.
Brock, John, 35.
Brooke, Capt. (later Commodore) Walter, 18, 19, 45, 49.
Brooks, Reuben, 38.
Brown, M. O., 122.
Brown, Thomas, 126.
Brown, Windsor, 9.
Buckner, Capt. William, 98.
Buckroe, 49.
Burke, James, 60.
Burwell's Ferry, 101, 107, 124.

C

Cagey's Strait, battle of, 131.
Callender, Capt. Eleazer, 12, 17, 57, 58, 60, 69, 80, 107, 136.
Calvert, Capt. Christopher, 20.
Calvert, Capt. John, 15, 16, 20, 44'
Calvert, Max., 12.
Cape Charles, 49, 58, 86.
Cape Francois, 17, 50, 58, 111, 123.
Cape Hatteras, 16.
Cape Henry, 18, 55, 70, 72, 86, 106, 115, 123.
Carrington, Richard, 121.
Cary, Robert, 9.
Carysfort (ship), 118.
Caswell (galley), 20, 53, 82, 92.
Caswell, Governor (N. C.), 20, 21, 68.
Catherine, Joseph, 9.

*This Index applies to the narrative, pages 5-136.

274 INDEX

Catlett, Lt. George, 35, 41.
Cerberus (ship), 105.
Chamberlaine, Lt. George, 35, 84.
Chamberlaine, Capt. Phillip, 12, 72.
Chamberlayne, Lieut. Byrd, 35, 41.
Chamberlayne, Mid. Edward Pye, 35.
Chandler, Lieut. Thomas, 80, 111.
Chandler, William, 38.
Chaplains, 78, 120.
Charles Town (Charleston, S. C.), 117, 23, 24, 84, 91, 103.
Chesapeake Bay, 57, 68, 71, 75, 76, 84, 87, 90, 122, 126.
Chick, John, 44.
Chickahominy shipyard, 80, 83, 94, 98, 101, 102, 135.
Chincoteague, 21, 48, 68.
Christian, Capt. George, 132.
City Point, 103.
Clark, Lieut., 122.
Clinton, Sir Henry, 101, 104.
Cobb, Seth, 47.
Cocke, Capt. James, 12, 15, 35, 42, 44.
Cocke, Capt. John Catesby, 136.
Coleman, Thomas, 44.
Collier, Sir George, 73, 77.
Colston, Raleigh, 23, 47, 52.
Confederacy (ship), 81.
Congress (ship), 9, 16, 41, 43, 44 (note).
Cook, Dawson, 45.
Cooke, Capt. Robert, 12.
Cormorant (ship), 120, 121, 122, 127.
Cornwallis (brig), 95, 96.
Cornwallis (galley), 74.
Cornwallis, Lord, 103, 105, 108, 110, 113, 118.
Cowper, Lieut. John, 111.
Cowper, Capt. John, 72, 136.
Cowper, Wills, 112.
Cox, Capt. John, 36, 104, 106.
Creyk, Capt., 75.
Crew, Lieut. John, 105.
Cropper, Col. John, 61 et seq.
Crow, Nathaniel, 11.
Culley, Armistead, 49.
Culley, Robert, 45, 49.
Cumberland shipyard, 44, 83.
Cunningham, Captain, 99.
Cunningham, Lieut. James, 72, 145.
Cunningham, Capt. Joseph, 83.
Cutler, W. R., 37.

D

Dabney, Col. Charles, 124.
Dale, Richard, 11, 12.
Dalton, John, 8, 12.
D'Anmours, Chevalier, 88, 89, 90.
Daniel, George, 58.
Dasher (galley), 135.
Davies, William, 130.
Dean, Silas, 41.
Defense (Maryland ship), 9, 16.
Defiance (ship), 12, 17, 35, 50, 53.
De Kay, Charles, 35, 41.
D'Estaing, Admiral, 54.
Dick, Capt. Alexander, 35, 39, 41.
Dickey, Lieut., 70, 71.
Diligence (galley), 21, 83, 85.
Dishman, William, 36, 38.
Disney, Capt. John, 95.
Dolphin (ship), 71, 72.
Dolphin (Bermudan ship), 105.
Douglas, James, 45.
Dragon (ship), 54, 55, 57 et seq.; 80, 83, 85, 87, 94, 98.
Dundas, Col., 97.
Dunleavy, John, 9.
Dunmore, Earl of, 5 et seq.
Dunmore (ship), 81.

E

Eagle (brig), 104.
East Florida, expedition planned against, 55.
Eaton, Capt., 53.
Edmondson, John, 11.
Eelbeck, Jonathan, 104.
Elégante (French snow), 51.
Elliott, Capt. George, 15, 21.
Elliott, Capt. (Robert), 105.
Emerald (ship), 59, 70, 76.
Eminence (sloop), 99.
Eskridge, Edward, 57.
Eskridge, Samuel, 57.
Evans, Mr., 132.
Experiment (ship), 195.

F

Fage, Capt., 102.
Fanny (ship), 6, 11.
Field (Feild), Theophilus, 57.
Fincastle (ship), 81.
Fiveash, Peter, 105.
Flags of truce, 103, 124.
Fleming, Mrs. Bridget, 9.
Fly (pilot boat), 135.
Folly Creek, 61, 64.

Fortune (Forton) Gaol, 38, 39, 40, 41.
Fortunatus (ship), 70.
Fowey (ship), 5, 13, 16.
Franklin, Dr. [Benjamin], 46.
Frazer, Mr., 57.
Frazer's Ferry (shipyard), 57, 135.
Fredericksburg, 57, 93, 135.
French fleet, 54, 96, 99, 118.
Frigates, to be built at Gosport, 17.

G

Galleys, 21, 40, 55, 90.
Galvan, Major, 89.
Gamecock (ship), 106.
Gardner, Lt. Samuel, 53.
Gates, General, 91.
General Monk (ship), 97.
General Warren (brig), 86.
Gérard (French Ambassador), 88.
Gerlach, Captain, 103.
Gibb, William, 132 et seq.
Gibson, John, 71.
Gillon, Commodore Alexander, 40.
Gloucester (prison galley), 46, 48, 83.
Goffigan, Lieut. Laban, 105.
Goodrich, Bartlett, 6, 10.
Goodrich, Bridges, 10.
Goodrich, John, 6, 7, 10.
Goodrich, John, Jr., 7, 10, 53.
Goodrich, William, 6, 7.
Goodriches, 13, 54, 68, 81.
Gooseley, Capt. George, 44.
Gosport (England), 38, 39.
Gosport (Virginia), 17, 135.
Gouverneur (ship), 29.
Graham, William, 27, 30.
Grand Tiger (ship), 86.
Grand Turk (privateer), 121.
Grande Terre, 35.
Grant, Thomas, 84.
Grasse, Count de, 106, 118.
Graves, Admiral, 99, 118.
Gray, Capt. James, 10, 48.
Gray, Lieut. Robert, 42.
Gray, Lieut. William, 49.
Grayson, Commodore, 69.
Green, Capt. William (of the Defiance), 12, 17, 39, 42, 53, 135.
Greenfield, Captain, 29.
Greyhound (ship), 49, 50.
Greyhound (pilotboat), 49.
Guadaloupe, 16, 36, 38.
Gwynn's Island, 12, 13.

H

Hall, Robert, 84.
Ham, Lieut [William], 90, 135.
Hambleton (Hamilton), Lieut. John, 57.
Hambleton, Robert, 35.
Hammond, Captain, 8, 13.
Hammond (ship), 81, 86.
Hampton (ship), 135.
Hampton, 12, 19, 56, 70, 84, 85, 90, 97, 98, 120, 122, 123.
Hampton Roads, 70, 85, 95, 112, 123, 125.
Handy, Capt. Joseph, 131.
Handy, Capt. Levin, 131.
Hany, John, 9.
Hardyman, Captain, 122.
Harris, Capt. John, 34, et seq.; 122.
Harrison (schooner), 127.
Harrison, Governor Benjamin, 120 et seq.
Harrison, Dr. Joseph, 49.
Harrison, Richard, 22, 36, 39, 46, 51.
Hatteras, 16.
Head of Elk (Maryland), 17, 121, 136.
Healey, Lieut. Samuel, 17.
Henry (galley), 15, 19, 58, 83, 85.
Henry, James, 121.
Henry, Governor Patrick, 5; 15 et seq.; 73, 77, 82.
Henry's Point, 65, 66.
Herbert, John, 34.
Herbert, Lieut. Pascow, 88.
Herbert, Capt. Thomas, 45, 46, 107.
Hero (galley), 12, 18, 19, 83, 91.
Hero's Revenge (barge), 104.
Hinton, Lewis, 60.
Hispaniola, 23, 123.
Hobbs Hole, 35.
Hog Island, 57, 84.
Hood's, 97, 98, 101.
Hope, Mr., 121.
Hope (sloop), 97.
Hopkins, Commodore Esek, 7.
Horn, Ralph, 36, 38, 39.
Hornet (sloop; name changed from "Liberty"), 10, 17.
Hospital (naval), to be established, 90.
Hotham, Commodore, 18.
Hughes, Edward, 17.
Hughes, John, 9.
Hunter, Capt. Caleb, 57.

Hunter, Dr. George, 9, 16.
Hunter, Mrs. Hannah, 9.
Hunter, John,
Huntington, Samuel, 86.
Hutchings, John, 135.
Hybernia (ship), 95.

I

Idea & Ann (ship), 46, 47.
Indigo, 17, 24, 28.
Industry (ship), 135.
Iris (ship), 119.
Iveson, Doctor, 39.
Ivy, Capt. William, 49.

J

James, Lt. Michael, 57.
Jamestown, 34, 84, 108.
Jane (ship), 45.
Jay, John, 80, 81.
Jefferson (ship), 83, 84, 87, 88, 89, 92, 96, 102.
Jefferson, Thomas, 13; 80 et seq.
Jeffries, Lt. Aaron, 49.
Jenifer, Daniel of St. Thomas, 14, 16, 93, 94.
Jennings, Michael, 84.
Jennings, William, 60, 106.
Jenny (boat), 22 et seq.
Joel, Capt. J. Edgar, 94, 98.
John (snow), 35.
Johnson, Governor, of Maryland, 52.
Jones, John Paul, 40, 209.
Joynes, Thomas R., Sr., 133.

K

Kautzman, Lt. John, V., 88.
Kemp, Captain, 56.
Kidd, Commodore, 61, 64, 132 et seq.
Kidnapper (barge), 131.
Kilby, John, 39, 40.

L

Lacraie, affair of, 89.
Lady Charlotte (ship), 13.
Lafayette, Marquis de, 33, 96, 97, 101, 102.

Landrum, Dr. Thomas, 57.
Lark (ship), 10.
Lattimore, Lieut. Edward, 17.
Laws, Timothy, 45.
Lee (pilotboat), 18.
Lee, Arthur, 40.
Lee, Richard Henry, 7, 13, 14, 15, 20, 21, 78, 81, 125.
Lee, William, 49, 52.
Lennis, Lt. Frank, 72.
Leslie, Major General, 112, 113.
Letter of Marque, 80, 95.
Lewis (galley), 17, 53, 54, 83, 91, 92, 102.
Lewis, Col. Fielding, 57.
Lewis, General, 13.
Lewis, Capt. William, 99.
Liberty (brig), 12, 15, 17; et seq.
Liberty (boat: schooner), 18, 69, 70, 71, 76, 83, 92, 97, 120, 121, 127.
Liberty (sloop), 49.
Lightburne (Lightburn), Lt. Henry, 17.
Lightburne (Lightburn), Lt. Stafford, 17.
Lilly (ship), 10.
Lilly, Capt. John, 12, 44, 45, 46, 48.
Lincoln, General Benjamin, 124, 125.
Liverpool (frigate), 12.
Livingston, Dr. Justice, 57.
Lookout boat, 83.
Lord Howe (ship), 59.
Lord North (ship), 81.
Loyalist (ship), 120.
Loyall, Paul, 122.
Lurty, Capt. John, 17, 58.
Luzerne, Chevalier de la, 82, 104.
Lyburn, Henry, 10.
Lynnhaven Bay, 55, 96, 123, 135.

M

McCarty, Charles, 11.
McCaw, Dr. James, 34, 39.
McCaw, General Walter Drew, U. S. A., 41.
McLane, Capt., 104.
McNickle (McNickel), Dr. Archibald, 39.
McWilliams, Joshua, 57.
Mahony, Captain, 23.
Mallory, Colonel, 86, 97.
Manchester, 93, 102.
Manly, Manley (galley), 16, 18, 19, 35, 83, 88.

Marbury, Lt. Samuel, 9.
Marines, 9, 12, 19, 34, 35, 45, 53 (note), 122.
Markham, Capt. James, 17, 18, 92, 102, 136.
Marquis Lafayette (privateer), 108 et seq.
Mars (ship), 99.
Marsden, Capt. James, 12.
Martinique, 12, 17, 18, 22, 36, 105.
Mason, Col. George, 8, 73.
Massenburg, Alexander, 45, 49.
Mathew, General, 74, 76, 77.
Mathews, Sampson, 136.
Mathews, Major, 77.
Maxwell, Capt. James, 87, 90, 96, 97, 120, 121.
May, Captain, 29.
Mercer, Samuel, 45.
Merchant Marine, 136.
Meredith, Captain, 112 et seq.
Meriwether, Lt. James, 48.
Metompkin Inlet, 21, 48, 61 et seq.
Milliner, Lt. Robert, 68 (note).
Minge's Ferry, 49.
Mitchell, Ross, 119.
Mitchell, Capt. William, 35.
Mitchell, William, 39.
Molly (boat), 17, 29.
Montague, James, 11.
Montgomery (ship), 37.
Moody, Lieut. John, 9.
Moore, Alexander, 39.
Morning Star (ship), 135.
Morris, Gouverneur, 122.
Morton, Lt. Edward, 53.
Moseley, Dr. Benjamin, 124.
Mosquito (brig), 9; 34 et seq.; 47.
Moxley, Thomas, 9.
Muddy Creek, 21.
Munroe, Captain, 119.
Muter, Capt. 12, 18, 48.

N

Nansemond Creek, 21.
Nansemond River, 53, 91, 108, 111, 112, 113.
Nantes, 40, 43, 46, 52.
Nash, John, 126.
Naval Descents, 78, 90, 93.
Nelson, Thomas, 92, 105 et seq.
New Point Comfort, 16.
Newport News, 90, 91, 98, 114, 115.
New Providence, 8.
Newton, Thomas Jr., 122, 135.

Nicholson (boat), 24, 89, 90, 107.
Nicholson, Capt. James, 9, 69.
Noble (ship), 36, 38.
Norfolk, burning of, 7 (note); 12, 74, 79.
Norfolk Revenge (galley), 15, 16, 19, 44, 53.
Northampton (boat), 15, 18, 19, 58, 59, 60, 87, 91.
Northumberland (ship), 106.
Nuttall, Iveson, 57.
Nuttall, John, 57.

O

Ocracock Inlet, 20, 53, 55, 68.
Oldham, George, 68.
Old Point Comfort (Point Comfort), 114, 115, 120.
Oliver (ship), 10.
Oliver Cromwell (ship), 41, 121.
Oliver Cromwell (ship, Capt. Courtier), 37.
Osborne's, 101.
Otter (ship), 13, 75, 81.
Oxford (ship), 11, 45.

P

Page (galley), 17, 18, 58, 83, 91.
Page, John, 13, 15 et seq.
Pain, Samuel, 25.
Palmer, Dr. W. P. 135.
Parker, Capt. Thomas, 131 et seq.
Parker, Lt. William Harwar, 57, 102.
Pasteur (Pasture), Capt. John, 17, 24, 106
Patriot (boat), 11, 12, 18, 59, 60, 83, 88, 89, 92, 108 et seq.
Patriot (built after the loss of the foregoing ship), 127.
Paullin, C. O., 136.
Paullin, John, 43.
Payne, Lieut. Merryman, 57.
Payne, William, 57.
Peace and Plenty (boat), 53.
Peers, Capt. Vallantine, 9.
Pepper Creek, 46.
Petersburg, 103.
Peyton, Sir John, 17, 18, 106.
Phenix (ship), 42.
Phillips, General, 101, 103, 104, 113.
Phill'ps, Captain, 95.
Pickering, Colonel, 106.
Pickett, Francis, 38.

Pierce, John, 57.
Pliarne, Penet & Co., 43.
Pocahontas (ship), 135.
Pollard, Lt. Benjamin, 12.
Port Royal, 35.
Portsmouth, 74, 76, 77, 91, 93, 96, 98, 99, 108, 135.
Potomac fleet, 9.
Potomac River, 10, 14, 125.
Prentis, Judge Joseph, 31.
Price, Captain, of Maryland, 14.
Prince George (ship), 38.
Pringle, Sir Thomas, 36.
Prince William (ship), 126.
Prize ships, 10, 11, 18, 24, 26, 27, 35, 36, 44, 46, 47, 48, 51, 57, 60, 71, 80, 81, 87, 88, 90, 96, 107, 126.
Protector (barge), 129, 131, 132.
Protector (galley), 18, 81.

Q

Queen's Creek, 16.

R

Rainbow (ship), 74.
Raisonable (ship), 19, 73, 74, 75.
Raleigh, Rawleigh (brig), 18, 20, 42.
Ralls, Capt. George, 27 et seq.
Randal (sloop), 86.
Rappahannock river, 10, 12, 18, 58, 95, 125.
Rattlesnake (ship), 87.
Rattlesnake (privateer), 55.
Reeves, Captain, 86.
Renown (ship), 99, 102, 105.
Reville, John, 132.
Reynolds, Dr. John, 60.
Reynolds, John, 34.
Rhodes, Henry, 9.
Richards, John, 9.
Richards, Richard, 9.
Richards, William, 57.
Richmond, 41, 84, 93, 101, 105.
Richmond (barge), 127.
Richmond (ship), 119.
Robins, Lt. John, 57.
Rochester (ship), 18.
Rodney, Commodore, 91.
Roebuck (ship), 8, 59.
Rogers, Capt. George, 34, 49.
Rogers, Lieut. John, 45, 49, 84.
Romulus (ship), 38, 104, 125.

Ronald, William, 44.
Rope-walk, 136.
Rose, Duncan, 29.
Ross, David, 122.
Row galleys, 8, 10, 12, 15.
Royall, Thomas, 126.
Royston, John, 44, 45.
Rust, Benjamin, 57.

S

Safeguard (galley), 15, 83, 91.
St. Christophers (St. Kitts), 28, 37.
St. Croix, 40, 49, 86.
St. Eustatius, 5, 23, et seq.; 49, 83, 105.
St. Pierre, 39, 51.
Sally Norton (ship), 104, 105.
Sandford, Captain, 16.
Saunders, Allen, 57.
Saunders, Capt. Celey, 12, 18, 21, 57, 136.
Saunders, Lt. Joseph, 60, 95, 102, 107.
Saunders, Capt. William, 12, 17, 19, 57.
Savage, Samuel Phips, 47.
Schemerhorn, Captain, 121.
Scorpion (ship), 9, 45, 49, 105.
Scotch prisoners, 11.
Seaford (ship), 28.
Sergeant, Capt. William, 29.
Selden, Lieut., 122.
Servant, Lieut. Richard, 55.
Signals (naval), 88.
Sinclair, Capt. John, 24.
Sisson, George, 95.
Skinner, Capt. William, 16, 43, 44.
Smith, Captain, of the Grand Tiger, 86.
Smith, James, 37.
Smith, John, 35.
Smith, Thomas, State Agent, 49, 58.
Smith, Wolling, 57.
Smith's Island, 60.
Smith river, 52.
Snale, Lieut. Thomas, 84.
Snead, Major Smith, 131, 132.
Snead, Capt. William, 132.
"Snow", definition (note), 35.
Solebay (ship), 42.
Soubies, Monsieur, 38.
South Quay, 20, 135.
Speedwell (ship), 10.

Stanley, Moses, 36, 38.
Staunton, 105.
Steele, Lieut. William, 57, 90, 102.
Steuben, Baron von, 93, 96, 98.
Stormont, Lord, 31, 52.
Stratton, Capt. Henry, 29, 83.
Strother, Mid, Benjamin, 57.
Sturdivant, Capt. Joel, 18.
Suffolk, burning of, 78, 112, 113.
Surinam, 17.
Susannah (ship), 10.
Swift (ship), 55.
Sybil (French frigate), 123, 124.
Sylph (ship), 28.

T

Tangier Island, 71, 86, 88, 129.
Tartar (ship), 54, 55, 57 et seq.; 83.
Taylor, Capt. Richard, 10, 18, 57, 59, 60, 136.
Tempest (ship), 57 et seq.; 84, 85, 87, 100, 102.
Thetis (ship), 44, 83, 85, 87, 88.
Thomas, Captain, of British schooner, 95.
Thomas, Captain, of ship Mars, 99.
Thomas, Captain John, 9, 16, 19, 44, 81.
Tilly, Captain de, 104.
Tompkins, Capt. Robert, 15, 35, 58.
Tories, 19, 126, 128.
Travis, Champion, 135.
Travis, Capt. Edward, 16, 18, 42, 100, 107, 111, 136.
Trimmer (schooner), 95.
Triplett, Lt. Daniel, 9, 44.
Tucker, Captain, 29.
Tucker, St. George, 22, 106.
Tupper, John, 57.
Turkey Island, 99.
Tutt, Mid. James, 57.

U

Umphlet [Humphlett], William, 109, 110.
Underhill, Capt. William, 21.

V

Valentine, Capt. Jacob, 34.
Valette, Chevalier de la, 124, 125.
Vallance, Captain, 84.
Van Bibber, Abraham, 22 et seq.
Van Bibber & Harrison, 22 et seq.
Van Bibber, Isaac, 32.
Victory (American barge), 130.

Victory (British barge), 66, 67.
Villebrun, Captain, 125.
Virginia (frigate), 77.
Virginia (sloop), 29.

W

Walker, Mr., 10.
Waller, Benj., 121.
Warwick, 136.
Warwick, Joseph, 35.
Washington, General, 8, 20, 28, 99, 101, 125.
Washington (galley), 20, 82.
Washington (ship), 111.
Watkins, George, 28.
Watkins, Lieut. James, 109, 110.
Watkins, William, 28.
Watson, Capt. Johannes, 21.
Watts, Samuel, 17.
Watts, Thomas, 17.
Webb, Lieut., 122.
Webb, Mid. Francis, 57.
Webb, George, 135.
Weedon, General, 111.
Westcott, Capt. Wright, 50, 53, 105.
Westham, 93.
Westover, 93.
Whaley, Commodore, 128 et seq.
Wheat, Sir Jacob, 105.
White, Joseph, 48.
Whiting, Thomas, 29, 54, 135.
Wilkes (ship), 87, 99.
Wilkes, John, 87.
Wilkinson, John, 57.
Williamsburg, 15, 29, 42, 84, 101, 135.
Willing Lass (ship), 99.
Willson, Joseph, 44.
Wilson, Captain, 135.
Wilson, John, 45.
Wilson, Capt. Willis, 20, 82, 92.
Wishart, Major, 90.
Wonnycutt, Capt. Edward, 10, 49.
Wrenn, Capt. Jos., 58.

Y

Yerby, Captain, 51.
York (barge), 127.
York (York Town), 5, 26, 92, 98, 106, 108, 118, 125, 126.
York River, 12, 19, 58, 106, 107, 125.
Young, Admiral, 28.
Younger, John, 72.
Younghusband, Capt. Isaac, 12, 34, 136.

www.ingramcontent.com/pod-product-compliance
Lightning Source LLC
Chambersburg PA
CBHW060351080526
44583CB00012B/266